Gillian Steinberg offers an approachable introduction to the poems of one of the most prolific and influential English writers, through an examination of wide-ranging selections from his work.

Part I of this invaluable study:

- provides clear and stimulating close readings of Thomas Hardy's key poems
- considers major themes in Hardy's poetry, including ghosts, God's role in the world, war, and the painful passage of time
- summarizes the methods of analysis and provides suggestions for further work.

Part II supplies essential background material, featuring:

- an account of Hardy's life and works
- samples of criticism from important Hardy scholars.

With a helpful Further Reading section, this insightful volume is ideal for anyone who wishes to appreciate and explore Hardy's poetry for themselves.

Gillian Steinberg is Associate Professor of English at Yeshiva University, New York City. Her previous publications include *Philip Larkin and His Audiences* (2010), also published by Palgrave Macmillan.

Analysing Texts is dedicated to one clear belief: that we can all enjoy, understand and analyse literature for ourselves, provided we know how to do it. Readers are guided in the skills and techniques of close textual analysis used to build an insight into a richer understanding of an author's individual style, themes and concerns. An additional section on the writer's life and work, and a comparison of major critical views, place them in their personal and literary context.

General Editor: Nicholas Marsh

ANALYSING TEXTS

General Editor: Nicholas Marsh

Published

Jane Austen: The Novels   *Nicholas Marsh*
Aphra Behn: The Comedies   *Kate Aughterson*
William Blake: The Poems   *Nicholas Marsh*
Charlotte Brontë: The Novels   *Mike Edwards*
Emily Brontë: Wuthering Heights   *Nicholas Marsh*
Chaucer: The Canterbury Tales   *Gail Ashton*
Daniel Defoe: The Novels   *Nicholas Marsh*
Charles Dickens: David Copperfield / Great Expectations   *Nicolas Tredell*
John Donne: The Poems   *Joe Nutt*
George Eliot: The Novels   *Mike Edwards*
F. Scott Fitzgerald: The Great Gatsby / Tender is the Night   *Nicolas Tredell*
E. M. Forster: The Novels   *Mike Edwards*
Thomas Hardy: The Novels   *Norman Page*
Thomas Hardy: The Poems   *Gillian Steinberg*
John Keats: The Poems   *John Blades*
Philip Larkin: The Poems   *Nicholas Marsh*
D. H. Lawrence: The Novels   *Nicholas Marsh*
Marlowe: The Plays   *Stevie Simkin*
John Milton: Paradise Lost   *Mike Edwards*
Shakespeare: The Comedies   *R. P. Draper*
Shakespeare: The Sonnets   *John Blades*
Shakespeare: The Tragedies   *Nicholas Marsh*
Shakespeare: Three Problem Plays   *Nicholas Marsh*
Mary Shelley: Frankenstein   *Nicholas Marsh*
Webster: The Tragedies   *Kate Aughterson*
Virginia Woolf: The Novels   *Nicholas Marsh*
Wordsworth and Coleridge: Lyrical Ballads   *John Blades*

Further titles are in preparation

Analysing Texts
Series Standing Order ISBN 978–0–333–73260–1
(*outside North America only*)

You can receive future titles in this series as they are published by placing a standing order. Please contact your bookseller or, in the case of difficulty, write to us at the address below with your name and address, the title of the series and the ISBN quoted above.

Customer Services Department, Macmillan Distribution Ltd, Houndmills, Basingstoke, Hampshire. RG21 6XS, UK

RICHARD TAUNTON
SIXTH FORM COLLEGE

Books should be returned on or before the last date shown.
To renew email **issues@richardtaunton.ac.uk** or ☎ **023 80514722**

**7 DAY
BOOK**

First published 2013 by
PALGRAVE MACMILLAN

Palgrave Macmillan in the UK is an imprint of Macmillan Publishers Limited, registered in England, company number 785998, of Houndmills, Basingstoke, Hampshire RG21 6XS.

Palgrave Macmillan in the US is a division of St Martin's Press LLC, 175 Fifth Avenue, New York, NY 10010.

Palgrave Macmillan is the global academic imprint of the above companies and has companies and representatives throughout the world.

Palgrave® and Macmillan® are registered trademarks in the United States, the United Kingdom, Europe and other countries

ISBN: 978–0-230–34912-4 hardback
ISBN: 978–0-230–34913-1 paperback

This book is printed on paper suitable for recycling and made from fully managed and sustained forest sources. Logging, pulping and manufacturing processes are expected to conform to the environmental regulations of the country of origin.

A catalogue record for this book is available from the British Library.

A catalog record for this book is available from the Library of Congress.

For my parents, Ted and Phyllis Steinberg

Contents

General Editor's Preface   x

Acknowledgments   xi

A Note on the Text   xiii

Introduction   1

The Scope of this Volume   1
Terms and Definitions   3
How to Read the Poems   5

PART 1   ANALYSING THOMAS HARDY'S POEMS

1   Poet as Storyteller   11
Stories   11
    At Casterbridge Fair   11
    "Ice on the Highway"   14
Setting   16
    "The Bride-Night Fire"   16
    "The Ruin'd Maid"   19
Character   23
    "Ah, Are you Digging on My Grave?"   23
    "The Country Wedding"   27
Dialogue   32
    "The Curate's Kindness"   33
Concluding Discussion   37
Methods of Analysis   40
Suggested Work   42

2   Ghosts   44
"Your Last Drive"   44
"I Have Lived with Shades"   48
"The Haunter" and "The Voice"   52
"Beeny Cliff" and "The Phantom Horsewoman"   59

Concluding Discussion   64
Methods of Analysis   70
Suggested Work   71

3   God, Man, and the Natural World   **72**
"Hap"   73
"The Darkling Thrush"   77
"Nature's Questioning"   81
"On a Fine Morning"   86
"To an Unborn Pauper Child"   89
"The Convergence of the Twain"   93
Comparative Discussion   99
Concluding Discussion   99
Methods of Analysis   103
Suggested Work   104

4   War and Its Casualties   **105**
"I Looked Up from My Writing"   106
"The Going of the Battery" and "A Wife in London"   110
"In Time of 'The Breaking of Nations'"   118
"The Man He Killed"   123
"Channel Firing"   128
Concluding Discussion   132
Methods of Analysis   135
Suggested Work   136

5   The Self and Time   **137**
"Afterwards"   138
"During Wind and Rain"   139
"The Self-Unseeing" and "At Castle Boterel"   144
"The House of Hospitalities"   151
"The Going"   154
"I Look Into My Glass"   159
Comparative Discussion   161
Concluding Discussion   162
Methods of Analysis   164
Suggested Work   165

PART 2 THE CONTEXT AND THE CRITICS

6	**Hardy's Life and Works**	**169**
	A Biographical Outline	169
	Novelist to Others; Poet to Himself	170
	A Man of Many Genres	172
	Reading a Literary Life	174
	Poems of 1912–13: How and Why We Read Poems	176
	Hardy's Place in Literary History	180
	Hardy the Victorian	181
	Hardy the Romantic	184
	Hardy the Modernist	186
7	**Critical Views**	**188**
	Early Twentieth-Century Critical Views	189
	Mid-century Criticism	192
	Poets on Hardy	194
	Four Critics in Depth	196
	Samuel Hynes	197
	Dennis Taylor	201
	Norman Page	204
	Susan M. Miller	207
Further Reading		211
Notes		219
List of Works Cited		226
Index		235

General Editor's Preface

This series is dedicated to one clear belief: that we can all enjoy, understand and analyse literature for ourselves, provided we know how to do it. How can we build on close understanding of a short passage, and develop our insight into the whole work? What features do we expect to find in a text? Why do we study style in so much detail? In demystifying the study of literature, these are only some of the questions the *Analysing Texts* series addresses and answers.

The books in this series will not do all the work for you, but will provide you with the tools, and show you how to use them. Here, you will find samples of close, detailed analysis, with an explanation of the analytical techniques utilised. At the end of each chapter there are useful suggestions for further work you can do to practise, develop and hone the skills demonstrated and build confidence in your own analytical ability.

An author's individuality shows in the way they write: every work they produce bears the hallmark of that writer's personal 'style'. In the main part of each book we concentrate therefore on analysing the particular flavour and concerns of one author's work, and explain the features of their writing in connection with major themes. In Part II there are chapters about the author's life and work, assessing their contribution to developments in literature; and a sample of critics' views are summarised and discussed in comparison with each other.

Some suggestions for further reading provide a bridge towards further critical research.

Analysing Texts is designed to stimulate and encourage your critical and analytic faculty, to develop your personal insight into the author's work and individual style, and to provide you with the skills and techniques to enjoy at first hand the excitement of discovering the richness of the text.

Nicholas Marsh

Acknowledgments

I am indebted to Nicholas Marsh for his work on the *Analysing Texts* series, his volumes of which first drew me to writing this book. His insights into Hardy's poetry have also been invaluable. I am grateful to Yeshiva University for encouraging my work, especially to Provost Mort Lowengrub for his support of faculty scholarship and undergraduate research assistants; Dean Barry Eichler for his generosity of time and spirit; and English Department Chair Adam Zachary Newton for his leadership and friendship. I also offer thanks to the Faculty Book Fund at Yeshiva College, sponsored by Dr Kenneth Richard Chelst, Dr Bertram M. Schreiber and Dr Fred Zwas. Thank you to Isaac Gewirtz and his assistants at the Berg Collection of the New York Public Library for providing access to the Hardy Collection of Papers.

Without the insights of several colleagues, this work would have suffered: Professors Chaviva Levin and Linda Brown read and commented upon nearly every aspect of this book and spent many hours discussing Hardy's poetry with me, for which I am extremely appreciative. Their friendship and collegiality is incomparable and will, I hope, continue for many decades to come. Professor Theodore Steinberg also read and helpfully commented upon this volume and provided me with the love of poetry that infuses all of my writing and teaching. Thanks, Dad!

My wonderful family is, of course, behind everything I do. My parents, Ted and Phyllis; my siblings and siblings-in-law, Dan, Miriam, Marc, Howard, and Adinah; my in-laws Andrea and Steven Davis; and my aunt Janet Steinberg have all bolstered me emotionally throughout this process and have served as excellent cheerleaders for my work. Mark Davis is the most remarkable husband anyone could ever have and the impetus for all my successes. And my two sons, Akiva and Gavriel, inspire me with their love of learning and joy in living.

Finally, I must thank four remarkable undergraduates who contributed so much of themselves to this volume. Charles Kopel offered tremendous insights into Hardy's theology; Dov Honick shared terrific thoughts on Hardy as a storyteller and on contemporary Hardy scholarship; Arel Kirshstein is a researcher extraordinaire and master of the Hardy section of the New York Public Library as well as a thoughtful, careful reader; and Daniel B. Goldberg contributed significantly to my thinking about Hardy's views of time and to the overall construction of this volume. I look forward to following the promising futures of all four of these young men and am grateful to them for learning and growing with me during the writing process.

A Note on the Text

All poems are referenced by page numbers from James Gibson's *Hardy: The Complete Poems* (Palgrave Macmillan, 2001), hereafter referred to as *CP*.

Introduction

When I mention to friends and acquaintances that I have been spending the bulk of my time lately thinking about Thomas Hardy, they almost inevitably expect that I am writing about his novels. Perhaps because novels are more widely read these days than poems, or because some of Hardy's novels include unforgettable plots and characters, like Tess Durbeyfield and Eustacia Vye, or because some of the novels are known for their film versions, most readers today think of Hardy primarily as a novelist. They are often not even aware that Hardy wrote poems, yet he actually composed more than 1000 poems, many of which are very highly regarded.

Hardy's career is frequently divided into halves based on these two genres: the first half is dominated by his 14 novels and the second half by his poems. In fact, the truth of this chronology is somewhat more complicated because Hardy wrote poems, including some of his best-known and most anthologized poems, during the first half of his writing career. While it is true that he never wrote a novel after 1897, his poetic aspirations began much earlier than the publication of his first volume of verse. Most of his poetic publication did occur in the latter half of his life, but his poetic composition follows a less stark trajectory, having begun when he was quite young and continued until his last years.

The Scope of this Volume

This volume considers poems from across Hardy's career, but rather than being organized chronologically, it is organized thematically.

Among Hardy's poems, written over about six decades, readers will find a number of recurring themes and images. The first section of this volume divides those overarching themes into four central categories: ghosts and the afterlife, God and nature, war, and the passage of time. These categories encompass the primary themes of nearly all of Hardy's verse by exploring the ideas that dominated the bulk of his work. Although at least two categories may seem noticeably absent here – love and rural life – they are folded into these other groupings. Hardy often pairs love, a common theme across English poetry generally, with one of these other categories, making his love poetry significantly darker than one might imagine love poems to be. Because his love poems are also typically about death, you will find that Hardy's many love poems are represented in the chapters about ghosts and about the passage of time and, to a lesser extent, the chapter about war. The other hallmark of Hardy's writings, rural life, permeates so much of Hardy's work that you will find it represented in many of the chapters and especially in his poems written, notably, in the voices of fictional characters.

Prior to examining the recurring themes of ghosts, God, war, and time in Chapters 2–5, the first chapter of this volume connects Hardy's poetry to his work as a novelist. Clearly, his poems, regardless of theme, exhibit many of his storytelling techniques, including detailed plots, interest in the lives of his characters, emphasis on particular settings, and use of evocative dialogue. By setting this groundwork and demonstrating the correlations among his genres, the first chapter should help to prepare us for studying the four themes that are the hallmarks of Hardy's verse. Rather than consider Hardy as though he is two separate writers – a novelist on one hand and a poet on the other – the first chapter examines the ways in which those two genres overlap in Hardy's work, particularly considering how his work as a novelist informs his poetry.[1]

In all five chapters of Part 1 of this book, and throughout the body of Hardy literary criticism, one overarching theme prevails: pessimism. Perhaps the single most important issue addressed by this volume, therefore, is the degree and depth of Hardy's pessimism. That Hardy possesses a worldview that regularly strikes readers as deeply, morbidly pessimistic is hardly debatable, but the extent to which that assessment is accurate is well worth considering. Each of the chapters in the first section of this volume aims to demonstrate that Hardy's pessimism is nuanced, varying, and well-considered. Because his mood is often reduced so generically to "depressive," readers of his verse may miss the complex and multi-faceted ways in which he employs that depressiveness. The broad-brushed approach irritated Hardy, who may have felt that all the nuance and power of his language and thought was diminished by the generic application of the "pessimist" label. As Harvey Curtis Webster notes, "Hardy's devotion to his right to be inconsistent made him angry with those who called him a pessimist, with those, indeed, who fitted his thought into any philosophical category whatsoever."[2]

This volume aims to move well beyond that basic assessment to see not only the wide variety of ways in which Hardy is indeed a bleak and despairing poet, but also the ways in which his verse is hopeful, joyful, and confident. Much of Hardy's verse, as we shall see, juxtaposes emotional extremities, positing hope alongside despair and pleasure alongside pain. This volume asks readers of Hardy's poems to consider not merely the basic truth of Hardy's bleak outlook but the complexity of his ideas and expressions as well as the ways in which his poems hover between anguish and anticipation.

The second section of the volume explores Hardy's life and works, specifically observing the manner in which his life has frequently been read into his poetry. It will also explore his connections to three literary periods and a specific poet within each era: the Romantic, the Victorian, and the Modern ages. The seventh chapter presents a number of critical responses to Hardy's verse, both from his contemporaries and from more recent literary analysts. Finally, the volume offers some suggested texts that can shed additional light on Hardy's verse and offer more comprehensive approaches to the study of his poetry.

Terms and Definitions

When we discuss the "form" of a poem, as opposed to its "content," we generally mean the structure of the poem, which can include its line lengths, rhyme, rhythms, stanza patterns, and other such compositional qualities. As we shall see throughout this volume, though, form is often not separable from content, and poets frequently use their formal choices to enhance and deepen their poems' meanings. Thus, the study of form is inherent to the study of content, and we will often examine Hardy's formal choices as well as the subjects and themes of his verse.

Meter, the most complex of the formal characteristics, is usually defined by "feet" and "stresses." A foot is the unit of rhythm within a line. For instance, in this line from "How Great My Grief," each foot is made up of two syllables, which I have indicated with separating lines: "How great| my grief,| my joys| how few." In these lines, from "At the Piano," each foot is made up of three syllables: "And the mould| of her face,| / And her neck,| and her hair,| / Which the rays| fell upon| / Of the two| candles there, . . ." The length of the foot is determined by the patterns of stressed and unstressed syllables, which are determined by how words are pronounced, individually or in conjunction.

In multi-syllable words, stresses are largely predetermined by common pronunciation. For example, the word "establish" is always pronounced with the stress on the middle syllable: es**tab**lish. If you tried to pronounce it another way, **es**tablish or establ**ish**, it would sound like a different word entirely. When the words are only one syllable long, though, the stresses are determined by each word's pronunciation in a context of other words. So the word "you" by itself might be stressed or unstressed, but in the line, "With you, my life is complete" the word "you" is stressed, while in the line "You wandered away from me," "you" is unstressed. In the first poetic line above, the stresses fall this way: "How **great** my **grief**, my **joys** how **few**." The line's words are all one syllable long, but in context, the stresses become clear. If you are not sure about where stresses fall, try reading the line in a variety of ways to see which seems most natural. If you reverse the stresses in this case, the line will feel quite unnatural: "**How** great **my** grief, **my** joys **how** few." Often unique and important words are stressed while prepositions, articles, and pronouns remain unstressed. This isn't a foolproof rule, but it is often true. (Incidentally, stresses can also be cultural or regional: for instance, Americans pronounce "garage" with the stress on the second syllable while the British pronunciation stresses the first syllable.)

The placement of stressed syllables within each foot often follows a pattern, and each of the different patterns has its own name. The most familiar of these in English poetry is "iambic," which means that the feet are iambs, two-syllable feet with stress on the second of the two syllables: "That **time** of **year** thou **may'st** in **me** be**hold**." A pattern of two-syllable feet with the stress on the first syllable is called "trochaic"; a three-syllable foot with the stress on the first syllable is a "dactyl"; a three-syllable foot in which the last syllable is stressed is an "anapest"; a two-syllable foot in which both syllables are stressed is a "spondee"; and so on. There are many such terms, but these are the most common in English verse.

In addition to determining the length of each foot and the placement of stresses within each foot, metrics includes counting the number of feet per line, which might remain consistent from line to line or might follow some other pattern (or, perhaps, no pattern at all). These line lengths are described by Latinate prefixes. A poem with four feet per line is written in "tetrameter" while a poem with five feet per line is written in "pentameter." If you are familiar with those numeric prefixes, you should be able to guess accurately at the names of each line length, from dimeter to octameter and beyond. Some poems retain a consistent line length throughout the poems while many poems, among them many of Hardy's poems, alternate or vary line lengths within a single poem.

The rhythm of a poem forms the basis of its unique music, and poets make choices based upon the rhythmic effects they wish to achieve. Patterns of rhyme also contribute to that music, as do line breaks (the places where lines end, whether or not those match up with punctuation marking), and the sounds of words in conjunction, as in alliteration, assonance, consonance, and echoing. Throughout this volume, we will see Hardy use all of these techniques in a variety of ways.

How to Read the Poems

You may be tempted, when reading some of Hardy's poems, to pull out a map and locate the places he discusses. Aside from London, though, the names of the British towns and villages are fictional. Not recognizing Hardy's fictional world of Wessex should not frustrate you, nor will it prevent you from understanding the poems. The name "Wessex" was taken from the early medieval Anglo-Saxon kingdom but is used to represent and fictionalize nineteenth- and twentieth-century southwestern England. Wessex served as the setting for Hardy's novels too, and he later identified the specific parallels between Wessex and real places in Dorset. Nonetheless, what he created for both the novels and the poems is a kind of alternate world that very much resembles his world but also exists outside of reality. Simon Gatrell, who has studied Hardy's Wessex extensively, argues that the Wessex of the novels can be very firmly rooted in the specific places of Hardy's childhood and of rural England, but he also remarks that, in the poems, "the idea of Wessex withdraws for the most part into Hardy's own imagination . . . The collective social and topographical implications of Wessex are often stripped away, to leave what was always there behind it, Hardy's personal response to the realities to hand about him."[3] According to Gatrell, then, as Hardy moved more entirely into the world of verse, his attachment to the firm accuracies of Wessex's locations lessened, and the correspondences between real and fictional places became more fluid and metaphorical. If you know that Wessex closely resembles Hardy's childhood province of Dorset and its surrounding locations in southwestern England, you need not necessarily try to locate each real-life concordance. You may also find that some of the dialect is difficult to understand, so if you are having trouble working out the language of Hardy's rural characters, try reading the poems aloud. That technique can make the dialect sound more familiar and recognizable.

In general, poems ask readers to pay attention to a multitude of details: the circumstances in which a poem takes place, the characters created, the ideas expressed, the sound and rhythm of the words, the location of line breaks, stanzaic patterns, allusion, metaphor, imagery, and more. Poems also ask readers to identify the speaker and the implied audience or audiences. It is important in all poems, but perhaps especially in Hardy's poems, to begin with the assumption that the "I" of the poems is often not the poet himself. If you begin each poem by asking what kind of speaker is talking, you will likely have an easier time interpreting the poems. Just as in a novel, you would not assume that the "I" voice is the unmediated voice of the author himself, so too in Hardy's poems, the "I" voice may be – and often explicitly is – a fictional character rather than an unfiltered representation of Thomas Hardy.

The same may be said for the audience of a poem. Of course, the poem's reader is always part of the reading experience, but sometimes the reader – that is, you – may exist only implicitly in the poem, just as the author literally wrote the poem's words but may not be an explicit character therein. In many poems, an additional audience exists within the poem, and the poem's current readers are voyeurs, observing conversations among others. As you read, consider where you fit into the lives of the characters and the structure of the poem. Are you being addressed directly by the poem's speaker? Is that speaker addressing someone else and allowing you to eavesdrop? Is the speaker's voice internal, existing only in his or her own mind, and do you become privy to it by reading the poem? All of these considerations are part of recognizing how a poem functions.

If you can read any poem with all of these structural possibilities in mind – its voice, audience, patterns, sounds, situations, and philosophies – your understanding of the poem can be increased. My approach throughout this volume is to consider each poem as its own world and, through close readings and examinations of the most notable aspects of each poem, to draw larger conclusions about Hardy as a poet. If readers approach Hardy's poetry with an open mind, they will see the vast range and scope of his poetic styles and sensibilities and the degree to which he is willing to experiment with scores of stylistic and substantive possibilities. Hardy seemed to desire recognition for his poetry more than for his prose,[4] and studying his poems can illustrate the countless ways in which his poetry contributed to his world and to ours.

PART 1

ANALYSING THOMAS HARDY'S POEMS

1

Poet as Storyteller

Stories

At Casterbridge Fair (*CP* 239)

We will focus on two parts of this seven-part poem. First, we will consider the sixth of the seven poems, entitled "A Wife Waits":

> Will's at the dance in the Club-room below,
> Where the tall liquor-cups foam;
> I on the pavement up here by the Bow,
> Wait, wait, to steady him home.
>
> Will and his partner are treading a tune,
> Loving companions they be;
> Willy, before we were married in June,
> Said he loved no one but me;
>
> Said he would let his old pleasures all go
> Ever to live with his Dear.
> Will's at the dance in the Club-room below,
> Shivering I wait for him here.

Written in four-line stanzas with alternating patterns of four feet and three feet per line, this poem's rhythm resembles the raucous dancing it depicts in the fair's dance hall. Hardy's emphasis is not merely on describing the place or the scene but on telling the story of William, whose wife reports that he once "said he loved no one but me" but who now dances with a different partner. The sadness of the poem's theme counteracts its festive rhythm, comingling William's gaiety with his wife's solitude.

The dance hall becomes a location at which this small drama can play out, as the wife reports that "Will's at the dance in the Club-room below, / Shivering I wait for him here." In just twelve lines, Hardy introduces three characters – William, his wife, and his dance partner – and tells the story of a dissolving relationship and the woman who is left behind. The setting highlights that sadness exists amid the fair's apparent joy while individualizing the whirling masses who populate a fairground scene.

After reading "A Wife Waits," readers may continue to contemplate the characters' micro-narrative despite knowing that they will never see William or his wife again. Tiny stories like this one highlight the fact that an extended reading experience is not essential to creating a relationship between readers and characters. Instead, readers are meant to empathize with these characters and recognize the universality – the ordinariness – of their situations. In addition, because their little story takes place at the fair, Hardy asks readers to recognize that the fair may be only superficially joyous and to note the ways in which human misery can exist even in the face of apparent frivolity. The ordinary ways that people behave, even in special circumstances, return again and again in Hardy's works. In his stories, regardless of genre, people constantly revert not just to their basest selves but to a kind of fundamental ordinariness illustrated in the simultaneously unique and representative characters of William and his wife.

The setting matters in *At Casterbridge Fair* to the extent that it anchors the various plots, but the plots themselves, the "narratives of events," and a sense of those events' causal effects, seem to be what interest Hardy most in this series. He imagines characters' inner lives and emotions as his speakers, for instance, ask the ballad-singer to "make me forget her name, her sweet sweet look – / Make me forget her tears" and then assert that the "former beauties" at the fair must not remember the charm they once possessed: "They must forget, forget! They cannot know / What they once were, / Or memory would transfigure them, and show / Them always fair." In each of these cases, Hardy uses the fair as a way to tell the stories of the fair's participants, developing their stories by reporting on their appearances, recalling their pasts, and anticipating their futures. This sixth section of *At Casterbridge Fair* follows other short poems, each of which capture a scene from the fair: a singer diverting his audience from its worries, a scorned maiden leaving her young man behind at the dance hall, a market-girl trying to sell her wares but finding love instead, and Patty Beech searching for John Waywood to whom she was once engaged. Each poem stands alone, but the cumulative effect of the seven poems paints a picture of the fair as a whole and the human dramas that play out there.

In "After the Fair," the final poem in *At Casterbridge Fair*, Hardy returns to some of the characters he considered earlier in the series:

> The singers are gone from the Cornmarket-place
> With their broadsheets of rhymes,
> The street rings no longer in treble and bass
> With their skits on the times,
> And the Cross, lately thronged, is a dim naked space
> That but echoes the stammering chimes.
>
> From Clock-corner steps, as each quarter ding-dongs,
> Away the folk roam
> By the "Hart" and Grey's Bridge into byways and "drongs,"
> Or across the ridged loam;
> The younger ones shrilling the lately heard songs,
> The old saying, "Would we were home."
>
> The shy-seeming maiden so mute in the fair
> Now rattles and talks,
> And that one who looked the most swaggering there
> Grows sad as she walks,
> And she who seemed eaten by cankering care
> In statuesque sturdiness stalks.
>
> And midnight clears High Street of all but the ghosts
> Of its buried burghees,
> From the latest far back to those old Roman hosts
> Whose remains one yet sees,
> Who loved, laughed, and fought, hailed their friends, drank their toasts
> At their meeting-times here, just as these!

Immediately, one notices that this poem's form differs significantly from the form of "A Wife Waits." While these line lengths do alternate, the do so with less regularity, and the long lines are so long that they seem almost not to want to end. Unlike the regularity of the dance hall's rhythm, "After the Fair" has a meandering, irregular pattern, capturing the sense of the night's dragging on.

As the fairgrounds empty, one might expect Hardy's thematic emphasis to shift to the location itself, but he remains focused on the characters and their lives, in this case moving on to discuss the "ghosts" of the town's "buried burghees." The speaker is most struck by the similarities of these ghosts to the fair's current participants, and the poem's ending with ghosts reminds readers (and fair-goers) how soon they themselves will be ghosts too. The story of these long-departed fair-goers encourages readers to think about the history of a place that feels full of life but that embodies tradition too, and to focus on the human dramas that take place there. And it asks readers to see everyone's story, just as Hardy does, in his careful telling of each individual's ongoing tale.

Hardy loves to follow characters through their daily lives and to explore the actions that lead to particular consequences. In 1878, after his success with *Far From the Madding Crowd* and *The Return of the Native*, Hardy wrote that a plot "should arise from the gradual closing in of a situation that comes of ordinary human passions, prejudices, and ambitions . . ."[1] Although this idea of plot may seem to apply particularly to novels, Hardy makes it true for his poems as well. Repeatedly, we see situations closing in around characters and feel their entrapment as he explores not only their environments but also the human choices that have led to increasingly claustrophobic feelings. His ability to capture that sense is part of what makes Hardy a great storyteller, not just in prose but also in verse.

"Ice on the Highway" (*CP* 734)

An enormous number of Hardy's poems demonstrate his ability to tell stories effectively, some with significant narrative intervention and others through relatively pure observation. This brief poem captures the details of seven women's brief experience in icy weather by presenting the distanced observations of a poetic watcher who does not participate in the action of the scene. Although the women are not alluded to in the poem's title, they are clearly its subject:

> Seven buxom women abreast, and arm in arm,
> Trudge down the hill, tip-toed,
> And breathing warm;
> They must perforce trudge thus, to keep upright
> On the glassy ice-bound road,
>
> And they must get to market whether or no,
> Provisions running low
> With the nearing Saturday night,
> While the lumbering van wherein they mostly ride
> Can nowise go:
> Yet loud their laughter as they stagger and slide!

The poem's first line begins with three trochees, "**seven bux**om **wom**en," and then hiccups into an iamb, "**abreast**," an interruption in pattern which reinforces the poem's meaning, as these stocky, solid women slip along the ice. Thus readers are engaged not only by the poem's images and ideas but also by its sound; even subconsciously, that extra beat created by the switch from trochaic to iambic verse destabilizes the reader as the women themselves are destabilized in their interactions with nature.

Initially, readers know only of the women's physical characteristics and their physical support of one another. Although Hardy's narrator never enters the women's minds, the external observations build to a story: they "must get to market" to prevent their, and presumably their families', starvation. Their relative poverty is emphasized by Hardy's mention of their dilapidated van. But the final line of the poem genuinely creates the story of the poem by taking these trudging, heavy-breathing, hard-working women and depicting their loud laughter in the face of their struggles.

The story in this poem, like the stories in *At Casterbridge Fair* and in the rest of *Human Shows*, in which "Ice on the Highway" was published, leave many details of the plot up to the reader but give enough information about character, circumstance, and events to establish intriguing outlines of stories into which much more complete information can be read. In just ten lines, readers are introduced to this group of women and led to make assumptions about them, at least one of which is that their struggles dominate them. By developing a narrative trajectory that ends with the women's raucous laughter, Hardy highlights the fact that stories' arcs are not predictable and that characters can react to circumstance in any number of ways.

The readers' surprise at the end of this poem is a result of Hardy's careful plotting. He challenges readers' preconceptions of these women by humanizing characters who might, without the final line, simply reinforce readers' stereotypes of poverty and struggle. These women's ability to laugh and to remain united in the face of a cruel natural world contradicts the common views of Hardy's pessimism and naturalism by depicting women who are emotionally triumphant despite their hardships. The plot development, over the course of only ten lines, accentuates Hardy's ability to move readers through the arc of a story – its exposition, rising action, and climax – while also attending to more traditionally poetic concerns like meter, rhyme, and line breaks.

Setting

The environment in which a story takes place is central to readers' interpretations of that story, and Hardy is one of the great writers of setting.

"The Bride-Night Fire" (*CP* 71)

The first of Hardy's two wedding night poems, "The Bride-Night Fire," is subtitled "A Wessex Tradition" and tells the story of Barbree, in love with Tim Tankens but forced by her uncle to marry Naibour Sweatly.[2] One of the first things readers may notice about this poem is its use of dialect, something Hardy alludes to in the poem's subtitle, and something that helps to establish and make real the narrative's setting; the language of the poem establishes its setting just as much as the physical descriptions of place do. Dialect helps to distinguish the voice of the narrator from the characters' voices and connect readers who lack this dialect to them through the "translator" narrator. The essential plot of the poem is presented by a third-person narrator whose grammatical knowledge is clearly standard, but he repeatedly uses the vocabulary of the rural characters, a technique that establishes the legitimacy of the dialect and discourages condescension towards the characters, whose unworldly speech is no less emotionally profound than it would be in more standard syntax. Within a primarily standard English syntax, just in the first stanza the narrator employs substantial dialect vocabulary, including "Zundays," "thirtover," "wight," and "sommat," demonstrating his proficiency with code shifting. That use of "Wessex" vocabulary bridges the gap between readers who are not familiar with this rural speech and the characters in the poem who may never have heard another mode of speech. The narrator's clear familiarity with both versions of English lends the poem an air of authenticity, suggesting that the poem is written by a fellow townsperson who is able and also willing to "translate" for readers by employing Wessex vocabulary within standard English syntax.

For example, these lines include multiple voices in close proximity:

> Like a lion 'ithin en Tim's spirit outsprung –
> (Tim had a great soul when his feelings were wrung) –
> "Feel for 'ee, dear Barbree?" he cried;

In this stanza, we see the narrator's use of Wessex vocabulary in the first line, the same narrator's perfectly dialectless parenthetical statement in the second line, and Tim's heavy dialect in the third line. Barbree's language is similarly more heavily accented than the speaker's:

> "I think I mid almost ha' borne it," she said,
> Had my griefs one by one come to hand;
> But O, to be slave to thik husbird, for bread, . . .

The narrator's self-conscious use of the characters' own dialect to tell Barbree's sad story presents her as worthy of the reader's sympathy and attention; language does not separate her from the narrator but instead connects them. While the narrator demonstrates his ability to write in dialectless language, his decision to employ Barbree's vocabulary, at least in places, suggests that her authenticity is worthy of emulation. Hardy's masterful use of levels of dialect makes evident the story's setting and its importance to the plot without overtaking the poem with descriptions of setting.

The sadness and resignation Barbree feels at her arranged marriage parallel Tim's frustration and powerlessness, and the "laughing lads" at the end of the poem resemble those mocking voices in any time and any place who question a woman's purity and belittle her. Certainly the details of the characters' lives are specific to a rural environment: maypoles, manure heaps, bridle paths, pigsties, thatched roofs, and so on. But the poem's fundamental situations are universal: a woman forced to marry someone she does not love; a hard-drinking husband; an accidental disaster; a rescue by the woman's true love; and, finally, a cautiously optimistic ending. More importantly, the poem's emotions are universal, and readers are encouraged to sympathize with, understand, and associate with these rural characters. For instance, as Barbree shivers and cries, unclothed in the winter night, and Tim looks desperately for something she can wear, the narrator agrees with Tim that "There was one thing to do, and that one thing he did, / He lent her some clothes of his own, . . . " The narrator's pointing out, twice in one line, that Tim made the only choice available to him urges readers to align themselves with Tim and recognize that no one in that situation or any setting would have had any other option. Tim's action is not born out of rude country manners or uneducated superstition but arises because he, like anyone, recognizes that "there was one thing to do."

The poem ends happily, with Barbree and Tim marrying, but they are only able to do so in the face of tragedy:

> Then followed the custom-kept rout, shout, and flare
> Of a skimmity-ride through the naibourhood, ere
> Folk had proof o' wold Sweatley's decay.
> Whereupon decent people all stood in a stare,
> Saying Tim and his lodger should risk it, and pair:
> So he took her to church. An' some laughing lads there
> Cried to Tim, "After Sweatley!" She said, "I declare
> I stand as a maiden to-day!"

Throughout the poem, the tone remains dark and ominous, and even in the relatively satisfying final moments of the poem, when the two lovers head to church to wed, Barbree must continue to defend herself against a mocking rabble. The cruelty of the "skimmity-ride" ritual, in which the lovers' effigies are ridden through town on a donkey, echoes a similar scene near the end of *The Mayor of Casterbridge* that results in a woman's death from shame and shock. Thus Barbree remains a victim from beginning to end, and Hardy exaggerates her weakness and subservience as a way to criticize not her but her forced role in the story, first as a victim of her uncle's controlling tendencies, then as a victim of Sweatley's drunkenness and carelessness, and finally as a victim of the gossiping youths who publicly deride her and question her virginity. While Hardy later dismissed this poem as an immature work written by "quite a young man," it reflects concerns that can be seen throughout his narrative poems. It especially highlights his sympathy for the most vulnerable members of society, who in this case – and in most cases – include women. The setting offers a starkly alternative view to the idealized rural lives of women in the Romantic poets' works, with Hardy emphasizing the misery that exists even in an environment that had been presented in earlier nineteenth-century Britain as utopian.

"The Ruin'd Maid" (*CP* 158)

"O 'Melia, my dear, this does everything crown!
Who could have supposed I should meet you in Town?
And whence such fair garments, such prosperi-ty?" –
"O didn't you know I'd been ruined?" said she.

– "You left us in tatters, without shoes or socks,
Tired of digging potatoes, and spudding up docks;
And now you've gay bracelets and bright feathers three!" –
"Yes: that's how we dress when we're ruined," said she.

– "At home in the barton you said 'thee' and 'thou',
And 'thik oon', and 'theäs oon', and 't'other'; but now
Your talking quite fits 'ee for high compa-ny!" –
"Some polish is gained with one's ruin," said she.

"Your hands were like paws then, your face blue and bleak
But now I'm bewitched by your delicate cheek,
And your little gloves fit as on any la-dy!" –
"We never do work when we're ruined," said she.

"You used to call home-life a hag-ridden dream,
And you'd sigh, and you'd sock; but at present you seem
To know not of megrims or melancho-ly!" –
"True. One's pretty lively when ruined," said she.

"I wish I had feathers, a fine sweeping gown,
And a delicate face, and could strut about Town!" –
"My dear – a raw country girl, such as you be,
Cannot quite expect that. You ain't ruined," said she.

In "The Ruin'd Maid," one of Hardy's best-known and most anthologized poems, Hardy creates two compelling characters who are, in some ways, "before" and "after" halves of the same character, an approach that highlights his storytelling techniques and, especially, his use of setting. This narrative functions both literally and metaphorically, with setting serving as the primary difference between the two women. This early poem presents a dialogue between a young country girl visiting town and 'Melia, a "ruined" girl who lives a life of urban luxury. It articulates the changes that have occurred in 'Melia's demeanor and dress and speech and presents ruin as an enviable social advancement. Issues of class and of how money alters behavior are subtexts in this brief poem, which is often read – probably falsely – as an unusually comic addition to Hardy's oeuvre.

The form of the poem resembles a song, as do many of Hardy's poems, especially in its regular line and stanza lengths and its use of a repeated choral element: "' . . . ruined,' said she." Rather than a narrative ballad, like "The Bride-Night Fire," "The Ruin'd Maid" follows a verse-and-refrain pattern. Each stanza is rhythmically and structurally parallel, and that structural parallelism extends to the speakers' voices and the stanzas' content. Each stanza begins with 'Melia's country acquaintance commenting, for two lines, on some aspect of 'Melia's former country life. The third line contrasts the early part of each stanza with her current, city existence. And in the fourth line of each stanza, which serves as the song's repeating chorus, 'Melia speaks, reminding her friend of the reason for her changed circumstances: "O didn't you know I'd been ruined?" The third, narrative voice in the poem appears only once in each stanza, with the final words "said she." While the narrator here might not seem to have a particularly important role – he says hardly anything at all – his regular reappearance at the end of each stanza reminds readers that there are external characters observing this interaction, and thus readers are aligned with that relatively quiet observer since readers, like the narrator, observe the dialogue and analyze the characters from an external vantage point. As outsiders, readers are able to see the ways in which the two characters speak different languages and exist in different locations, reflecting on the same ideas but unable fully to communicate.

What we notice especially in the characters of these two women is their potential interchangeability. Although 'Melia is now decked out and newly sophisticated, a sexually-corrupted version of Eliza Doolittle, she was once as rustic and naïve as her interlocutor, who clearly has the potential, as well as the desire, to become ruined herself. "Ruin" here is presented as a privileged state, and as perhaps the only escape from the poverty and hardship of country life. Each stanza emphasizes another way in which 'Melia has improved herself: in the first stanza, she is newly prosperous; in the second, the focus is on her gay and bright clothing; the third highlights the new sophistication of her speech; the fourth stanza shows 'Melia's improved physical state; and the fifth is about her happier manner and attitude. Although each stanza returns in its last line to 'Melia's ruin, the final stanza presents the country girl's explicit envy of 'Melia's new life: "– 'I wish I had feathers, a fine sweeping gown, / And a delicate face, and could strut about Town!' –"

Many critics read this poem as humorous, and there is indeed a note of dark comedy in the play on the word "ruin" and in the characters' almost willful misunderstanding of one another. Clearly, for 'Melia and her acquaintance, "ruin" hardly means what readers are supposed to think it means; if anything, ruin for these characters signals a significantly better life. And the irony of 'Melia's improved life, not just in her appearance and material well-being but even in her self-satisfaction, underscores the humor that grows from the confounding of readers' expectations. Particularly because Hardy's poems are so often bleak, readers might anticipate that a poem called "The Ruin'd Maid" will offer the same unremitting pessimism as some of his other poems. Instead, though, readers are treated to a relatively happy poem, such as it is, with a character who seems, unlike the more obviously manipulated Barbree in "The Bride-Night Fire," content with her lot and her position in life. Her change of locale has led her to deeper, more satisfying changes.

Nonetheless, the humor that some readers see here may be a misreading. Certainly the tone does differ from some of Hardy's other poems, but that tone only serves to emphasize the tragedy of the characters' circumstances, regardless of setting. What readers are asked to recognize in "The Ruin'd Maid" is that, despite its surprises, it is as bleak and miserable as "The Bride-Night Fire," because 'Melia and her friend are both essentially hopeless despite 'Melia's relative self-satisfaction. In "The Bride-Night Fire," Barbree is fully trapped by circumstance and selfish male decision making. "The Ruin'd Maid," too, shows that women are offered only very limited options: to suffer interminably or to be exploited by men. The fact that 'Melia herself does not recognize the tragedy of her circumstances but seems only to notice that she has chosen the better of the two options does not lessen the catastrophe of the situation. Actually, one might argue that 'Melia's inability to perceive any other options for her life makes this poem even more miserable than some of Hardy's other poems, where at least some level of knowledge on the part of the characters might lessen the reader's unhappiness on their behalfs. The locations of the two women determine the type of misery to which they are subject, and so readers see, as country and city collide, the ways in which the characters are shaped and manipulated by their environments. Readers recognize that neither is really better off, regardless of the characters' possible feelings to the contrary, but they suffer in different ways. By juxtaposing two settings, Hardy allows each woman's location to determine her circumstances and character, a technique that highlights the locations' importance to the women.

Hardy's novels are known for their beautifully descriptive passages about the English countryside, and the characters are carefully placed into environments that enhance, mirror, and complement their situations. Often for Hardy, setting is not incidental to the poems but central to characters' actions and interactions, a fact that has long been noted in novels like *The Return of the Native* and *The Mayor of*

Casterbridge. The same is obviously true in the narrative poems we have just considered.

Hardy's poetic settings achieve both a particularizing, by making the characters unique beings in specific surroundings, and a universalizing, by showing that even characters in these particular places experience fundamental human emotions that are shared regardless of environment. Even as Hardy emphasizes characters and their stories in his poems, readers are drawn to the settings in which the narratives occur. By creating characters, like 'Melia and Barbree and Tim, whose emotions and reactions are universal, even if their setting is notably particular, Hardy encourages readers to feel connections with characters who may exist outside their familiar circles. The strangeness of the characters' circumstances is belied by the commonness of their emotions and the familiarity of the stock characters who exist around them.

Character

"Ah, Are You Digging on My Grave?" (*CP* 330)

"Ah, are you digging on my grave,
        My loved one? – planting rue?"
– "No: yesterday he went to wed
One of the brightest wealth has bred.
'It cannot hurt her now,' he said,
        'That I should not be true.'"

"Then who is digging on my grave?
        My nearest dearest kin?"
– "Ah, no: they sit and think, 'What use!
What good will planting flowers produce?
No tendance of her mound can loose
        Her spirit from Death's gin.'"

"But some one digs upon my grave?
        My enemy? – prodding sly?"
– "Nay: when she heard you had passed the Gate
That shuts on all flesh soon or late,

She thought you no more worth her hate,
      And cares not where you lie."

"Then, who is digging on my grave?
        Say – since I have not guessed!"
– "O it is I, my mistress dear,
Your little dog, who still lives near,
And much I hope my movements here
        Have not disturbed your rest?"

"Ah, yes! *You* dig upon my grave. . . .
        Why flashed it not on me
That one true heart was left behind!
What feeling do we ever find
To equal among human kind
        A dog's fidelity!"

"Mistress, I dug upon your grave
        To bury a bone, in case
I should be hungry near this spot
When passing on my daily trot.
I am sorry, but I quite forgot
        It was your resting-place."

While some of Hardy's characters may wonder why they were born, they at least have the advantage of being alive to consider the question. The main character in "Ah, Are You Digging on My Grave?" is in a far worse position than many of Hardy's miserable sufferers, and the tremendous pathos of this poem, spoken from the perspective of a dead young woman, explores this ghostly character by imagining her continued posthumous existence. Even from the title, readers are made aware of the pathos of the poem as well as the fact that it is written in a voice other than that of the poet. Here, readers are privy to a ghostly voice, a technique Hardy frequently employs, as we will see in later chapters. This ghost, despite her fairly hopeless position, is neither haunting a human speaker nor particularly troubled. Instead, she wonders optimistically who is digging on her grave. Hardy presents this speaker as blinded by her death and burial – that is, she cannot see who is digging on her grave – but either she is still capable of hearing the digging or she is able to feel the vibrations and scratching above her. Of course, the literal place and physical abilities of this ghost are less important to the poem than the fact that she maintains a hopeful attitude, despite having died young, and embraces the belief that her family and friends are still thinking of her and visiting her grave. The storytelling here is heavily moralistic, and the characters created through the poem ask readers to find obvious fault with some and tremendous sympathy for others. By creating a pathetic character with whom readers are asked to identify through a highly unusual narrative perspective, Hardy demonstrates one approach to characterization. Significant pieces of the speaker's former existence and current personality can be deduced from this presentation.

As the reader progresses through the stanzas, the speaker's initial sense of hope fades. At the beginning, the ghost hopes that her lover is visiting her, mourning her loss, but we hear through the narrator that the lover has just wed another. His statement, "It cannot hurt her now, / That I should not be true" is a fairly widely-held belief, but because Hardy writes this poem with so much pathos, that lack of fidelity is presented as a real flaw on the part of the lover. While most readers probably feel comfortable with the idea that a young man might yet wed following the death of his first love, here he is called "untrue" for doing so. The young man is expected not only to mourn for his lost love, a reasonable expectation, but also to remain true to her, apparently forever. Hardy sees the ghost as so alive here that her lover's marriage indicates his abandonment of her.

In the following stanza, the ghost hopes that the digging she perceives is being done by her family, but she is soon disabused of that notion by a report of the family members, who "sit and think, 'What use! / What good will planting flowers produce?'" As in the previous stanza, the family is presented as being at fault for disregarding her grave. Of course, their belief that planting flowers will not undo her death is perfectly true, but Hardy nonetheless implies that they are callous and uncaring. They do seem to lament her death, but they do not behave in a way that he feels is sufficiently respectful of her memory. Particularly because the narrator is aware of the ghost's continued "existence" while the family members are not, he seems to respond most emotionally to her posthumous abandonment, or perhaps this narrator simply approaches the dead woman's questions with straightforward truth, not attempting to sweeten the situation.

The next stanza follows a similar pattern: does an enemy dig on the grave? No, the enemy "thought you no more worth her hate, / And cares not where you lie." While this might be a positive development, even this abandonment of hatred is presented in this poem as misguided. The poem seems to proclaim that all of these people are mistaken in their belief that the young woman has died and that they should instead continue to live their lives holding on to their love, their familial responsibilities, and even their hatred; anything less is a denial of her existence, such as it is.

Eventually, readers, along with the ghost, discover that her old faithful dog digs at the grave. Finally, the reader might reasonably feel, there is some relief from the unrelenting misery of this poem. Even if humans have not felt sufficient responsibility towards this dead woman, her dog has not forgotten her. Unfortunately, even that small hope is misplaced here: the last stanza reports that the dog was simply digging to bury a bone. This final twist of the knife demonstrates that the poem's issue is not simply with human insensitivity but with a kind of earthly forgetting; even loyal animals forget their masters. The whole world has forgotten her too soon, the poem suggests. It is not clear from the poem just how soon this forgetting has taken place: is it merely months? Years? The poem hints that any amount of time is too soon, though, and that readers should feel guilty for any similar offenses toward the dead.

The sympathy in this poem clearly lies with the ghost, with whom the narrator empathizes. And after the final stanza, readers realize that the narrator was all along the dog, who plays a sad guessing game with the young woman. No one but the narrator and the dog even acknowledge the existence of the ghost, and only the dog has an awareness of her continued otherworldly existence simply because he happened to be in the graveyard and could hear her. The lover and the family speak of her only in the third person, neglecting to address her because they do not realize she continues to reside in the cemetery; the enemy does not speak of her at all, having decided that her former hatred was no longer worth her time. The ghost is the most human (and humane) character in this poem, which may make readers feel her loss, and others' forgetfulness, more acutely.

The dog/narrator is positioned as the single observer who recognizes her plight, and the reader is privileged to overhear their conversation. This animal-speaker's voice appears in this poem as a storyteller; his awareness of both the ghost's existence and the happenings of the living world allows him to serve as an intermediary, telling her, and simultaneously the reader, about the actions of her lover, her family, and her enemy. This perspective creates a heightened sense of pathos as well as a bitter joke because the ghost is alone, except for a dog who, despite feeling at least a bit apologetic, has also forgotten her.

Hardy's use of characterization here is an extreme version of what we saw in "A Wife Waits" and "After the Fair." In an effort to give voice to the voiceless, Hardy goes to some extremes, but a person does not get much more voiceless than when she is dead, so here he embodies the dead woman, imagines her concerns, and articulates them for readers, who are put in the uncomfortable position of both knowing people who have died – and possibly treating them with the same "disrespect" confronted by this ghost – and facing the prospect of eventual death themselves, perhaps wondering if their families, friends, enemies, and even pets will be equally forgetful. The central character of the poem is not "real" in the usual sense of that term, but the real fears about death that Hardy explores – "When I am alive and another is dead, is it ethical for me to 'move on'?" "When I am dead, will I be remembered?" – are captured by his creation of this pathetic (and pathetically hopeful) character whose situation is obviously quite strange but whose fears and desires are universal.

"The Country Wedding" (*CP* 650)

A parallel poem to "The Bride-Night Fire," and a poem that again explores characterization, is another country wedding poem that was written at the end rather than the beginning of Hardy's career and that features similarly compelling, multi-dimensional characters despite its brevity.

The Country Wedding
(*A Fiddler's story*)

Little fogs were gathered in every hollow,
But the purple hillocks enjoyed fine weather
As we marched with our fiddles over the heather
 – How it comes back! – to their wedding that day.

Our getting there brought our neighbours and all, O!
Till, two and two, the couples stood ready.
And her father said: "Souls, for God's sake, be steady!"
And we strung up our fiddles, and sounded out "A."

The groomsman he stared, and said, "You must follow!"
But we'd gone to fiddle in front of the party,
(Our feelings as friends being true and hearty)
And fiddle in front we did – all the way.

Yes, from their door by Mill-tail-Shallow,
And up Styles-Lane, and by Front-Street houses,
Where stood maids, bachelors, and spouses,
Who cheered the songs that we knew how to play.

I bowed the treble before her father,
Michael the tenor in front of the lady,
The bass-viol Reub – and right well played he! –
The serpent Jim; ay, to church and back.

I thought the bridegroom was flurried rather,
As we kept up the tune outside the chancel,
While they were swearing things none can cancel
Inside the walls to our drumstick's whack.

"Too gay!" she pleaded. "Clouds may gather,
And sorrow come." But she gave in, laughing,
And by supper-time when we'd got to the quaffing
Her fears were forgot, and her smiles weren't slack.

A grand wedding 'twas! And what would follow
We never thought. Or that we should have buried her

On the same day with the man that married her,
A day like the first, half hazy, half clear.

Yes: little fogs were in every hollow,
Though the purple hillocks enjoyed fine weather,
When we went to play 'em to church together,
And carried 'em there in an after year.

The form of this poem, which readers might expect to resemble a song or ballad, as so many of Hardy's poems do, instead adopts a complex and uncommon pattern of rhymes. The middle two lines of each stanza rhyme with each other, which usually creates a sing-songy feeling; but, unusually, the first and last lines of each stanza do not rhyme with each other but with the first and last lines in each stanza. After the first four stanzas, the rhymes change from a first line ending with a long "o" and a lasts line ending with a long "a" to consonant endings: "father," "rather," and "gather" in the first lines and "back," "whack," and "slack" in the last lines. Those harsher ending sounds may begin to prepare readers for what is to come, and when the last two stanzas return to opening rhymes of long "o" sounds but end with "clear" and "year," the rhymes seem to have progressed from the open-ended possibilities of the early stanzas to the closed finality of the last line.

Although the poem has a happier, lighter tone throughout than "The Bride-Night Fire," its morbid ending and oddly unsatisfying rhyme scheme suggest a darker poem overall. The narrative is offered from the perspective of a fiddler, whose job is to make happy events even more joyous through music. In this case, though, the bride complains that too much happiness might "jinx" her wedding. Of course, as it turns out, the bride's concerns were not misplaced, and the final two stanzas of the poem lament the bride and groom's deaths just a year later, in what readers can only assume was some terrible tragedy that would have caused two premature deaths on the same day.

While in "The Bride-Night Fire," the speaker is not identified, and so readers might assume that it is Hardy himself, in "The Country Wedding," the speaker is identified as another fictional character, telling a story to the readers. Naturally, Hardy has created the fiddler as well as the bride and groom, and, in doing so, he has removed himself farther from the story, asking readers to approach the bride and groom's story through the fiddler's narrative. The creation of an additional level of remove from the narrative highlights the qualities of all these characters, not just the couple but the seemingly incidental fiddler as well. Readers thus consider the fiddler's life and situation as well as the couple's. While the bride's primary emotions on her wedding day were worry and anxiety, the fiddler remained confident; now, though, at the time of his retelling of the story, he clearly feels regret and sadness at remembering that day.

At the time of the wedding, the fiddler uses his music to prompt the bride to push aside her misgivings, and he dismisses her concerns as foolish and superstitious. Clearly this apparently mistaken attitude continues to haunt him, though, as he remarks, only a stanza later, "And what would follow / We never thought." The character's inability to have recognized the rightness of the bride's superstitious feeling is here mildly mocked, implying that he should have trusted her and made the music less gay in order to ward off the "clouds" that she feared. But, as in "The Bride-Night Fire," the woman's views are insufficiently attended to, and an unwillingness on the part of male characters to consider the woman's feelings leads, inevitably, to tragedy. The fiddler seems, years later, to have concluded that the bride was correct and therefore to have internalized some of the superstition that he once derided.

Although the subtitle of "The Country Wedding: A Fiddler's Story" might feel misplaced – this is the story of the lovers, after all, not really the story of the fiddler – it becomes his story because of the way that the events of the marriage and its subsequent tragedy have stuck with him. That use of titling and subtitling is part of Hardy's strength as a storyteller, and he uses those places of narrative distance to point readers in the right interpretative direction, leading them to focus on the characters towards whom he directs them. This is, ultimately, the fiddler's story, despite the fact that readers might not initially recognize that fact in the text itself. It is a story from his distant past, as is evidenced by the fiddler's early exclamation "How it comes back!" as he retells it. He remembers every detail, from the weather to the bride's relatives to each of the instrumentalists' names. And the sad outcome continues to plague him, making these strangers' story into his story and again allowing him to serve as an intermediary between the characters of the narrative and readers, who are asked to feel a similar level of empathy. Because readers see the lovers through the fiddler's eyes, they recognize that his version of their story may differ from the lovers' version; his sense of guilt at having played a part (literally) in their misfortune puts him rather than them at the center of this retelling.

In this wedding poem as well as in "The Bride-Night Fire," Hardy highlights the distinctions between male and female characters. The woman's voice in both wedding poems is showcased through her speech, but the narration and the occurrences within the poem are controlled by men, whose intuitive sense of how the world works is presented as inevitably and tragically misguided, always to the detriment of the female characters. Each poem's wisdom lies with the woman, but she is, almost as a matter of course, not listened to by the characters in the poem, a fact that Hardy highlights in his sympathetic presentation. This presentation also reflects Hardy's narrative sensibility, which offers readers the opportunity to interpret and evaluate the poems' characters at the same time that Hardy manipulates readers to identify with certain characters and not with others. By creating a hierarchy of characters, some round and others flat, Hardy again applies his rich background as a storyteller to his verse.

Just as Hardy's use of setting both particularizes and universalizes his stories, so too does his creation of characters within the poems. His characters often differ starkly from himself – in age, gender, experience, profession, voice, and circumstance – but his universalist notions of humanity suggest that there is something of him, and of everyone, even in the most obscure characters. What is interesting about each of his characters is not just how they diverge from himself or from his readers but how they mirror him, and, by extension, us.

In this poem, as in "Ah, Are You Digging on My Grave?" we see how Hardy cultivates and develops his characters to embody generic human traits and, at the same time, to be kind and fair to ordinary characters by giving voice to the voiceless. Benjamin Sankey argues that Hardy's plots in the novels are not "a straightforward expression of his conception of the universe, but rather an intentional exaggeration, even a caricature, of it," but he also notes that Hardy's characters are credible not "by a sustained attention to what is special about them, but by a knack of embodying ordinary traits distinctly, and by a habit of fairness to run-of-the-mill human motive."[3] According to Sankey, then, the novels' characters embody the same dichotomy we see in the poems' characters: an emphasis on individuality that is ultimately subsumed by commonality. By understanding and then illustrating these average human motivations, Hardy draws connections among all people in various circumstances to create an overarching sense of humanity.

In studying Hardy's use of character, we should begin consistently to notice the perspective from which a poem is spoken. This is always an important first step in reading any poem, but it is especially essential when reading Hardy. While many readers of poetry assume that the speaker of a poem and the author of the poem are inevitably one and the same, in fact, poets frequently create characters who serve as narrators, just as novelists do. Hardy is especially adept at this kind of character development, and while many critical readers of Hardy assume that he is necessarily the speaker of his own poems — and chances are that some of his poems are more autobiographical than others — we can see from the poems in this chapter that he also approaches poems as opportunities to tell stories and create fictional narrators just as he had done in his novels. Thus the universal aspects of his characters should be noted, but so should the characteristics that make each character unique.

Dialogue

In addition to creating remarkable characters and stories and putting them into thought-provoking settings, Hardy is also a master of constructing dialogue. While many readers might consider dialogue a hallmark of prose fiction rather than poetry, Hardy's poems often include complex and multilayered conversations among characters, whose distinct voices create connections between themselves and their readers without the constant intermediary of a narrator's voice. Dialogue's play with language and voice helps Hardy to enact all of his other storytelling techniques: it advances a plot, exposes readers to the characters' environments in their own words, and enhances and deepens characterization.

"The Curate's Kindness" (*CP* 208)

An excellent example of Hardy's use of multiple layers of conversation is "The Curate's Kindness: A Workhouse Irony," a poem that offers readers a dynamic and compelling speaker who engages and entertains readers despite his surprising views.

> The Curate's Kindness
> *A Workhouse Irony*
>
> I
> I thought they'd be strangers aroun' me,
> But she's to be there!
> Let me jump out o' waggon and go back and drown me
> At Pummery or Ten-Hatches Weir.
>
> II
> I thought: "Well, I've come to the Union –
> The workhouse at last –
> After honest hard work all the week, and Communion
> O' Zundays, these fifty years past.
>
> III
> "'Tis hard; but," I thought, "never mind it:
> There's gain in the end:
> And when I get used to the place I shall find it
> A home, and may find there a friend.
>
> IV
> "Life there will be better than t'other,
> For peace is assured.
> *The men in one wing and their wives in another*
> Is strictly the rule of the Board."
>
> V
> Just then one young
> Pa'son arriving Steps up out of breath

To the side o' the waggon wherein we were driving
To Union; and calls out and saith:

VI
"Old folks, that harsh order is altered,
Be not sick of heart!
The Guardians they poohed and they pished and they paltered
When urged not to keep you apart.

VII
"'It is wrong,' I maintained, 'to divide them,
Near forty years wed.' 'Very well, sir.
We promise, then, they shall abide them
In one wing together,' they said."

VIII
Then I sank — knew 'twas quite a foredone thing
That misery should be
To the end! . . . To get freed of her there was the one thing
Had made the change welcome to me.

IX
To go there was ending but badly;
'Twas shame and 'twas pain;
"But anyhow," thought I, "thereby I shall gladly
Get free of this forty years' chain."

X
I thought they'd be strangers aroun' me,
But she's to be there!
Let me jump out o' waggon and go back and drown me
At Pummery or Ten-Hatches Weir.

As in the two wedding poems, readers must initially attend to both the title and subtitle before moving on to the verses. In this case, "The Curate's Kindness" intimates one kind of poem while "A Workhouse Irony" suggests another. Holding the title and subtitle in their minds, readers can approach the poem with the question of whether the curate was truly kind or whether his kindness was the irony. The title might lead readers to believe that this was a truly kind curate, but the subtitle might make them think that he was actually a cruel curate with the word "kindness" being used ironically. The dialogue then helps readers to understand and interpret the motivations of each speaking character.

Eventually readers see that, although the poem is fairly simple in its vocabulary, Hardy has created a complicated web of emotions that speak to his understanding of humanity, each strand of which exists in a different character's voice. In this poem, no character is intentionally cruel, and so the "curate's kindness" is not ironic at all. In fact, the curate goes out of his way to be kind. The irony, instead, lies in the interpretation of the word "kindness," which the curate understands to mean that he goes to great lengths to keep the speaker and his wife together. For the speaker, though, "kindness" would have meant separation from his wife, a fact the curate could hardly have been expected to realize and that readers only learn through their exposure to the poor man's internal dialogue.

Hardy's use of dialogue creates dramatic irony in this poem, in which the irony is known only to the poem's readers and to Hardy, because only readers are privy both to the words of the curate and to the musings of the narrator, who expresses to readers his innermost thoughts. The speaker longs to be separated from his wife, to "get free of this forty years' chain." But the curate of the workhouse, in his effort to offer some kindness to the speaker, has allowed for a change in the rules in order that the man and his wife might continue to live together. While this sort of misunderstanding might be read as humorous, Hardy presents it as having more sinister overtones, not just for this individual speaker but also for how life works in general. Each character's voice communicates to the poem's readers, but the characters neglect to communicate fully with each other.

The poem's dialogic construction allows readers to see the story from several sides and thus gives them knowledge to which none of the poem's characters are entitled. First, Hardy presents the speaker's voice in his own head, which begins to tell the speaker's story before introducing the other characters. The first two lines could certainly be read, initially, as an exclamation of relief. Hardy thus sets readers up for a surprise as they uncover the poem's irony for themselves. The next three stanzas also confide the thoughts of the speaker directly to the reader, but they do so in a more self-referential way; the speaker tells readers what he had been thinking in the past, and those thoughts appear in quotation marks: " 'Life will be better than t'other, / For peace is assured. / *The men in one wing and their wives in another* / Is strictly the rule of the Board.' " The speaker's past thoughts are framed by his unquoted opening (current) thoughts, so readers are privy to the speaker's unmediated thoughts and then to feelings that occurred in the past and that are more carefully prepared, almost as spoken monologue. In addition, readers can see the speaker quoting the rules of the Workhouse Board, which appear in italics within the quotation marks of the man's thoughts. All of these different voices in the opening stanzas – the speaker with his recent revelation, the speaker with his past beliefs, and the Board as quoted in a rulebook – require that readers not only decipher the different emotions but also negotiate the various tales being simultaneously told and that they hear each voice individually.

The fifth stanza again employs the voice of the unmediated narrator, but in this case the voice describes external actions of another rather than his own musings, so he serves as a narrator of his own story. The sixth stanza quotes the curate, and the seventh stanza, a bit confusingly, is written in the voice of the curate quoting himself and then quoting his supervisors.

Important aspects of this poem to note are the quotation marks themselves, which serve as markers to distinguish who is speaking and in what circumstance. The seventh stanza offers multiple sets of quotation marks to help readers differentiate among the curate speaking now, the curate speaking in the past, and the Workhouse Board members speaking in the past. Stanzas eight through ten finally return to the simpler unquoted narrator, who speaks to readers without any intermediary.

The primary irony of the poem is that the speaker is being done a "kindness" that he does not want, and part of what Hardy highlights is that people, even perfectly well-intentioned people, do not understand one another. A kindness from one person's perspective is a cruelty from another, and, in almost every case in Hardy's verse, as well as in the novels, circumstances result in greater cruelty being perpetuated. Perhaps this regular result demonstrates people's unwillingness to be satisfied, but Hardy seems more strongly to be arguing that, in fact, everyone's fate is ultimately misery. The world is simply tilted towards sadness, and the great irony of "The Curate's Kindness" is that the world's unfortunate leaning will have its way in spite of man's best intentions and most noble efforts. An additional irony here is that only readers – those who exist outside the poem and who cannot communicate with the participants to clarify their positions – can have full knowledge, which leaves readers in a situation of impotence and frustration. Perhaps they can be humored by this little tale, but they are also stymied by it and by the truth of its revelation: despite layers of speakers and many efforts at dialogic communication, full communication can never be realized, and that fundamental truth leaves humans frequently miserable.

Concluding Discussion

Throughout his works of any genre, Hardy is attentive to issues most frequently associated with narrative: plot, setting, character, and dialogue. These aspects of Hardy's writing might be seen as hallmarks of prose fiction that Hardy adapts and reshapes into prosody, but they are also markers of great storytelling, and Hardy is a quintessential storyteller. His poems are not merely the later works of a beloved novelist but the writings of an author who cares about the stories he tells at least as much as the philosophies he espouses, an approach to poetry that is, in itself, a literary philosophy.

The poems in this chapter serve as representative, but far from comprehensive, examples of Hardy's storytelling techniques. Each poem chosen here could easily have been replaced by any number of other examples, but I selected these to draw attention to the various ways in which his poems tell stories. In each case, the categories might also be complicated by noting that poems about interesting characters also feature significant settings, poems whose hallmark is skillful dialogue also include intriguing characters, and so on.

Hardy the storyteller is not a common voyeur but someone who wants to understand others and offer momentary windows into their lives. By voicing the concerns and telling the stories of the voiceless, he finds fundamental humanity in each of his characters. The pathos of his often powerless, unfortunate, or mistreated characters emphasizes the many ways that they are trapped in their lives and their locations, but they are seldom treated patronizingly or with condescension. Instead, the tragedies that beset them are not particularly different from those that Hardy believes beset everyone, and their experiences only differ from those of more empowered characters in their details, not in the depth of their feelings.

As Hardy creates and develops characters, readers observe his concerns with gender and its accompanying imbalance of power, which become clearer in the poems of love and death that follow shortly. For characters like 'Melia, Barbree, the dead bride, and the neglected ghost, gender remains consistently the identifying feature that weakens and traps them. While male characters – like Tim Tankens and the husband in "The Curate's Kindness" – are also imprisoned in their own lives, the women are treated by Hardy's narrators sympathetically and with a consistent sense that they could do better for themselves if only they were not commodified, ignored, discounted, and abused.

The plots that Hardy constructs repeatedly show characters trapped by circumstance, sometimes of their own making, sometimes caused by the carelessness or malice of others, and sometimes by the whims of the world, or fate, or God. None of his stories, even the ones with ostensibly "happy endings," like "The Bride-Night Fire," really feels joyful or optimistic. Instead, the poems reflect the various kinds of miseries to which people are constantly subject, but they do so with a sense of resignation and a realization that each story's characters are unique and individual. They also sometimes demonstrate, as "Ice on the Highway" does, that painful circumstances need not lead to pained reactions. The most common trajectory for Hardy's poems is a cyclical pattern of hope followed by disappointment, but the hopes and disappointments vary, and occasionally characters do escape from that pattern.

Hardy's careful construction of setting also helps him to underscore his characters' basic humanity and the universality of their stories. For instance, the superstition and primitivism of country life are presented not as necessarily better or worse than the emptiness and vapidity of city life, as readers can see in "The Ruin'd Maid." 'Melia was given the opportunity to make a "choice" for herself as Barbree was not, but neither city nor country represents the kind of idealized freedom and mastery of self that one might hope for. And the rural women in "Ice on the Highway," who by any objective measure suffer with their circumstance, nonetheless laugh together and support one another through their trials. By making setting a vivid part of his poems, Hardy emphasizes his empathy for suffering humanity anywhere and argues for his apparent belief that human life is comparable across the various geographical boundaries that people may establish for themselves.

His use of distinctive and varied voices also reinforces this humanitarian sensibility. The poems, through their articulation of individuals' voices, feel like one – usually the only – outlet where otherwise silenced voices can be heard. Ghosts, for instance, seldom have a chance to air their concerns in real life (so to speak), yet Hardy vividly imagines their pain and gives voice to the voiceless. Only one step beyond these maltreated ghosts, are the similarly abused women, whose lives are nearly as doomed as those of the woman who died young. Throughout Hardy's poetic narratives, regardless of the tone or approach, a person who would ordinarily not be heard – whose appearance or lack of education or poverty might make her an unlikely subject for poetry – is given an opportunity to speak.

Hardy's use of voices separates his poetry from many others'. His poetry asks that readers pay special attention to language, dialect, and the varied voices of the speakers. While Hardy's speakers often face similar problems, the characters are developed through their modes of speech. Look, for instance, at the divergent speech patterns of the dismayed husband and the "kind" curate in "The Curate's Kindness." The husband's words are cut short and signal certain qualities: his lack of education, his poverty, and his powerlessness relative to the articulate and polished curate. As the husband says, colloquially, "Let me jump out o' waggon and go back and drown me . . . ," the curate speaks forcefully and with a sense of his own importance: "'It is wrong,' I maintained, 'to divide them, / Near forty years wed.'" The differences in these two characters' voices point to aspects of the poem worth noting: that the husband's incapacity to change his lot both grows from his inarticulateness and is perpetuated by it. While the ostensible topics of the poem are the plight of the speaker, his relationship with his wife, and the curate's ineffective effort to fulfill the speaker's needs, an additional topic of the poem is language itself. The power of language becomes clear when the curate expresses pride in his own ability to convince the Guardians that the husband and wife should remain together, and in the concurrent inability of the husband to argue otherwise. The curate proudly quotes himself, using the forceful "I maintained" to demonstrate his communicative ability, at the same time showing readers how fully he has misunderstood the husband's wishes. Language equals power in this poem, as is so often the case in Hardy's verse.

Not only are the characters' voices important, though; the voice of the narrator, who might often be assumed to be Hardy, is also consistently significant. The narrator serves as a kind of moral compass, pointing readers towards the appropriate emotions and reactions to each poem. This narrative quality may be most evident in "Ah, Are You Digging on My Grave?" in which the narrator pushes the poem's readers towards responses they might not otherwise have. Because the poem seems to feel so strongly about the neglect of the young woman's grave, readers are similarly pushed in that direction, even though they might (reasonably) not have felt that neglecting her grave was so, well, grave. The perspectives of the narrators, especially those who are distanced from the poems' actions, present the speaker as reporter, and yet the narrator seldom achieves complete objectivity.

Methods of Analysis

Because these poems include multiple voices, paying attention to voice is a methodology most useful for Hardy's work. One technique we have used consistently in this chapter is an examination of voice. Who is speaking at any given moment? What can we learn not only from that person's words but from his or her manner of speech? Hardy asks us to notice quotation marks and quotations within quotations.

We have also begun to explore the idea of narrative in verse, asking what it means for a story to be told in the form of a poem.

Different kinds of stories are being told here, and we want to differentiate among them, too. The story of "The Ruin'd Maid" takes place between two characters, and readers are given the opportunity to overhear their dialogue. Other narrative poems, though, offer multiple layers of narrative, like "The Curate's Kindness," "The Bride-Night Fire," or "The Country Wedding." In those poems, not only does a narrative exist at the center of the poem – the story of Barbree and Tim or of the curate's defense of marriage or of the ill-fated bride and groom – but there is an additional narrative layer between some character and the reader. In the case of "The Country Wedding," the musician speaks to the reader or some other, unnamed, internal character to recall that wedding from long ago. Is the poem's primary story the tale of a bride and groom who died tragically? Or is it the story of a musician haunted by superstition and the possibility of his role, however unlikely, in their untimely deaths? As readers of these poems, we must be able to see the simultaneous stories being told and determine which one has primacy and, more importantly, why they are being told together. The filters through which a narrative is presented necessarily affect the way in which we read the narrative, so here we have practiced attending to such details.

One literary technique that we may also consider more a part of novels than poems is an emphasis on setting. But in Hardy's poems, as we have already seen, setting shapes character, tone, and voice, and therefore understanding setting is essential to understanding other aspects of the poem. By focusing in this chapter on the locations of the characters in addition to their stories, we are able to observe how setting provides clues to the narrative. For instance, the juxtaposition of settings in "The Ruin'd Maid" is essential to understanding 'Melia's development over time. There, though, the setting is referred to explicitly, so even without examining setting we would understand its centrality to the themes of the poem. But in a poem where setting is less explicitly stated, like "The Bride-Night Fire," it is nonetheless central to our understanding of the characters, their motivations, and their interactions.

In addition to these storytelling principles, we have begun to note how form and content interact, by looking at line lengths, stanza forms, rhyme schemes, and patterns of stressed and unstressed syllables. All of these concerns will carry through the rest of our readings, and we will continue to consider how form and content complement each other.

Finally, in this chapter we have learned how important it is to read the poems' titles. Often the titles give clues to our interpretation that would not be clear from the poem itself. In some cases, the title simply prepares us for what is to come, as in "The Bride-Night Fire." Before we begin reading this poem, we already know at least two of the events that will occur. In other cases, the title intentionally does not prepare us for the poem, as in "The Country Wedding," which we would imagine to be an uplifting poem, and "The Ruin'd Maid," which we might expect to be much sadder than it seems on first reading. Sometimes, as in "After the Fair," the title merely sets the scene, but even there, information is doled out to us with great consideration. And, in still other cases, the title may provide information that is not given to us in the poem, or speak in a voice that does not exist in the poem. "The Curate's Kindness: A Workhouse Irony," for instance, includes information, voice and tone that do not all occur in the poem. We are never told, in the poem itself, that the tone is ironic, so the subtitle both prepares us for and confirms our suspicions of the poem's irony; the title itself reinforces that irony with the word "kindness." For Hardy, titles can set the scene, introduce characters, begin to establish plot, and influence readers' interpretations of characters' voices, all of which we will see Hardy do in the following four chapters, which explore the central recurring themes of Hardy's verse.

Suggested Work

"A Wife Waits" and "After the Fair" are the last two poems in the series *At Casterbridge Fair* (*CP* 239). Read the other poems in the sequence to see how they fit, tonally and stylistically, with these two selections and with Hardy's other "fair" poems.

"In the Servant's Quarters" (*CP* 382) emphasizes Hardy's interest in dialect, here as a subject of the poem rather than as its written language. In this poem, the characters mock certain dialects and use dialect as a way to implicate a character in the poem: "'Why, man, you speak the dialect / He uses in his answers; . . . His syllables / Are those you sound yourself when you are talking unawares.'" While the person being addressed tries to deny his connection to the accused criminal, his dialect has given him away. Consider whether dialect's correlation with socioeconomic class is more evident in this poem than in the poems that are actually written in dialect. You might also consider whether dialect in Hardy's poems, like setting and social oppression, traps people in their circumstances.

Consider "The Peasant's Confession" (*CP* 31) and "The Pine Planters" (*CP* 271) as two additional poems that obviously speak in others' voices. Then read several of the poems that seem to speak in Hardy's voice, such as "A Meeting with Despair" (*CP* 57), "I Found Her Out There" (*CP* 342), and "Architectural Masks" (*CP* 160), to see how they employ some of the same techniques as the poems that obviously adopt others' voices.

2

Ghosts

This chapter focuses on Hardy's depictions of death and what happens after death, topics that preoccupy Hardy throughout his writings. Often, these concerns manifest themselves in ghost characters, a variety of whom we will consider now.

"Your Last Drive" (*CP* 339)

Here by the moorway you returned,
And saw the borough lights ahead
That lit your face – all undiscerned
To be in a week the face of the dead,
And you told of the charm of that haloed view
That never again would beam on you.

And on your left you passed the spot
Where eight days later you were to lie,
And be spoken of as one who was not;
Beholding it with a heedless eye
As alien from you, though under its tree
You soon would halt everlastingly.

I drove not with you. . . . Yet had I sat
At your side that eve I should not have seen
That the countenance I was glancing at
Had a last-time look in the flickering sheen,
Nor have read the writing upon your face,
"I go hence soon to my resting-place;

"You may miss me then. But I shall not know
How many times you visit me there,
Or what your thoughts are, or if you go
There never at all. And I shall not care.
Should you censure me I shall take no heed,
And even your praises no more shall need."

True: never you'll know. And you will not mind.
But shall I then slight you because of such?
Dear ghost, in the past did you ever find
The thought "What profit," move me much?
Yet abides the fact, indeed, the same, –
You are past love, praise, indifference, blame.

From the first line of this poem, a reader can sense the ghostliness of the poem's sound. The pattern of stresses helps to emphasize the "oo" sounds of "moorway" and "you" by beginning with a stressed syllable followed by two unstressed syllables: "**Here** by the **moor**way **you** re**turned**." The trochee followed by three iambs leads readers to pause subtly on "moor" and "you," which, in conjunction with those long vowels and the syllables' stresses, emphasize the ghostly "oo" even before the ghost is fully introduced. Those "o" and "oo" sounds continue throughout the poem, with rhymes on "view" and "you," "know" and "go," as well as repeated stresses on words like "true" and "soon."

The ghost of "Your Last Drive" is less corporeal than some of Hardy's other ghosts, and yet she possesses many typically ghostly qualities, at least as Hardy sees them; she is calm, accepting, prescient, and non-judgmental. While the living speaker is tormented by self-doubt, lack of foresight, and loneliness, the dead speaker seems to suffer from no such problems. The ghostly voice in this poem is exceptionally insightful while the living speaker recognizes that he lacks similar insight. In fact, the speaker comments that he would not have noticed the apparent awareness, written in his love's face, of her impending death even had he been given the chance to notice it. He says, "I should not have seen / That the countenance I was glancing at / Had a last-time look in the flickering sheen . . ." But the beloved was, according to the speaker, aware that death fast approached.

The most confusing aspect of "Your Last Drive" may be the placement of the dead love, who speaks as a ghost but not exactly from beyond the grave. Instead, the voice of the dead love is an imagined voice from life; the monologue represents her prescient realization, before death, that death is imminent and also that, after death, she will have no more awareness, no more cares, no more regret. The voice's prescience is only imagined, of course, since the speaker reports that this is merely what the dying love *might* have said, and even had the speaker recognized it, these would not have been articulated words but "writing upon your face," that is, a look of foreknowledge.

Although the speaker of the poem clearly agrees with the ghostly voice's view of death's finality, he is not fully willing to accept it, and so he says both that the dead love is "past love, praise, indifference, blame," underscoring death's absolute separation from life, and also that he will continue to visit the grave anyway because he will not "slight" the ghost. In this split between "knowing" that the dead love will completely lack awareness and hoping, nonetheless, that some awareness remains, we feel again one of the primary tensions of Hardy's poems. To address a lost love as "dear ghost," despite knowing that the ghost "shall take no heed" of anything, is to recognize the finality of death and simultaneously to hope for a different kind of end. Unlike the tormented ghost of "Ah, Are You Digging on My Grave?" this ghost seems to believe that the actions of the living have no impact on the dead, and therefore whether mourners visit their loved ones' graves is of no matter. But despite the speaker's naked attachment to this ghostly voice, he will continue to act in defiance of her belief that she "shall not care."

In this poem, the speaker seems to believe strongly in the power of love and its potential for a true connection between people whether living or dead, but he, importantly, does not believe in love's power to repel death. The beautiful descriptions of the dead before death – "the borough lights ahead that lit your face," "the charm of that haloed view" – and the apparent understanding shared by these two people speak with some enthusiasm to the possibilities for human love. And yet the poem is, as always in Hardy's verse, tainted by death's presence and by the reality of mortality. This poem makes evident Hardy's sense that mortality is not a distant concept but something immediate and ever-present. The kind of happiness that exists in the first lines of this poem cannot exist unspoiled even for a single stanza; it is always, inevitably, colored by death's presence, and so the ephemeral beauty of the loved one is necessarily haunted by the fact that it will "be in a week the face of the dead." In some ways, though, the love in this poem is so true that death is only a minor impediment to its continuation. Even in the last stanza, the speaker's love seems to persist; the speaker will continue to visit the beloved's grave and will continue to be a victim of death's interference, regardless of the dead woman's lack of belief in a continued, ghostly existence.

It is worth noting here that I have interpreted gender in "Your Last Drive" in a fairly conventional way: I assume in my analysis that the speaker is male and the deceased love is female. Male speakers and deceased female lovers represent an explicit pattern in Hardy's poems, particular the *Poems of 1912–13*, from which "Your Last Drive" comes. And yet this poem articulates no gender for either the speaker or the dead character. While there are compelling reasons to read the poems in their published contexts – to see the speaker of "Your Last Drive" as male because the speaker of the previous poem calls himself a man, or to see the dead love as female because the dead figure two poems later is called "she" – readers should note that no gender is ever articulated in this particular poem. Readers may also be tempted to read Hardy's biography onto these poems, for understandable reasons. Readers may know, for instance, that Hardy's most poignant and romantic poems were written after the death of his wife, and therefore may assume that, in all of his poems, Hardy himself is the speaker and Emma is the ghost. As we will explore more fully in Chapter 6, while the poems do exist in a context – both within a poetic collection and within a writer's life – they also exist on their own, and readers should learn to approach them both ways. Hardy often writes from a female perspective, and so a reader cannot necessarily assume that the speaker is Hardy or even resembles Hardy. This particular poem works with both a male or a female speaker, and it might be an interesting experiment for readers to reread the poem imagining the genders reversed to see how, or even if, the poem reads differently.

"I Have Lived with Shades" (*CP* 184)

I
I have lived with shades so long,
And talked to them so oft,
Since forth from cot and croft
I went mankind among,
    That sometimes they
    In their dim style
    Will pause awhile
    To hear my say;

II
And take me by the hand,
And lead me through their rooms
In the To-be, where Dooms
Half-wove and shapeless stand:
    And show from there
    The dwindled dust
    And rot and rust
    Of things that were.

III
"Now turn," they said to me
One day: "Look whence we came,
And signify his name
Who gazes thence at thee." –
    – "Nor name nor race
    Know I, or can,"
    I said, "Of man
    So commonplace.

IV
"He moves me not at all;
I note no ray or jot
Of rareness in his lot,
Or star exceptional.
    Into the dim
    Dead throngs around
    He'll sink, nor sound
    Be left of him."

V
"Yet," said they, "his frail speech,
Hath accents pitched like thine –
Thy mould and his define
A likeness each to each –
But go! Deep pain
Alas, would be
His name to thee,
And told in vain!"

In "Your Last Drive," Hardy chooses a conversational, dialogic structure, and the speaker of the poem discusses death with a lover, who speaks as well, albeit before death, with prescience about impending death. In "I Have Lived with Shades," written in 1899, Hardy continues the dialogic structure, but in this case the conversation occurs on two levels: both between the ghosts and the speaker and between the speaker and the poem's reader. This poem too, like "Your Last Drive," accentuates the use of "o" vowels, in rhymes like "rooms" and "dooms" as well as lines like "since forth from cot and croft," which not only rhymes with "so oft" but whose assonance almost sounds like internal rhyme. The third-person voice here addresses the poem's readers, but it also presents a dialogue between the shades and the speaker, which the speaker then reports to his readers. The speaker begins by directly addressing the readers, framing the dialogue that will appear in the third stanza, and he explains the long relationship he has had with ghosts, "since forth from cot and croft / I went mankind among . . ." That is, although this speaker lives among mankind, he has a special relationship with the dead, which, in this poem, is more real than his relationship with mankind. He refers only to his relationships with ghosts, and no living humans aside from the speaker appear in the poem; thus, the majority of his life seems to be lived among shades.

The ghosts here are friends to the speaker, kind souls who guide the speaker through life. In fact, even the title uses the word "lived" to juxtapose life and death: to have "lived" with ghosts is a puzzling notion but one that feels organic to Hardy's poems. The ghosts themselves seem to be alive, and despite the fact that their single defining quality is their lack of life, in many ways they are more real to him than living people. Their abilities to show him truths about the world and to lead him by the hand through this world and to the very edge of the next illustrate his closeness with them.

In this poem, the ghosts are both frightening and kind. They are frightening in the way that they show the speaker the "To-Be" (a wonderful phrase, straightforward yet terrifying) and kind in their willingness to "take [the speaker] by the hand" and in their reluctance to cause the speaker any pain. Like the ghosts of "Your Last Drive" and "Ah, Are You Digging on My Grave?" they retain many human qualities, including compassion, which we see most clearly when they exclaim, "But go!" not wishing to cause the speaker any emotional trauma. Unlike the ghosts of "Your Last Drive" and "Ah, Are You Digging on My Grave?" these ghosts have a community together and are, therefore, less alone than the speaker of the poem. In other poems, the ghosts are lonely and reach out to humans for some comfort and connection, but these shades have one another while the speaker of the poem has no one but them. While the shades attempt to help the speaker come to some realization, they decide ultimately to allow him to remain innocent in his understandings, another demonstration of their kindness.

When, in the third stanza, the actual dialogue is introduced, Hardy does not eliminate the conversation his speaker had begun with readers, and the poem thus takes on a kind of double dialogue. By including the speaker's voice in the signal phrases of the conversation with the shades, Hardy continues to remind readers of their active presence in the poem: "'Now turn,' they said to me / One day: 'Look whence we came . . .'" Hardy's use of phrases like "they said to me one day" reminds readers that the speaker of the poem continues to address them and that this narrative is being reported for their benefit.

One important technique to note in this poem is dramatic irony. The speaker here has less awareness than either the readers or the shades do. This poem is also one of the important instances in which we see the distinction between a speaker who may strongly resemble Hardy, and Hardy himself. Clearly the poet in this poem knows far more than the speaker of the poem, and so the speaker and the poet simply cannot be one and the same. The shades try with some diligence to help the speaker wake from his reverie and recognize something important about his own mortality, but he refuses to do so.

By pointing the speaker towards his own future ghost and asking him to "signify his name / Who gazes thence at thee," they try to insist on the speaker's education and self-awareness. He rejects the shades' efforts and instead insults his potential ghost-self. The shades clearly know that the man whom they display this way is the speaker himself, and they try to hint as much by identifying their similarities. But ultimately these compassionate shades decide that trying to get the speaker to recognize himself will cause him pain but no real awareness, and so, that work would be "in vain." The poem ends, then, with a suggestion that the speaker will be incapable of making himself any more rare or exceptional, so forcing him to see himself mirrored in this unimpressive shade will simply cause him unwarranted pain.

The readers, however, who have been included in the poem both directly and indirectly all along, clearly share knowledge with the shades of this oblivious speaker. Thus Hardy succeeds in joining the readers with the shades and giving them some shared knowledge of a speaker who claims to possess a special insight and is, simultaneously, ignorant and obtuse. Readers can practically see these shades throwing up their arms in defeat, realizing that this speaker is just not quite bright enough to get it. And readers may be feeling the same way; in fact, if readers feel sympathy for anyone in this poem, it may be the shades, who cannot adequately convey their knowledge to this man who is so incapable of seeing the truth about himself.

Perhaps more importantly, though, by including readers in this poem from the very beginning, Hardy insinuates that there is something to be learned from these shades as well. Even if readers have not "lived with shades," their voices can give readers some insight too: human self-perception may be as flawed as that of the poem's speaker, and readers might be equally unimpressed with themselves if only given the opportunity to view themselves from an external vantage point. When the speaker of this poem is given the chance to see himself, along with other "things that were," he does not recognize himself, and the poet (but probably not the speaker, who is a bit too dense) implies that readers should learn from such an experience. Would readers, too, look so commonplace to themselves? The poem uses its obtuse but supernaturally-aware speaker to suggest that readers, given the opportunity, might observe their own lack of exceptionality and, if they are wise enough to notice it, make some meaningful change.

"The Haunter" and "The Voice" (*CP* 345 and 346)

These two poems, often read, logically, as a pair, depict the same situation from two different perspectives. In "The Haunter," a female ghost nightly haunts her former love, while in "The Voice," a male lover suspects that he is haunted by his dead love. Both poems are poignant and moving, and both depict death as a necessary and unavoidable corollary to love. Just as "Your Last Drive" presents love as inevitably – and immediately – connected to death, so both "The Voice" and "The Haunter" include death as an ever-present element in any loving relationship. In fact, as we shall see, these relationships seem to be made more meaningful by death's inclusion.

The Haunter

He does not think that I haunt here nightly:
    How shall I let him know
That whither his fancy sets him wandering
    I, too, alertly go? –
Hover and hover a few feet from him
    Just as I used to do,
But cannot answer his words he lifts me –
    Only listen thereto!

When I could answer he did not say them:
    When I could let him know
How I would like to join in his journeys
    Seldom he wished to go.
Now that he goes and wants me with him
    More than he used to do,
Never he sees my faithful phantom
    Though he speaks thereto.

Yes, I companion him to places
    Only dreamers know,
Where the shy hares print long paces,

Where the night rooks go;
Into old aisles where the past is all to him,
    Close as his shade can do,
Always lacking the power to call to him,
    Near as I reach thereto!

What a good haunter I am, O tell him,
    Quickly make him know
If he but sigh since my loss befell him
    Straight to his side I go.
Tell him a faithful one is doing
    All that love can do
Still that his path may be worth pursuing,
    And to bring peace thereto.

"The Haunter," like "I Have Lived with Shades," presents a level of dramatic irony in that readers are privy to special information that the subject of the poem does not have. The ghost in this poem is real, and yet the subject of the poem is not fully aware of her existence. Thus she actually exhorts the reader to "tell him!" how well she does her haunting despite his lack of awareness thereof. She is frustrated by her ghostliness and its ineffectiveness on this particular lover. In other poems, notably "I Have Lived with Shades," the speaker is even more aware of ghosts than he is of real people; he knows and recognizes ghosts more than he knows even himself. But in "The Haunter," the speaker of the poem – the ghost – realizes that her still-living lover remains unaware of her existence, a state that is very troubling both to her and to him. The ghost knows that her lover speaks to her and waits for her, and the readers know that the ghost is constantly hovering near her living love, but the male lover is sadly unaware that the ghost is still with him. Her dilemma is how to make him aware that she stays with him at all times, haunting not only his daytime wanderings but also his dreams.

Ultimately, she realizes that the only way to make him aware is to ask the poem's readers to let him know. In this case, unlike in "I Have Lived with Shades," the reader serves as an intermediary between the human and the ghost. The human in "The Haunter" is not in touch with the ghosts surrounding him as the speaker of "I Have Lived with Shades" is, and so the reader, who is both able to hear from the ghost and, apparently, speak with the living, is asked to "tell him" that she stays with him at every moment, what a good haunter she is, and that she is working to bring him peace and make the rest of his life worthwhile. In poems, readers are often asked to act, as in Wordsworth's "The World is Too Much With Us," where readers are reminded that they may be behaving badly and should change their ways. But seldom are readers imparted with as much responsibility as they are in "The Haunter," which asks readers to intervene with fictional characters, serving as the intermediary communicants in a curtailed relationship.

As with so many of Hardy's love poems, the pervading sense is one of misery and despair, but there remains a level of hopefulness even in a poem as suffused with death as this one. Yes, the loving relationship has been ended by death, as is almost always the case in Hardy's poems, but the love actually lives on. The frustration of the poem is not with death, exactly, but with the two characters' inabilities fully to connect with one another. In fact, this poem suggests strongly that such connection remains possible, if only the haunted one were more attuned to his lover's presence. And, if readers intervene successfully, the relationship can continue as before (though with less physical contact). Somewhat encouragingly, in this poem, the emotional relationship between these two lovers continues unabated; death has not erased their love. Unlike the surviving male lover in "Ah, Are You Digging on My Grave?" this lover has remained true, even after his beloved's death, and he continues to sigh and pine for her, apparently as Hardy feels a true love should. While this scenario might not fit everyone's definition of happiness, this is one of the poems in which we see Hardy's hopefulness, that death need not interfere with love and that love has the possibility of outliving what feels to many of us like an unequivocally terminal experience. Certainly misery exists in this poem, but only in the form of thwarted communication and not because of any abatement of feeling.

"The Haunter" becomes – dare I say it? – an even happier poem if it is read in conjunction with "The Voice," which may present this same relationship from the surviving man's perspective.

> Woman much missed, how you call to me, call to me,
> Saying that now you are not as you were

When you had changed from the one who was all to me,
But as at first, when our day was fair.

Can it be you that I hear? Let me view you, then,
Standing as when I drew near to the town
Where you would wait for me: yes, as I knew you then,
Even to the original air-blue gown!

Or is it only the breeze, in its listlessness
Travelling across the wet mead to me here,
You being ever dissolved to wan wistlessness,
Heard no more again far or near?

Thus I; faltering forward,
Leaves around me falling,
Wind oozing thin through the thorn from norward,
And the woman calling.

This poem's meaning focuses on sound, with the speaker suspecting that he hears the voice of his lover's ghost but distrusting his own senses, and so its technique also emphasizes sound. Hardy reflects the poem's theme in its form, using echoes, for example, to mimic the elusive sound of the ghost's voice. In the first line, he writes, "Woman much missed, how you call to me, call to me." Clearly that repetition mimics the sound of her ghostly calling and underscores the frequency with which he thinks he hears her voice. But he takes that sound even farther in the third line, which offers repetition and rhyme together: "When you had changed from the one who was all to me." The rhyme here is technically "me" rhyming with "me," a not very sophisticated poetic technique. But, in fact, the whole phrase rhymes: "call to me" with "all to me." By elongating the rhyme to encompass three words rather than the traditional one, Hardy emphasizes the ghostly sound of "the voice" and recreates for readers the speaker's sense of hearing something familiar and resonant. Hardy repeats that elongated rhyme through other lines; in the second stanza, he rhymes "view you, then" with "knew you then," and in the third stanza "listlessness" rhymes with "wistlessness." Those three-syllable rhymes are followed in the last stanza by a two-syllable rhyme: "forward" with "norward." Those rhymes are in the first and third lines of each stanza, but Hardy extends the sound of echoes further by also having rhyme in the second and fourth lines of each stanza. Thus the second stanza, for instance, has repetition and extended rhyme ("let me view you, then" and "as I knew you then") and an additional second and fourth line rhyme ("town" and "gown").

In addition, the rhythm of the poem contributes a soothing, waltz-like pattern, with its unusual use of dactylic feet. That pattern, a three-beat foot that starts with a stress and then has two unstressed syllables, has a rocking sensibility, especially when combined with the alternating line lengths of twelve syllables in the first and third lines (four feet each) and only ten in the second line (three feet plus an extra stress). Because the second line ends with a stress, and those two last unstressed syllables are absent, the reader is forced to pause in the space where those two unstressed syllables would otherwise be. One then anticipates ten syllables in the fourth line as well, but Hardy upends that very regular, rhythmic pattern in the fourth line, which has only nine syllables and extra stresses in the final words, "day was fair." Again, the reader is forced to pause to accommodate those missing syllables, and the pattern reflects the meaning of the poem, which is neither perfect nor soothing. Something missing within the content of the poem – the lost love – is echoed by something missing within the form of the poem – those heavily patterned dactyls. And as readers are lulled by the repetitive pattern of the first lines of each stanza, they are jarred from that hypnotic state by the last line.

Furthermore, as the poem progresses, the fourth lines become less and less regular: the second stanza continues with perfect dactyls in the first and third lines, a ten-syllable dactylic second line, and a jarring fourth line of iambs, trochees and eleven mismatched syllables. The third stanza follows the same pattern, with three perfectly dactylic lines (four feet in the first and third lines and, again, three feet plus a stress in the second line) and then a fourth line whose rhythm is hard to place and harder to read: "Heard no more again far or near?" The reader might try to read dactyls there, and can almost do it with the first three words, "heard no more," but "again" requires one to read the syllables as unstressed followed by stressed, which makes reading "heard no more" as a dactyl almost impossible. And "far or near" is almost certainly read as stressed, unstressed, stressed, suggesting a trochaic reading. But it only has eight syllables and so feels, again, incomplete, fractured, and misplaced.

Finally, the last stanza completely upends the pattern established in the first three stanzas. The first, second and fourth lines have six syllables each, which is, not coincidentally, half the length of the rhythmic, lulling lines in the earlier stanzas. The third line of the last stanza has ten rhythmically irregular syllables, a choice which both makes it too long for the rest of the stanza's lines and very difficult to read in a way that feels appropriately poetic. The strong rhythms that break down in the poem's last lines, and whose breakdown has been foreshadowed by the last lines of each earlier stanza, reflect the poem's concurrent hope and pessimism. The regular rhythmic sections of the poem suggest that the voice may be real, lulling, and comforting the speaker, who recognizes the ghost's regular calling. But the final lines, particularly those that discuss the speaker's "faltering" and the leaves' analogous "falling," disrupt that rhythm and therefore highlight the speaker's pessimism and distrust of his own senses. It is possible, in this poem, for him to be lulled into supernatural belief, but he is also very ready to have that belief supplanted by skepticism.

"The Haunter" and "The Voice" were published side by side, and their themes are clearly related, but Hardy offers no other evidence that they represent two halves of the same relationship. What "The Voice" shows readers that "The Haunter" did not is that the male lover is, in fact, aware of the ghost's presence. While the speaker in "The Voice" doubts his interactions with the spirit world, he nonetheless suspects that the voice he hears is that of his dead love: "Can it be you that I hear?" he asks. The speaker's problem in "The Voice" is that he does not fully trust his own senses, and so he hopes that an additional sense will confirm for him what he suspects to be true. It is possible, he tells himself, that the voice he hears is really just the breeze, and so he pleads, "Let me view you, then, / Standing as when I drew near to the town / Where you would wait for me." If only he were able to *see* her, he would believe that the sounds he hears are supernatural rather than merely natural. Without that ocular proof, though, the speaker hesitates to trust his own perceptions.

Hardy again puts readers into a particularly privileged position, in that they are allowed to see the poems as potential complements to one another. The speaker in each poem does not know that the other poem exists, just as the ghost does not know that the man feels her presence and the living man doubts whether the voice he hears actually belongs to his love. As in "I Have Lived with Shades," this pairing of poems asks readers to attune themselves to their own lives and losses. Is it possible, these poems ask, that readers' loved ones hover around this world too? Might readers be too confident in their belief that death is permanent? Might they be too ready to move on when a beloved dies? Because readers – and only readers – can see the truth of the poems' relationship, they are asked to consider the possibility that love can exist even with death as its third member. The fluidity of movement between the worlds of the living and the dead suggests that these two worlds work in tandem and that people with enough sensitivity can transcend their separation; Hardy presents this view as an alternative to the more conventional view that death is an unbreachable terminus.

Of course, it is also possible that the poems are not meant to be read as a pair, in which case they are less affirming. If they are not paired, rather than emphasizing the hope and continued love of the relationship, they each emphasize aborted communication and the inability of love to continue meaningfully after death. "The Haunter," read alone, shows the isolation and misery created by death, as love remains but communication disappears. And "The Voice" similarly, when read on its own, suggests that a person may feel "haunted" but will never be able to confirm his suspicions and will, therefore, continually distrust his own senses. The poems, taken together, offer comfort through the readers' knowledge of both perspectives of the relationship; but if the poems represent merely similar situations rather than two halves of the same relationship, then the poems reinforce the sense that death does present an unbridgeable divide and that, whether one acts the part of the living mourner or the departed ghost, he or she will be continually miserable and alone. That the poems were written and published at the same time offers some justification for the paired reading, but the fact that Hardy did not make them two halves of a single poem but two separate entities requires that we consider the despair of dying oneself *and* of losing one's love to death. In these two poems, we feel the pull of Hardy's fervent wish for comfort on one side and the pain of existential ignorance on the other.

"Beeny Cliff" (*CP* 350) and "The Phantom Horsewoman" (*CP* 353)

Another set of ghost poems that can be powerfully paired are "Beeny Cliff" and "The Phantom Horsewoman." Also both published in *Poems of 1912–13*, these two reinforce the pain of lost love at the same time that they demonstrate the unique nature of ghosts in Hardy's verse. The first of the poems discusses a death but not a ghost while the second, which may or may not mean to comment on the first, includes the ghostly image of a very similar woman. By offering two different views of the same situation, one from the perspective of the lover left behind and the other from the perspective of an observer, watching the man mourn, Hardy offers readers a potentially fuller perspective on this love story. He asks readers to consider how "real" this ghost might be; and, even if she is not real to an outside observer, readers must grapple with the fact that she is absolutely real to the man who lost her.

Beeny Cliff

O the opal and the sapphire of that wandering western sea,
And the woman riding high above with bright hair flapping free –
The woman whom I loved so, and who loyally loved me.

The pale mews plained below us, and the waves seemed far away
In a nether sky, engrossed in saying their ceaseless babbling say,
As we laughed light-heartedly aloft on that clear-sunned March day.

A little cloud then cloaked us, and there flew an irised rain,
And the Atlantic dyed its levels with a dull misfeatured stain,
And then the sun burst out again, and purples prinked the main.

– Still in all its chasmal beauty bulks old Beeny to the sky,
And shall she and I not go there once again now March is nigh,
And the sweet things said in that March say anew there by and by?

> What if still in chasmal beauty looms that wild weird western shore,
> The woman now is – elsewhere – whom the ambling pony bore,
> And nor knows nor cares for Beeny, and will laugh there nevermore.

These lines seem to stretch on forever, and Hardy's choice of the unusual heptameter structure (seven feet per line) elongates each thought. In fact, this pattern does not differ substantially from his more frequent choice of four-foot lines alternating with three-foot lines, but rather than including those line breaks here, Hardy combines the four-foot and three-foot lines to create greater fluidity, which complements the poem's imagery of waves and breezes and "ceaseless babbling."

Despite its beautiful and exuberant opening, readers immediately sense foreboding in the poem. While the first line uses no verbs and the second line uses only a gerund for its action, the third line draws attention to its two past tense verbs: I *loved* her, and she *loved* me. That early hint of love's having ended colors the poem's tone and offers a clue of what is to come. As is so often the case for Hardy, happiness, especially in love, cannot exist without some indication that it is about to end in the way that all loves end.

The second stanza offers a similar hint at morbidity in its last line as the speaker notes, again in ominous past tense, that "we laughed light-heartedly aloft." The word "March" in this line echoes the poem's subheading, "March 1870–March 1913," written as the dates on a gravestone or obituary are written. The light-hearted laughter, in Hardy's world, is a clue that something bad is about to happen because none of Hardy's characters can ever escape the trap of having been light-hearted, even for a moment. To be light-hearted seems to tempt or tease death, and so the tone in the second stanza is dark and portentous, as characters forget momentarily about death and are therefore doomed to experience it.

The next two stanzas rehearse the couple's temporary happiness together, and they lead into the final stanza by asking whether the speaker and his love might revisit this spot to recreate that March day. Eventually, the speaker leads readers into the final stanza, which confirms what they suspected from the beginning:

> The woman now is – elsewhere – whom the ambling pony bore,
> And nor knows nor cares for Beeny, and will laugh there nevermore.

As in "Your Last Drive," this poem hints at the possibility that death has severed the woman's consciousness and, as in that poem, she no longer "cares" about the things that once mattered to her. Naturally, that apparently happy laughter returns in the final lines. Her laughter is referred to as a last disparagement of her light-heartedness, a reminder that she should never have laughed in the first place.

Because Hardy is so interested in perspective, though, we must also consider the possibility that another poem in this collection approaches the same situation and the same characters from another perspective. Just as in the possible pairing of "The Voice" and "The Haunter," "Beeny Cliff" might reasonably be paired with "The Phantom Horsewoman." Unlike the pairing of "The Voice" and "The Haunter," "The Phantom Horsewoman" does not offer tremendous hope for the couple's relationship, and does not provide the possibility of communication between the dead and the living, but it demonstrates how a living human might lose himself in his memories of a ghost and therefore mitigate his pain. This poem is told, unusually, not from the perspective of either lover but from the point of view of an outside observer who watches the living man watch the ghost of his love.

The Phantom Horsewoman

Queer are the ways of a man I know:
He comes and stands
In a careworn craze,
And looks at the sands
And the seaward haze
With moveless hands
And face and gaze,
Then turns to go . . .
And what does he see when he gazes so?

They say he sees as an instant thing
More clear than to-day,
A sweet soft scene
That was once in play
By that briny green;
Yes, notes alway

Warm, real, and keen,
What his back years bring –
A phantom of his own figuring.

Of this vision of his they might say more:
Not only there
Does he see this sight,
But everywhere
In his brain – day, night,
As if on the air
It were drawn rose bright –
Yea, far from that shore
Does he carry this vision of heretofore:

A ghost-girl-rider.
And though, toil-tried,
He withers daily,
Time touches her not,
But she still rides gaily
In his rapt thought
On that shagged and shaly Atlantic spot,
And as when first eyed
Draws rein and sings to the swing of the tide.

Despite pairing so well thematically with "Beeny Cliff," this poem employs an altogether different metrical pattern. Unlike the elongated lines of "Beeny Cliff," "The Phantom Horsewoman" has the shortest lines possible: except for the first and last line of each stanza, which is written in tetrameter, each line has only two feet. The choppiness and brevity of each line draw attention to the contrasts between the two poems, which share a setting but explore that setting in very different ways and with drastically different metrics and tones.

The speaker of the poem begins by introducing the strange man who stares into the haze, "And what does he see when he gazes so?" "They say he sees an instant thing . . . A phantom of his own figuring." This phantom very much resembles the woman of "Beeny Cliff," and so we might assume that the man is the speaker of "Beeny Cliff," reflecting on his lost love. Readers are put in the unusual position of observing the man observing the ghost; while readers cannot "see" the ghost, they realize that the man can. Readers recognize how real the ghost is to him, but, rather than being placed in the man's mind, as they are in "The Voice," they are placed outside the haunted man's mind. Nonetheless, they can still see how real the haunting is to him.

The woman whom he sees, this phantom horsewoman, is described as a "ghost-girl-rider" who "rides gaily / . . . On that shagged and shaly / Atlantic spot." She could very well be the same woman described in "Beeny Cliff," but this is one poem in which the ghost is presented only as half-real. That is, the speaker of the poem feels comfortable that the girl-ghost-rider is a figment of the man's imagination, and readers are aligned with that speaker; when the speaker calls the ghost "a phantom of his own figuring," readers probably agree with the assessment of the ghost as part of the man's mind rather than part of the "real" world. At the same time, readers see how real this ghost seems to the man who watches her, and, particularly when reading it in the context of other Hardy poems, they may feel that the ghost is indeed real but visible only to her lover.

As with Hardy's other ghosts, this one is untouched by human troubles. The dichotomy drawn between the two lovers in this poem is particularly stark: while the man ages and declines, the woman remains not only physically vibrant but also joyous, riding and singing as she did many years earlier. He is "toil-tried" and "withers daily" even as "time touches her not." The poem offers the possibility that "time touches her not" because she is merely a figment of the man's imagination; but she may also remain untouched not because she is imaginary but because, in death, she is beyond the ravages of time. In this poem, although she is death's victim, he suffers far more than she does. The external view readers are allowed in this poem shows that Hardy recognizes the tenuous hold on sanity that some of his male characters seem to have in the eyes of outside observers and offers a troubling rather than fully romanticized view of the ghost-obsessed lover. The choppy, short lines of "The Phantom Horsewoman" reinforce the sense of the man's suffering as the poem practically chokes on its own words.

The male character in "The Phantom Horsewoman," despite his terrible suffering, acts according to Hardy's plan for left-behind lovers: he remains true to her, so much so that he has half-exited the world of the living in his devotion. In both "The Phantom Horsewoman" and "Beeny Cliff," we see that love has reached its only possible conclusion – the death of one half of the couple – and that the ghost who lives on after their love is justifiably light-hearted, carefree, and eternally youthful. In this way, death is idealized in Hardy's verse at the same time that it is dreaded and mystified. Still, the mourning seems to be more for the living than the dead, who are not troubled by the problems of life, most of which are tied to death anyway. And so this strange spiraling philosophy continues: death is simultaneously the cause of and the end of all our human troubles.

Concluding Discussion

In the midst of a wide range of poetic views about death, ranging from "hope in God's grace" to "death is a meaningless void," Hardy exists in a unique space. In the seventeenth century, John Donne idealizes the afterlife in "Death Be Not Proud" and uses his belief in its exist-ence to mock and deride death, which, he claims, can have no sway over the life that awaits believers. Two hundred years later, John Keats moves away from explicitly religious pronouncements about death but similarly proclaims that life is a dream and death an awakening into reality. "Can death be sleep when life is but a dream?" Keats asks in "On Death." Just before Hardy's time, Alfred Lord Tennyson and Robert Browning both explore death at length, and, in places at least, both determine that death can be read as hopeful and as proof of God's existence. And, just after Hardy, Philip Larkin, who claims Hardy as a great influence, writes almost compulsively about death, but for him it offers nothing but painful and absolute finality.

As we have seen, Hardy's view of death does not remain entirely consistent across the poems: in some of his work, death does seem to have some finality, especially when the speaker considers his own impending death. But that more conventional approach is relatively rare in Hardy's verse. More often, death is only a small but impor-tant step away from life; it changes something in people's particular characteristics more than it alters their daily existence. As we have seen in this chapter, Hardy's ghosts are often more emotionally stable than living humans, more insightful into human nature, and better equipped to handle setbacks. Hardy's imagined ghosts can be sad and lonely, as human beings can be, but their sadness is less pervasive and less heavy than human sadness, and it often accompanies a greater sense of the wide view of life. While Hardy's living humans are often plagued by the mysteries of life and the sense that no one can understand the workings of the world, Hardy's ghosts are more self-assured, more confident, and less troubled by their own ignorance than are Hardy's living characters.

These ghosts, with their altered personalities, populate Hardy's poems, and they are often able to interact powerfully with the living. Especially when the deceased – almost always women – are in loving relationships, death seldom acts as an end to the relationship but serves as a kind of barrier to full communication between both parties. Instead of death serving as an end to the relationship, in many of Hardy's poems, it is merely a minor impediment to true love, one that causes some communication difficulties and often sadness, but one that does not prevent relationships from continuing despite the barrier death creates.

Readers might imagine that positivity would be absent from poems in which one half of a loving couple is dead. For Hardy, though, some sense of affirmation lies in two possibilities: that both halves of a couple – the living and the dead – will remain true to each other after one partner's death; and that they will still be able to communicate with each other in some meaningful and mutually understandable way, either verbally or through other, subtler, means. Since these poems include an already deceased person, the potential for comfort lies not in hope for continued life but for some other kind of fulfillment. These poems reflect a tainted satisfaction at best, but it is a kind of satisfaction nonetheless.

Another notable aspect of Hardy's unusual view on death is that he begins every love poem, even the most conventionally romantic, with the notion that death is imminent. Sometimes death occurs just a couple of lines into the poem while in other cases it takes a bit longer for death to appear, but the possibility that a relationship between two people might exist, even briefly, without the constant, looming specter of death seems never to have crossed Hardy's mind. Although Hardy has been criticized for this unflinching view, the reasons for this gloominess might be apparent to some readers: death actually *is* looming for all of us. Hardy's view, therefore, is not pessimistic but realistic. Even so, the reality of this perspective does not make it any more popular, and Hardy seems actively to oppose the idea that poetry might lead to a kind of immortality (as Shakespeare and other Renaissance poets frequently claim) or that love is so powerful that it can make lovers feel immortal (as Donne has suggested in some poems).

Hardy has no time for this sort of self-delusion. On the contrary, he not only constantly faces the reality of death but refuses to consider even a moment in which death is not a third figure in any relationship. To pretend that death is not part of every couple's life together seems to Hardy either childishly naïve or simply inconceivable. Death's omnipresence hangs over every loving relationship, and if mortality does not feature prominently in a love poem, its absence must only be because a death has already occurred. Life and love seem to exist, for Hardy, only in their proximity to their inevitable end. Perhaps understandably, then, Hardy is often considered a dark, depressive, and miserable poet. But if readers can move beyond death's omnipresence in his love poems, they may be better able to accept his apparent depression and read instead to explore his unique and, frankly, rational approach to life. Hardy's active poetic confrontation of the details of human existence that most readers would rather ignore makes Hardy depressed in the identical way that most readers' desire to disregard death, or to believe that love triumphs over death, makes them delusional. Perhaps neither is an ideal approach to the truths of human mortality, but Hardy's sharp-eyed view, while not entirely popular, is no less valuable than more conventional views and reflects Hardy's willingness and even insistence on pursuing truth in the face of pain.

In addition to death's acting as an additional character in each of these poems, the reader also plays an important role, serving as the speakers' confidant and as the only figure capable of observing the full truth of love and loss. Hardy leaves much up to the reader, from the possibility that only the reader knows the full truth of the circumstances in "The Haunter" and "The Voice" to the fact that the reader is exhorted by the ghost in "The Haunter" to act on her behalf. We also see the reader aligned with the poet – but not the speaker – in "I Have Lived with Shades," where the reader is privy to information that the speaker of the poem cannot, or will not, see for himself. In "The Phantom Horsewoman," the reader is aligned with an observer rather than the mourner and is therefore able to see what some of Hardy's other characters look like from the outside.

Hardy's ghost characters often feel as present as, or even more present than, living people. A lover's emotional force is almost negligible when compared with the power of her ghost. For instance, even when the ghost of "The Haunter" laments her lover's ignorance of her, she does so from a perspective less of despair than of frustration with his deficiency of insight. She knows, for instance, that he still longs for her, and she realizes that he searches for her: "Hover and hover a few feet from him / Just as I used to do, / But cannot answer the words he lifts me – / Only listen thereto." She can hear his words and is fully aware of them – in contrast to his suspicions and doubts in "The Voice" – but she cannot make him understand what she knows: she is, essentially, with him just as she was in life. Death has changed his ability to recognize her presence, but it has changed nothing else: not her love for him, not his love for her, not even their proximity to one another. The issue of corporeality is put aside in these poems, and the dead speakers in some of the poems seem even to possess bodies; the only difference between them and the living is that they are harder for the living to perceive.

Living speakers, on the other hand, seem often to inhabit an intermediate dream state. Living people outside of the relationship are seldom encountered, and, when they are, they have less presence than the ghosts. Ghosts speak in voices of clarity and knowledge, unlike living people, who are often shortsighted or misguided. Ghosts serve as a means for Hardy to present information that other humans, those within the poems and the readers who exist outside the poems, cannot see for themselves, and so the ghosts are another kind of poetic voice, one that can serve as a kind of liaison between the present and the absent.

While shades in Hardy's poems can be male or female, the ghosts of love are almost always female, and male lovers are almost exclusively left behind. "Your Last Drive" seems consciously to avoid gendered pronouns, opening the possibility that the ghost and the living lover might belong to either gender, yet most of the love poems speak from the perspective of a man who has lost his female love. And the ghostly voice is a knowledgeable female voice, which speaks with a sense of nostalgia to the reader and, sometimes, to the living lover. Perhaps because of Hardy's own masculinity as well as his position as the lover left behind after a woman's death, he tends to present poems from that perspective. But, as we saw in the previous chapter, Hardy held these views well before his wife's death, and he is often deeply respectful of women, so his frustration in many of the narrative poems is with women's voices being insufficiently attended to.

That concern is extended in the poems that feature female ghosts, which heighten his impatience with men who are deaf to the presence of wisdom greater than their own. Even in "I Have Lived with Shades," in which the ghosts are not gendered, the male speaker displays a frustrating level of ignorance that Hardy never assigns to a female speaker. "Your Last Drive," while not explicitly gendered, does seem to imply a male speaker and dead woman, and that implication fits with this pattern: the woman is unusually prescient, ready to acknowledge her own impending end with no more evidence than a kind of suspicion, while the man possesses – and admits to – extreme cluelessness. Like the men in the narrative poems we considered in the previous chapter, the men in these ghost poems rely heavily on women, love women, and need women, but they also do not listen very carefully to women. The female ghosts are elevated even beyond their usual prescience by the additional fact of their deaths, which seem to give them a wide view of the realities of life as well as a comfort and satisfaction that the left-behind men do not get to experience. Men are thus presented as victims of circumstance and as victims of their own self-absorption.

While the dead are clearly victims in these poems, in some ways ghosts are seen less as victims than as having been saved from the tragedy of continued existence. The people who suffer most in these poems are not the departed ghosts but the people left behind, who must endure life. And it is not simply life bereft of their loved ones that torments them but life of any sort. The living in Hardy's love poems suffer endlessly: the speaker of "I Have Lived with Shades" is both obtuse and self-defeating; the speaker of "Beeny Cliff" is tormented by regret and lost opportunities; the speaker of "The Voice" is miserable, alone, and filled with doubt; the speaker of "Your Last Drive" is self-critical, cynical, and painfully isolated; and the man in "The Phantom Horsewoman" is delusional and wasting away. Ghosts, on the other hand, seem actually to have gone to the proverbial "better place," where they are sure of themselves and their roles in the world, where their love continues unabated, and where they have a uniquely truthful perspective on the living world. In "I Have Lived with Shades," for instance, the ghosts have confidence, insight into living people, and community amongst themselves; in "Your Last Drive" and "The Haunter," the deceased lovers possess foresight, wisdom, and a sense of purpose. And in "The Phantom Horsewoman," the dead woman blithely and obliviously rides her horse, singing and enjoying the scenery, while her living lover withers and attempts to endure what little is left of his life until he can join her.

Finally, we may notice that some of the most powerful and moving ghost poems appear in Hardy's *Poems of 1912–13*. Many readers have noted the strength of these poems and their unique articulation of Hardy's view of ghosts, especially ghosts in love. But these are far from the only ghost poems in Hardy's work, and we can see both earlier and later poems that reflect similar ideas. In the four "She to Him" poems of 1866, Hardy already explores ideas of a woman's death, her prescience in predicting the nature of her death, and the fact that her death will not undermine their love: "I will be faithful to thee; aye, I will! And Death shall choose me with a discerning eye. . . ." In 1890, Hardy composed "Thoughts of Phena: At News of Her Death," in which his speaker exclaims at hearing of a woman's death, "Thus I do but the phantom retain / Of the maiden of yore / As my relic." Ghosts also frequently appear in the war poems of 1899–1901, as in "A Christmas Ghost Story" and "The Souls of the Slain." Ghosts are given voice in "The To-Be-Forgotten," written around 1899, and "Channel Firing," written in 1914. Clearly, then, these ghostly figures and the unique ideas about death were part of Hardy's writing well before and also after the loss of his wife that is often thought to have precipitated the *Poems of 1912–13*. While that event may have brought out some of Hardy's most poignant ghosts, they existed in his writing in powerful ways long before those years.

Methods of Analysis

In this chapter, we continued to read the poems closely, observing the ways in which Hardy creates characters and noting that, while characters in the poems may strike us as being very like the poet, they may not be exactly the poet. Again, we noted the voices of the poem, considering who is speaking at any given time and considering how those voices are layered. We paid special attention to the use of quotation marks and signal phrases, and we noticed the ways in which characters, like those in "The Haunter" and "The Voice," openly addressed one another, *as though* they were conversing with each other but without really communicating, and in monologues that may have been heard by no one but the reader. In this chapter, we also noticed when living characters spoke, when dead characters spoke, and when characters who were about to be dead spoke in imaginary voices about their impending deaths (as in "Your Last Drive"). Noticing each of these techniques helped us to understand the themes of these poems.

By looking at how the various voices of the poem speak to one another and to an unnamed audience, we are able to see the inclusion of the reader in the poetry as well, a technique that Hardy uses to several ends. First, the poetry becomes instructive, encouraging readers to learn from the situations of the characters. It also encourages readers to feel some stake in the poems since they have been addressed directly and therefore implicated in the actions of the poems. And, finally, in some of the poems readers are asked to act on behalf of the characters, giving the readers a kind of agency and level of participation from which they would otherwise be excluded.

We also paid close attention in this chapter to Hardy's use of sound, especially his rhythmic concerns and his attention to rhyme and repeated sounds; and we noted how those foci help to reinforce a poem's theme rather than serving merely as a neat trick of language. In analyzing rhythm, we looked not only at how the rhythms fit into patterns but, perhaps more importantly, where the rhythms broke their patterns. By noticing Hardy's formal choices, and especially by considering form in conjunction with meaning, we can see how the structures and sounds of a poem reinforce and enhance its theme.

Suggested Work

Compare "Her Immortality" (*CP* 55) with "Your Last Drive" to consider the different treatment of ghosts, especially as one speaks from beyond the grave while the other is given voice only before her death. Now compare "Her Immortality" with "The Haunter" and "The Voice." In "Her Immortality," the living man and the female ghost are able to communicate with each other, and the man is given the weighty task of continuing to live so that the ghost's memory – and "her spirit" – can remain on Earth. The concerns in "The Haunter" and "The Voice" seem more personal and less communal, but the characters in those two poems also lack the ability to communicate with one another. "Her Immortality" seems to solve that problem, but another problem replaces it. Why do you think Hardy shows so many different possibilities for life after death? Some of the options we have seen so far include the existence of ghosts and their full ability to speak with and hear from the living; the existence of ghosts and their inability to communicate with the living; and the absolute absence of ghosts, with no afterlife whatsoever.

"Her Immortality" asserts that "A Shade but in its mindful ones / Has immortality; / By living, me you keep alive, / By dying you slay me." This is not an entirely uncommon view in poetry, and many poets throughout history have argued as much. Shakespeare, Edmund Spenser and many other Renaissance poets have presented the living as maintaining the memories of the dead, and they have also presented their own poems as maintaining those memories. Emily Dickinson's poems often state the same thing. Usually, though, it is not simply the living partner who keeps the dead alive but future, living readers. For Hardy, despite his frequent inclusion of readers in the verse, the ghost in "Her Immortality" rests the full weight of responsibility for her memory on another character within the poem rather than on the poem's readers. Why are the readers excluded here? Try to find other poems, especially in Hardy's *Poems of 1912–13*, that similarly suggest that a living partner has particular responsibilities to the dead. Why do you think Hardy so strongly emphasized that idea in this poem but works against it or ignores it in others?

3

God, Man, and the Natural World

Hardy's poems, which resemble some earlier poetic styles both formally and thematically, explore faith, spirituality, and belief, in notably modern ways, as we began to see in the previous chapter. Unlike earlier religious poems, in which God is loving, omnipotent, and deeply concerned with humanity, in Hardy's poems, God is far from benevolent or healing and is, instead, either maliciously malignant or cruelly, intentionally absent. Hardy struggles with these two poles but seems not to be able to discern any other model based on his observations of the world. Certainly his poems contain no blessing and no sense of humans prevailing over evil. Instead, Hardy consistently underscores the notion of entrapment between two unpleasant possibilities: either God intervenes in the world but so hates it that He actively works to punish its inhabitants, or God does not intervene in the world and instead leaves it to function on its own, which it does with an inevitable inclination towards punishment of its inhabitants. Obviously, both possibilities result in extreme human misery, and Hardy spends many of his poems trying to determine which view might be the truer one. That there might be any other option is hardly considered, since no other option – at least, none that involves happiness, reward, or human achievement – apparently seems true to Hardy's experience of the world.

"Hap" (*CP* 9)

If but some vengeful god would call to me
　From up the sky, and laugh: "Thou suffering thing,
Know that thy sorrow is my ecstasy,
　That thy love's loss is my hate's profiting!"

Then would I bear it, clench myself, and die,
　Steeled by the sense of ire unmerited;
Half-eased in that a Powerfuller than I
　Had willed and meted me the tears I shed.

But not so. How arrives it joy lies slain,
　And why unblooms the best hope ever sown?
– Crass Casualty obstructs the sun and rain,
　And dicing Time for gladness casts a moan. . . .
　These purblind Doomsters had as readily strown
Blisses about my pilgrimage as pain.

William Wordsworth's Romantic influence is especially evident in this poem, which begins with a Wordsworthian set-up: a lone figure ponders God's relationship to the natural world and articulates for the reader, and for himself, his musings. In addition to resembling Wordsworth's poems thematically, though, "Hap" also shares many of his poems' stylistic characteristics. It is a sonnet, specifically a Wordsworthian sonnet, a formal choice which both invokes the Romantic worldview and undermines that view by taking a philosophical approach very different from Wordsworth's. As in Wordsworth's sonnets, the first eight lines (an octet, composed of two quatrains) offer a proposition about nature and God's role in the world, and then the turn (or *volta*) in the ninth line reverses and challenges that first view as it moves into the final six lines (sestet). Generally, for Wordsworth, that structure allows him to criticize human behavior while presenting a benevolent natural world. For instance, in his sonnet "The World is Too Much With Us," Wordsworth posits "the world" against "Nature," criticizing humans for being "out of tune" with Nature's primal connection to

God: "Little we see in Nature that is ours." Hardy, though, takes Wordsworth's structure and presents an entirely different idea: a cruel, malicious and, most importantly, random world in which there is no central, controlling God and in which nature is either malevolent or meaningless or, perhaps, some combination of the two. By borrowing Wordsworth's form and theme but upending Wordsworth's meaning, Hardy attaches himself to a poetic tradition at the same time that he undermines it.

"Hap" is one of Hardy's earliest theological poems and the most skeptical of the poems we will consider, and it uses its sonnet form to present a debate between two theological positions, emphasizing the speaker's pain in considering either possibility. Written early in Hardy's career, in 1866, this poem argues that a cruel God is better than an absent one. "Hap" presents two choices for the world's functioning, and even if they seem oppositional, neither of them involves a benevolent God. While many philosophers have found ways to explain away misery and suffering – by defining it as divine punishment for human sin, by reading suffering as preparation for eternal reward, or by seeing it as educational and morally improving – this speaker has no patience for those moralizing views. Instead, he relies entirely on his worldly observations to help him determine absolute truth: people suffer meaninglessly and with no hope for future solace. Therefore, the debate in this poem focuses on the only two possibilities that seem feasible: God loves human suffering, or the world is controlled by mere chance.

The octet begins with the word "If," presenting the whole statement as a plea, almost begging for the first option to be true: if only God were cruel and vengeful, that would give the speaker some comfort. The idea that the speaker would wish for a vengeful God may seem, perhaps, surprising, since people do not generally wish for that kind of cruelty. But, given the two options that this poem presents, the speaker would prefer vengefulness. Why? Because at least it would serve some purpose. The purpose, in this case, would be to satisfy a cruel but superior being. The speaker's desire to "know," as he writes at the beginning of the third line, could, if fulfilled, give him some satisfaction even if knowledge were forever accompanied by suffering. The speaker wants to believe that the world works according to some plan, even if that plan is based on hatred and torment.

The second quatrain explains why the speaker has this seemingly perverse wish: to feel confident in one's knowledge that the world functions with logic and to know that a cruel god wishes for the speaker's misery would at least "half ease" his pain. The speaker here laments his inability wholly to believe, and while he does not specifically mention Christianity here, the implication of the poem is that he cannot believe absolutely in a specifically Christian theology, which asks for people to suffer on Earth in return for a better afterlife. While the speaker admits that he would not be *entirely* comforted by that belief, it would steel him and half ease his mind, allowing him to continue to live, miserably but with the knowledge that the world is ordered.

The sestet, though, begins with a stark refutation of that earlier hope: "But not so." Here the speaker does not question himself but instead states unequivocally that the world does not work according to the plan he has just described. He knows something more powerful than the belief for which he wishes in the first eight lines: "Crass Casualty obstructs the sun and rain, / And dicing Time for gladness casts a moan. . . . " The misery of the world remains as real as it was in the first lines, but in the latter part of the poem it is not mitigated by divine intention. Instead, misery is random, haphazard, arbitrary, and inevitable. The fact that the speaker's suffering is not caused by a malicious god proves more painful to the speaker, who feels that his life might just as easily have been filled with celebration as suffering, but only random circumstance has put him in this agonizing position. He would like to suffer with meaning. To ask for an absence of suffering seems too much for him, and not in keeping with his views of how the world works, but to suffer meaninglessly is much more painful than to suffer with a belief that one's suffering is desired by a higher power.

The speaker's suffering lies in randomness, not in meaning, not in the promise of a better future, and not for any purpose or reason. This realization brings greater pain than the suffering itself. The failure here is a failure of the speaker's Christian belief, in suffering for the sake of heaven. That point is highlighted by Hardy's choices in capitalization in this poem. Notice that "god," a word generally capitalized both for respect and for specificity, is here consciously lower case, to emphasize that this is not "the God" but merely "some god."

In the last lines of the poem, though, Hardy purposefully capital-izes "Casualty," "Time" and "Doomsters" to highlight the reality of *their* existence and the real power of those influences on Earth. God is only capitalized to the extent that he is "Powerfuller," but the genuine powers, as far as this poem is concerned, are those of "hap" or "happenstance." Despite the firmness of these apparent beliefs, though, the speaker continues to search and wish for faith and for some indication of divine intention.

Wordsworth's view of God is that He is most evident in nature and that the natural world is constantly in concert with God's mood and reflective of God's concerns. The man who separates himself from nature also, necessarily, separates himself from the divine. Wordsworth's "Tintern Abbey" is perhaps the best example of the Romantic belief in a compassionate God who is most visible through the natural world:

> Nature never did betray
> The heart that loved her . . .
> She can inform
> The mind that is within us, so impress
> With quietness and beauty, and so feed
> With lofty thoughts, that neither evil tongues,
> Rash judgments, nor the sneers of selfish men,
> Nor greeting where no kindness is, nor all
> The dreary intercourse of daily life,
> Shall e'er prevail against us, or disturb
> Our cheerful faith that all which we behold
> Is full of blessings.

For Wordsworth's speaker, God's benevolence trumps any mundane human concerns, and communing with nature reinforces the speaker's sense of God as perfectly in control, of life as fundamentally blessed, and of the natural world as enthusiastically congruous with God's feel-ings. Hardy's speakers, on the other hand, always doubt either God's presence or God's benevolence, and seem never to experience a single moment in which "all which we behold / Is full of blessings." Despite the many similarities in the two poets' works – the use of natural imagery, the frequent solitary wanderings and philosophical pon-derings, the considerations of man's relationship to the divine – the glimpse into the mind of God offered by the natural world is much more troubling and worrisome for Hardy than it is for Wordsworth and his contemporaries.

As we saw in the previous chapter, pinning down Hardy's view of death and the afterlife is difficult, but in this chapter we will find that determining Hardy's ideas about God is practically impossible. The reasons for this near impossibility lie not only in the depth of Hardy's theological and philosophical considerations but also in the fact that Hardy's poems do not express a consistent theological position. Instead, the poems experiment with various possibilities and waver among various beliefs, testing a range of options as a way to uncover some of the world's veiled mysteries. In some, like "Hap," God is a wished-for nonentity; in others, God controls the world entirely; and in still others, God is present but uncaring. Despite this variety of approaches, two consistent views exist across Hardy's theological poems, as we see in "Hap": one is that human life necessitates suffering. Just why that suffering occurs, though – whether it is because of God's cruelty and malice or because of His absence – varies from one poem to the next. The other unwavering characteristic of Hardy's poems is that his speakers *want* to believe even when they feel incapable of doing so. How they can reconcile that desire with the suffering they observe is one of the great emotional trials of Hardy's poetry.

"The Darkling Thrush" (*CP* 150)

I leant upon a coppice gate
    When Frost was spectre-grey,
And Winter's dregs made desolate
    The weakening eye of day.
The tangled bine-stems scored the sky
    Like strings of broken lyres,
And all mankind that haunted nigh
    Had sought their household fires.

The land's sharp features seemed to be
    The Century's corpse outleant,

His crypt the cloudy canopy,
   The wind his death-lament.
The ancient pulse of germ and birth
   Was shrunken hard and dry,
And every spirit upon earth
   Seemed fervourless as I.

At once a voice arose among
   The bleak twigs overhead
In a full-hearted evensong
   Of joy illimited;
An aged thrush, frail, gaunt, and small,
   In blast-beruffled plume,
Had chosen thus to fling his soul
   Upon the growing gloom.

So little cause for carolings
   Of such ecstatic sound
Was written on terrestrial things
   Afar or nigh around,
That I could think there trembled through
   His happy good-night air
Some blessed Hope, whereof he knew
   And I was unaware.

About thirty-five years after composing "Hap," Hardy wrote "The Darkling Thrush" on New Year's Eve of 1900. The form, unlike that of "Hap," maintains a regular eight-line stanza structure but with alternating line lengths. Hardy's sonnet, in keeping with Wordsworth's style, employed iambic pentameter, but the form of "The Darkling Thrush" is less derivative of the Romantic style and more typical of Hardy's other poems. By alternating four-foot lines with three-foot lines, Hardy creates a full stop at the end of each even-numbered line, where that fourth foot "should" be. That four-and-then-three pattern creates a halting feel for the reader, who must pause four times in each stanza, a regular interruption that echoes both the "strings of broken lyres" of the first stanza and the "ancient pulse . . . shrunken hard and dry" of the second stanza.

The poem, while mostly bleak, attributes to nature some possibly secret knowledge that gives its speaker hope. The poem addresses the same question as "Hap," wondering how the world works and why life must be made up of so much pain and sorrow. But the intervention of the bird here provides some comfort and at least a possibility of reassurance that is entirely absent from "Hap." While the initial environment of this poem is bleak and barren – "grey," "hard and dry," "fervourless" – in the second half of the poem, a singing thrush appears and mitigates the poem's potential hopelessness.

In the first two stanzas, the speaker is alone, observing the desolation of a winter day. All of the images of those first stanzas are ghostly and dead. The lack of music is emphasized by the analogy of tangled bine-stems "like strings of broken lyres." Nothing living surrounds the speaker, since "all mankind that haunted nigh / Had sought their household fires." Not only have all people deserted this spot, but, even had they been present, they would have been ghost-like in their "haunting" of the world. The whole earth is dead: only the speaker remains to mourn for it, and even he does so unenthusiastically.

As in "Hap," the turning point in this poem comes suddenly, and at the beginning of a stanza. Here, the third stanza announces the change in tone: "At once a voice arose . . ." When the tone of the poem changes, thanks to the bird's song, the Earth very notably does not change. Instead, Hardy takes pains to point out the ways in which the Earth remains as it was in the first two stanzas: "the bleak twigs" and "the growing gloom" remind him that "So little cause for carolings . . . Was written on terrestrial things." Unlike in many Romantic poems, the Earth does not reflect the bird's joyous song and, almost defiantly, remains cold and bare as the bird sings. The bird may therefore seem delusional because its mood is so different from that of the Earth, but "The Darkling Thrush" also suggests that the Earth's appearance may not accurately represent truth and uses the thrush's song as potential proof for a different option, one that is not offered in "Hap."

In "The Darkling Thrush," the speaker hints that the world might have some goodness in it after all, but the speaker is not privy to it. Even this mild possibility is tempered by Hardy's speaker, who admits only that "I could think" that some hope existed because of the surprising song. He is not certain of the hope but sees, in the world's mystery, some possibility for a sliver of optimism. Readers might wish for greater confidence and surety on the speaker's part, but since he has no hope whatsoever prior to his hearing the bird's song, even a glimpse at a possibility of a chance of hope represents a move in a positive direction.

The real question of the poem is whether that hope is realistic or whether it exists entirely in the speaker's desperate imagination. As we saw in the previous chapter, one of Hardy's preoccupations is the difference between what one can see and what might "really" exist. For instance, in "The Voice," the living speaker cannot perceive the ghost who is truly there, and only through the poem is that truth revealed. Unlike in the ghost poems, though, in "The Darkling Thrush," the special knowledge is possessed by a bird, who has reason for "some blessed Hope." The secret knowledge in this poem is less supernatural than in the ghost poems, but it nonetheless highlights living humans' inability to share in secret knowledge, whether it is possessed by an animal or a ghost. Hardy's speaker wants to know if the bird has knowledge that is not available to people or if the speaker's wish for hope leads him to misread apparent joy in the bird's song as a sign of insight.

The speaker's frustration in the early stanzas is eventually mitigated by the voice of the bird, which acts as the mediator between that mystery world in which hope resides and the desolate world that the speaker observes. Since the bird seems initially to be part of nature, nature seems to be working against itself. Romantic literature often presents nature as being in concert with itself, but the darkling thrush and the Earth do not express the same message, and so in this poem the bird functions less as part of nature than as a ghost or spirit, with greater knowledge of the world than the world itself has. And, in the same way that ghosts might offer some hope to humans, as the ghost in "The Voice" can, so this bird acts as a conduit between the world of knowledge and the world of ignorance inhabited by the speaker.

This poem raises the question of nature's place in God's world by asking if the bird is indeed a part of the natural world, which is, otherwise, "the Century's corpse," or if the bird serves as a connection to something more otherworldly, a Godly voice speaking through a bird. The optimism in this poem lies in the possibility that the speaker might differentiate between what he sees and what he hears.

If his aural perception is truer than his visual perception, then it is indeed possible that what he thinks he observes – and believes to be fully true – might only be illusory. And he holds fast to this possibility because, as in so many of Hardy's poems, that deep desire to believe in what one cannot see exists here too. While in "Hap" the stark reality of one's vision overrides any other options, in "The Darkling Thrush," Hardy allows room for a more hopeful possibility in the face of a harsh visual reality.

The fact that this poem was composed at the turn of a new century further highlights Hardy's break from the poetic traditions that came before as well as the fundamental tension that exists in borderlands. At the precise boundary between one century and another, Hardy's speaker considers the potential for hope on the cusp of a new age. At the same time, the poem also doubts God's role in the world, which suggests not only that the twentieth century will require a new approach to the natural world and to views of God but also that human nature has changed; what people are capable of perceiving has been irrevocably altered since the time of the Romantics, at the turn of an earlier century. In keeping with the nineteenth-century "disappearance of God" tradition that Hillis Miller outlines, Hardy enters the twentieth century full of doubt but not entirely doubting, lacking hope but not entirely hopeless. Of course, other writers handled this *fin de siècle* quite differently, and the British artists whom we most associate with the turn of the twentieth century – Oscar Wilde, Aubrey Beardsley, William Butler Yeats – approached the changing times with a new attitude towards formal and aesthetic development. Hardy had no less profound views on the move into modernity, but he expressed them, as in "The Darkling Thrush," with boundary-pushing ideas that still fit within the poetic formalism of an earlier age.

"Nature's Questioning" (*CP* 66)

When I look forth at dawning, pool,
  Field, flock, and lonely tree,

All seem to gaze at me
Like chastened children sitting silent in a school;

Their faces dulled, constrained, and worn,
    As though the master's ways
    Through the long teaching days
Had cowed them till their early zest was overborne.

Upon them stirs, in lippings mere
    (As if once clear in call,
    But now scarce breathed at all) –
"We wonder, ever wonder, why we find us here!

"Has some Vast Imbecility,
    Mighty to build and blend,
    But impotent to tend,
Framed us in jest, and left us now to hazardry?

"Or come we of an Automaton
    Unconscious of our pains? . . .
    Or are we live remains
Of Godhead dying downwards, brain and eye now gone?

"Or is it that some high Plan betides,
    As yet not understood,
    Of Evil stormed by Good,
We the Forlorn Hope over which Achievement strides?"

Thus things around. No answerer I. . . .
    Meanwhile the winds, and rains,
    And Earth's old glooms and pains
Are still the same, and Life and Death are neighbors nigh.

As in "The Darkling Thrush," the stanzas here each follow a slightly
jarring repeated pattern; in this case, each stanza's first tetrameter lines
is followed by two curtailed lines of trimeter and an uneasily long final
hexameter line. Again, the discomfort raised by the poem's themes is
echoed in the awkwardness of the poem's form.

The speaker of "Nature's Questioning" begins with his own
voice, but in the third stanza he turns the poem's perspective to

the natural objects around him, "pool / Field, flock, and lonely tree," allowing them to voice questions similar to those asked in "Hap" and "The Darkling Thrush." As in "Hap," the questioners in "Nature's Questioning" offer multiple possible answers to their own questions, but here they ask not exclusively about suffering but more generally about the reasons for existence at all. While in "The Darkling Thrush" the natural world (aside from the thrush itself) was analogized to a corpse and was, therefore, silent, in "Nature's Questioning," the natural world is analogized to children and is, therefore, inquisitive. Of course, this being Hardy, the children are not happy and playful but "chastened," "silent," "dulled," "constrained," and "worn." Despite their unhappiness and introspection, these symbolic children are able to wonder aloud about their existences. As we will see shortly, the sympathy we have already seen in Hardy for ignored and maltreated women parallels his sympathy for unwary children, brought into the world without knowledge of the pain they will face. He uses children in this poem as analogies for puzzled trees and birds, an analogy that demonstrates Hardy's kindhearted feelings for any beings, human or otherwise, that are brought into the world without volition and forced to remain in the world without knowing why.

Unlike the binary position Hardy sometimes presents about God's role in the world – that He is present but cruel, or absent and indifferent – personified Nature in this poem articulates four distinct ways in which part or all of this binary could be true. In the fourth stanza, Nature wonders if "some Vast Imbecility" created it as a joke and has now left it entirely to its own devices, combining an incompetent God with a distant one. In the fifth stanza, the natural things consider whether they were created by "an Automaton / Unconscious of our pains," again suggesting a completely disconnected and disinterested creator. Later in the stanza, they wonder whether they were not created at all but are "live remains / Of Godhead dying downwards," implying that God is even more distant, actually unaware of their accidental existence. That image reverses the Neoplatonic ideal of a universe overflowing with divine creation, and instead presents a universe overflowing with the death of God. Finally, in the sixth stanza, Nature speculates that perhaps there is "some high Plan betides, / As yet not understood, / Of Evil stormed by Good . . . " Of these four choices, three of them – an incompetent god, absolute randomness, and life as a waking dream – all suggest that God is absent or illusory, while the last – a scheming and malicious god – points to the worst but perhaps most realistic option. All of these, ultimately, represent Hardy's hopeless binary, his typical approaches to the world, the tension he feels about life's purpose, and the wish he has to resolve his questions and know the truth.

While "Hap" presents two possibilities and then settles firmly on the bleakest of them, and "The Darkling Thrush" presents two possibilities and then ends tentatively on the more hopeful of them, "Nature's Questioning" remains less resolved than either of those poems. Hardy returns to his speaker in the final stanza, leaving Nature's questions echoing emptily. The speaker asserts that he will not answer these questions, and Earth does not answer them either. The great pain in this poem lies in its speakers' unending ignorance: "We wonder, ever wonder, why we find us here!" The speakers seem to have landed, totally unawares, in a hostile, foreign environment, and they cannot conceive of their purpose or the meaning of their presence in this setting. Each of their proposed options seems viable: they might exist because of a vast joke; by random chance; as the residue of some divine death; or for some larger, albeit mysterious and possibly malicious, purpose.

We can see the echoes of these choices in "Hap" and "The Darkling Thrush" too. The two options in "Hap" are the "high Plan," in this case an evil plan, for which the speaker hopes, or the "Vast Imbecility," in which the speaker ultimately believes. The two choices in "The Darkling Thrush" are the "Automaton" or the "high Plan," in this case a hopeful but hidden plan, which bolsters the speaker's spirit. In each of those poems, the human speaker is capable of reasoning a way through the choices, and leaning towards one or the other. But by repositioning the speaker's voice from the human speaker to natural objects in "Nature's Questioning," Hardy also avoids the decision-making process that occurs in "Hap" and "The Darkling Thrush." Of course, the natural objects here take on the speaker's voice, particularly since readers know that the speaker merely imagines their questions rather than hears them literally, and so these questions are the speaker's own, presented as coming from the trees and fields. Nonetheless, the fact that the poem presents the questions as posed by innocent, naïve nature allows them to remain unanswered.

In "Hap," the speaker is completely isolated, and his pain is compounded by his separation from everything. He is alone in his observations of the world, so he feels not only abandoned by God (or Chance) but also by any other living beings that might share his concerns. "The Darkling Thrush" makes that isolation even more explicit, emphasizing the fact that every person, other than the speaker, has sought another place and that nature itself is a "corpse." When the thrush eventually sings and lends some warmth to the wintry scene, the speaker, while comforted and bolstered by the thrush's song, remains separate from it in his continued ignorance. The thrush seems to possess some knowledge that the speaker lacks, and the thrush's song tries to communicate that secret, but the speaker cannot comprehend it except to feel some vague hope and to believe that a meaning might exist, without knowing what that meaning might be.

The pain in "Nature's Questioning" comes from the same ignorance and isolation that cause pain in the other two poems, but here that ignorance is more acute because the questions are never answered, and the silence in response to those questions is overwhelming. And yet the hope here is that one might move, as the speaker does, from an initial separation from nature to a feeling of communion with it. Indeed, "Nature's Questioning" is also significantly more comforting than either "Hap" or "The Darkling Thrush" because the sense of loneliness in those poems is mitigated here by the speaker's connection with the natural world. While the speaker does not state that he feels comforted by that connection, the poem nonetheless makes clear that the speaker's isolation is neither as pointed as in the other two poems nor as frustrating.

At the beginning of the poem these natural "pupils" consider the speaker himself as though he is their schoolmaster, but by the end of the poem they have become equals, as the speaker says in response to their questions, "No answerer I. . . ." He thus indicates that he does not wish to be the schoolmaster but that he and Nature together wait for an answer from the real Schoolmaster. That connection, however small and however imaginary, prevents the speaker from having the same feeling of isolation that afflicts the speakers of the other two poems. Instead, the questions are lent legitimacy by being shared among many. The silence and stasis at the end of the poem cause less pain to the speaker because he stands among others who share his questions; and so while this poem is still bleak and still poses uncomfortably unanswered philosophical and theological queries, it does so from a position of communal, rather than individual, curiosity.

"On a Fine Morning" (*CP* 129)

> Whence comes Solace? – Not from seeing
> What is doing, suffering, being,
> Not from noting Life's conditions,
> Nor from heeding Time's monitions;
>   But in cleaving to the Dream,
>   And in gazing at the gleam
>   Whereby gray things golden seem.
>
> Thus do I this heyday, holding
> Shadows but as lights unfolding,
> As no specious show this moment
> With its iris-hued embowment;
>   But as nothing other than
>   Part of a benignant plan;
>   Proof that earth was made for man.

"Whence comes solace?" begins the speaker of "On a Fine Morning," almost as though this poem picks up where "Nature's Questioning" left off. But rather than focusing on questions, this poem begins with that singular query and then moves on to an answer, which is that humans should find solace by willfully ignoring reality. Certainly, the first stanza explains, one cannot find solace by actually seeing the world as it is, "Not from noting Life's conditions, / Not from heeding Time's monitions." The speaker then explains that, while reality is absolutely incompatible with any kind of comfort, one can find comfort "in cleaving to the Dream, / And in gazing at the gleam / Whereby gray things golden seem." In other words, the speaker's advice for his listeners is that they should not look too hard at the real world but instead should focus on something imaginary; do not consider what you see, the speaker suggests, but instead look at some "light" at the margins of reality, which gives a glow to the things at which you do not stare. This may seem like very strange advice indeed, but "On a Fine Morning" intimates that this approach to life is the only way that people can have an optimistic outlook. If one sees the world as it really is, one cannot possibly feel happy or reassured, but if one looks only peripherally, one can ignore reality and therefore live with some comfort.

After describing, in the first stanza, how one might live with this approach to the world, the speaker goes on to explain how he uses this technique, pretending that shadows are not darknesses, worries, doubts, or mysteries but merely "lights unfolding." The speaker looks at the margins not for speciousness, not to prove that something is good while knowing that it has no merit, but because fooling himself in this way helps him to believe in "a benignant plan" and find "proof that earth was made for man." Such proof, of course, is the very thing that the speakers of "Hap," "The Darkling Thrush," and "Nature's Questioning" so desperately want to have and labor so hard to figure out. Yet here, the speaker presents his answer as the most obvious thing in the world; of course the world is made for man! The only catch is that one must ignore reality in order to believe that statement, but the speaker here seems adept at doing so, even pleased to pass his technique along to others.

This poem, like the previous three, poses philosophical questions and presents a worldview that highlights life's suffering, misery, and hopelessness. Written in 1899, just a year before "The Darkling Thrush," "On a Fine Morning," unlike the other poems we have examined in this chapter, offers a concrete solution to the problems he observes. The speaker presents his solution with a kind of brutal honesty and realism that gives this poem a bluntness reminiscent of the tone of the other poems even though its subject is more optimistic than theirs. The poem does not at all abandon its belief in the supreme existence of the world's horrors. Instead, it argues that people must consciously overlook those horrors as a way to survive them. It also ignores God as the world's primary mover, focusing instead on how humans should approach the world rather than who controls it.

Of these four "meaning of life" poems, "On a Fine Morning" may have the most notably different form. "Hap," "The Darkling Thrush," and "Nature's Questioning" all follow a pattern of alternating rhyme: in "Hap" and "The Darkling Thrush" the rhyme is a b a b c d c d etc.; "Nature's Questioning" uses outer and inner couplets, with each stanza following an a b b a pattern. But "On a Fine Morning" has only two stanzas, each of which follows this pattern: a a b b c c c. The heavy rhymes in the last three lines of each stanza, in particular, give the poem a sing-songy, childish, almost joking tone. Of course, the subject matter is not light-hearted at all, but the form of the poem makes it feel far less serious than the other poems addressed in this chapter. In addition, each of the four lines in the quatrain has eight syllables, while each of the three lines in the triplet has only seven syllables, giving a sense that each line of the triplet is missing a beat, and therefore drawing greater attention to that thudding rhyme at the end of each line. The first four lines of each stanza here include four complete trochaic feet, but the last three curtailed lines end on a stressed syllable, leading, again, to forced pauses and to an irregularity – not only in the seven- rather than eight-line stanzas but also in the seven- rather than eight-syllable lines – that feels congruent with the poem's theme: something is off-balance, imperfect, discomfiting.

The fact that this poem so noticeably uses a less sophisticated form and rhyming pattern and that it does so in the context of a poem about denial rather than reality stresses that this is a less serious, perhaps less heartfelt poem than the others and that, perhaps, Hardy is mocking the view his speaker espouses in this poem. Particularly when readers reach the last line, after having read so many proximate rhymes, "Proof that earth was made for man" sounds like a punchline rather than a poetic proclamation.

Just as "Nature's Questioning" gives symbolic children's voice the opportunity to question God and the meaning of existence, so in "On a Fine Morning," the speaker's voice – and the poem's complementary form – present an immature approach to seeing the world. When the last two lines of the poem are read out of context, this poem is by far among the most hopeful and conventionally optimistic of Hardy's works; but when read in context, those lines merely highlight the naïveté of a person willing always to approach the world by looking only at the periphery. As we know of Hardy, and as he demonstrates through most of his poetic speakers, he is not a man who works much to shade himself from painful reality. But this speaker's blithe willingness to engage in and recommend this obfuscating technique feels contrary to Hardy's speakers' customary behavior and attitude. While this margin-focused approach is presented in "On a Fine Morning" as a genuine option for living well, it is evidently not an option that Hardy recommends sincerely but one that he mocks, using this speaker to point out to readers the near ridiculousness of living with one's eyes constantly searching the fringes of life for delusions of joy.

"To an Unborn Pauper Child" (*CP* 127)

Also written before the turn of the century, this poem increases the pathos we have so far seen in Hardy's theological poems by addressing his concerns for the meaning of life and the world not to his living readers but to a fetus. And, of course, he chooses not just a fetus but a "pauper" fetus, to emphasize the suffering and misery in the world that will, undoubtedly, befall this child once he or she is born.

Breathe not, hid Heart: cease silently,
And though thy birth-hour beckons thee,
Sleep the long sleep:
The Doomsters heap
Travails and teens around us here,
And Time-Wraiths turn our songsingings to fear.

Hark, how the peoples surge and sigh,
And laughters fail, and greetings die:
Hopes dwindle; yea,
Faiths waste away,
Affections and enthusiasms numb;
Thou canst not mend these things if thou dost come.

Had I the ear of wombed souls
Ere their terrestrial chart unrolls,
And thou wert free
To cease, or be,
Then would I tell thee all I know,

And put it to thee:
Wilt thou take Life so?

Vain vow! No hint of mine may hence
To theeward fly: to thy locked sense
Explain none can
Life's pending plan:
Thou wilt thy ignorant entry make
Though skies spout fire and blood and nations quake.

Fain would I, dear, find some shut plot
Of earth's wide wold for thee, where not
One tear, one qualm,
Should break the calm.
But I am weak as thou and bare;
No man can change the common lot to rare.

Must come and bide. And such are we –
Unreasoning, sanguine, visionary –
That I can hope
Health, love, friends, scope
In full for thee; can dream thou'lt find
Joys seldom yet attained by humankind!

The form of this poem, perhaps because it is addressed to a child, uses even more proximate rhymes than "On a Fine Morning," with every couplet rhyming. Yet the line lengths, while consistent among stanzas, vary widely within each stanza: the first couplet is in tetrameter, the second in dimeter, and the last has, in most of these stanzas, one line of tetrameter and a final line of pentameter. Why Hardy chooses this particular pattern is open to speculation, but again the juxtaposition of some regularity – among the stanzas and certainly with the heavy rhymes – and irregularity – with the drawn-out final lines and unmatched final couplets – creates a sense of something out of place or dysfunctional. In addition, the poem's asymmetry gives a greater weight to the last line of each stanza, which seems to summarize the most significant points and central arguments of the poem. In each stanza, the momentum builds to that final, solidly philosophical line, which states a painful truth in the face of the speaker's wavering hopes and beliefs.

The primary tension in this poem lies not in the speaker's concerns for himself, or even for humankind generally, but for the most vulnerable and least responsible of all beings: the almost born. And, as we have seen frequently in Hardy's verse, the poem is also caught between its speaker's belief in the world's unending horrors and his apparently irrational hope that some respite from those horrors might be possible.

The speaker's first wish in this poem sets the awfully morbid tone for the rest of the poem; he requests that the fetus abort itself and end its own life rather than join the living on Earth. As in the previous poems, wherein life's purpose is hidden or nonexistent and life is all suffering and misery, here the speaker applies that principle to the unborn child and begs that it not subject itself to the pain experienced by the already living. After that cynical beginning, the speaker goes on to explain just why non-life would be better than life: people suffer and are afraid; "laughters fail, and greetings die." The speaker then warns the fetus that "Thou canst not mend these things if thou dost come," and he poses one of his philosophical questions: If you were able to end your own life before it begins, and you knew the real truth of what life entails, "Wilt thou take life so?" In the last two stanzas, the speaker wishes valiantly to find some place where the child might live without misery, but he gives up very quickly on such a plan since "I am weak as thou and bare." Instead, the speaker acknowledges that the child will indeed have to be born, and will almost certainly have to suffer, but the speaker's humanity – like all humans, he possesses futile optimism and irrationality – allows him to continue to hope that the child will find some happiness, even though almost no human being before has ever done so.

That final line, "Joys seldom yet attained by humankind!" is almost comical in its extreme effort to reinforce the poem's argument. For a poem that tells an unborn child's heart to stop beating for its own good and then offers a heartfelt prayer for the child's happiness, that final reminder from the speaker – that happiness probably won't manifest itself – hardly seems necessary. But Hardy's speaker, as is so often the case, cannot quite stop himself, and so, rather than ending the poem with the prayer for the child's happiness, he sticks in one last line to reiterate his abiding doubt, even in the face of his earnest prayer. We see the speaker's back-and-forth with himself throughout the poem, as when he requests that the fetus' heart stop beating and then acknowledges that the heart cannot do so. The speaker thus admits that his dramatic monologue is really only a monologue, because the fetus cannot hear what he says, no matter with how much feeling he expresses it. The speaker's self-positioning, as a powerless intermediary who nonetheless offers advice, traps him between his own observations of a meaningless world and his wish for another's happiness. And the poem is again presented in the debate format that Hardy seems to favor for his theological poems.

While this poem might be read as an even more pathetic expression of the same ideas presented in this chapter's previously discussed poems, it might also be read as more explicitly allusory and, consequently, more terrible and more heretical. The most famous of babies is, of course, the Christ child, and several aspects of this poem intimate an address to that particular unborn pauper rather than any other: the repetition of the antiquated words "thou and thy" hints at biblical language; and the line "Thou canst not mend these things if thou dost come," especially the word "come," suggests a revision of the Christian narrative, in which the child's coming could indeed mend worldly things. While the whole poem may not imply such a reading, to look at the poem through this revisionist Christian lens gives it an even bleaker interpretation. The one place to which the hopeless can look for some comfort, the promise of a better life through salvation, is denied here with such resignation and such surety that the poem's hopeless outlook becomes even more apparent than it would be were the audience any ordinary innocent child.

In keeping with the impotent Christ figure of the poem, its apocalyptic images resemble the destruction as described in Revelation, wherein "lo, there was a great earthquake; and the sun became black as sackcloth of hair, and the moon became as blood" (6:12) and "there followed hail and fire mingled with blood" (8:7). In Hardy's stanza IV, "skies spout fire and blood and nations quake." Of course, Revelation also includes an unborn child who has the potential to save the world but whose birth is fraught: "and the dragon stood before the woman which was ready to be delivered, for to devour her child as soon as it was born" (12:4). In Revelation, Satan is put aside so that Jesus can ascend to heaven and rescue Christian believers, but the birth itself, and the moments before the birth, suggest that the story might result in either salvation or destruction. Revelation ends with salvation, but "To an Unborn Pauper Child," while wishing to end with paradise, instead ends with destruction.

Hardy's poetic conception of God, as we have seen in many poems already, is that He is either absent – the world is controlled by "Doomsters" and "Time-Wraiths" rather than a deity – or impotent, particularly if this unborn pauper child serves as a re-envisioning of the Christ child who cannot solve the world's problems. Unlike the New Testament narrative, this poem's apocalypse is not followed by salvation or a second coming. It is followed, instead, by futile dreams of an unattainable Edenic paradise. That is, the speaker, despite the exceptional misery and hopelessness of this poem, still holds out hope for a possibility that he strongly suggests is unachievable but that he nevertheless refuses fully to abandon.

"The Convergence of the Twain" (*CP* 306)

I

    In a solitude of the sea
      Deep from human vanity,
And the Pride of Life that planned her, stilly couches she.

II

    Steel chambers, late the pyres
      Of her salamandrine fires,
Cold currents thrid, and turn to rhythmic tidal lyres.

III

    Over the mirrors meant
      To glass the opulent
The sea-worm crawls – grotesque, slimed, dumb, indifferent.

IV

    Jewels in joy designed
      To ravish the sensuous mind
Lie lightless, all their sparkles bleared and black and blind.

V

    Dim moon-eyed fishes near
    Gaze at the gilded gear
And query: "What does this vaingloriousness down here?" . . .

VI

    Well: while was fashioning
    This creature of cleaving wing,
The Immanent Will that stirs and urges everything

VII

    Prepared a sinister mate
    For her – so gaily great –
A Shape of Ice, for the time far and dissociate.

VIII

    And as the smart ship grew
    In stature, grace, and hue,
In shadowy silent distance grew the Iceberg too.

IX

    Alien they seemed to be:
    No mortal eye could see
The intimate welding of their later history.

X

    Or sign that they were bent
    By paths coincident
On being anon twin halves of one august event,

XI

    Till the Spinner of the Years
    Said "Now!" And each one hears,
And consummation comes, and jars two hemispheres.

This poem, subtitled "Lines on the Loss of the *Titanic*," presents one of the twentieth century's best-known events through the lens of Hardy's efforts to explore theology. While many artists have presented the *Titanic* disaster as an illustration of the folly of human pride – a modern-day Tower of Babel – Hardy's unique presentation focuses dually on the human recklessness and the divine malice involved in the crash. Hardy's eleven short stanzas examine the boat's destruction from multiple perspectives, seeing it not as mere tragedy but as pre-destiny and as a perfect illustration of the way that God works. Unlike the other theological poems we have considered in this chapter, "The Convergence of the Twain" is not constructed as a debate or a question but as a confident, unquestioning statement of God's role in the world.

Hardy's structure throughout this poem involves three-line stanzas that could, very easily, be four-line stanzas. Each of the first two lines has three feet while the third line has six feet. Obviously, Hardy might have split those six-foot lines into two, making a more even and Skeltonic pattern for each stanza. Instead, he uses the long last line, as he did in "To an Unborn Pauper Child," to make a more emphatic and philosophical point. In "The Convergence of the Twain," his lengthening of the final line of each stanza has the additional effect of making each stanza into a tiny boat. This illustrative effect not only emphasizes the subject of the poem but ridicules it a bit too, showing how easily one might recreate the majestic ship, and how, miniaturized, it takes on entirely different characteristics.

The second through fifth stanzas show two alternating perspectives: the first two lines of each stanza explain what the boat was intended to be, and the last line describes it as it exists now. In each case, Hardy's imagery in the third line reflects the irony of the boat's current state. The mirrors that should have reflected opulence now reveal "grotesque" and "slimed" worms; the jewels that should have entranced passengers with their glow are now dull. At the end of the fifth stanza, the fishes ask why the boat – "this vaingloriousness" – is here. This question might remind readers of the queries posed by fields and ponds in "Nature's Questioning," except that in that case, nature wanted to know its own purpose, and the speaker stood alongside nature, wondering the same thing. Here, nature seems content with its role – the worms are doing their slimy thing, the tidal currents are flowing with purpose and rhythm – and nature's question, as expressed by moon-eyed fishes, is about something out of place, an object of human vanity in a space that should be reserved for natural things.

The fishes' question leads into the second part of the poem, which maintains the same stanza structure as the first part but offers a new pattern within each stanza. Stanza six begins to answer the fishes' question, and thereafter Hardy maintains the two line / one line split between subjects in each stanza, but with a change in the subject of the lines. In stanzas seven and eight, the first two lines refer to the ship and the third, longer line refers to the iceberg. By juxtaposing these two objects, Hardy creates a sense of their existence as a pair, not as two separate entities that accidentally collide but as two halves of the same object or, as Hardy writes, "twin halves of one august event." They were created concurrently and meant for one another. Their separation within each stanza, between the first half dedicated to the ship and the second half dedicated to the iceberg, highlights their relationship to one another and the fact that, in this poem's view, one could not exist without the other.

Hardy's philosophy, in this poem perhaps more explicitly than in others, is that the anthropocentric view of many people is misguided. The humans' actions in this poem are hardly Hardy's emphasis. Instead, he is interested in the actions of the "Immanent Will," Hardy's term for the divine Being who tricks people into a sense of their own centrality while preparing to shock them with the truth. As people created the prideful ship, God created the iceberg concurrently for the specific purpose of joining with the ship, a juxtaposition that is uniquely Hardian. Most people consider the crash an unfortunate coincidence or, at most, divine punishment for human pride. But Hardy's view is much more intricate; the world does not work on a logical system of reward and punishment but in a more sinister, less comprehensible way. Human autonomy, in this poem at least, is an illusion to which humans continue to subscribe, but, as this poem makes clear, "no mortal eye could see / The intimate welding of their later history." Only a divine power could have the foreknowledge of that which humans can see only in hindsight; the reasons for the collision remain hidden or, more likely, absent, but the objects' fatedness for one another stakes a theological claim.

The poem's title, "The Convergence of the Twain," may allude ironically to Rudyard Kipling's 1889 poem "The Ballad of East and West," which begins, famously, "Oh, East is East and West is West, and never the twain shall meet." That poem, of course, is also about "two hemispheres," but in a more localized, human, cultural context. Kipling, in explaining the contrast between India and England, argues that these two antitheses will never collide "Till Earth and Sky stand presently at God's great Judgment Seat." Hardy turns that popular idea on its head, proposing not only that two earthly hemispheres can indeed collide, but also that God's Judgment Seat is not a distant, otherworldly concept but a regular part of life on earth. In "The Convergence of the Twain," unlike in many of Hardy's other theological poems, God is real and present, and His judgment affects people constantly and in ways they do not expect.

The coincidences that occur in "The Convergence of the Twain" are not coincidences at all but preplanned, highly ordered events. In fact, "The Convergence of the Twain" offers the precise world that Hardy's speaker wishes for in "Hap," presided over by a possibly vengeful god who "Had willed and meted me the tears I shed." We might suppose that the difference in years between these poems – a full half-century – produces those philosophical differences, but in fact Hardy struggles throughout his poems to reach conclusions about these theological inquiries. Unlike poets whose philosophies change steadily over years, Hardy writes each poem as its own self-contained philosophical world; each one is internally consistent, but the distinctions from one to the next point to a poet with ongoing questions and a variety of possible answers, each applied in a different setting.

We have thus far seen many of Hardy's terms for the world's controlling force, which he sometimes calls "god" and sometimes reframes: "a Powerfuller than I," "Crass Casualty," "some Vast Imbecility," "an Automaton," "the Doomsters," or "Time-Wraiths." But "The Convergence of the Twain" offers two of the most evocative of these terms: "the Immanent Will" and "the Spinner of the Years." These terms capture some of Hardy's opinions about how the world works, the former emphasizing God's interiority and indifference to human suffering or desires and the latter highlighting God's control over time's passage. More centrally, though, they revise God's relationship with man, making Him a force rather than a being, and reiterating Hardy's belief that there was, in the words of Nathan Scott, "a very strong unlikelihood . . . of life's being providentially ordered by any gracious Deity."[1] "The Immanent Will" almost completely depersonalizes God, but the "Spinner of the Years" suggests a God with human motivations and human abilities (speech, for one) whose fundamental attitude towards humankind might be described as authoritarian detachment. Scott claims that it was Darwin who influenced Hardy to think this way and to believe that, "even if the theistic premise is to be retained, God cannot be assumed to have any real concern for Man's welfare."[2]

Hardy uses the term "Immanent Will" elsewhere in his work as well, perhaps most notably in his epic drama *The Dynasts*, a very long poem written in multiple voices, in the style of a play but not intended for staged performance. This work, a large-scale depiction of the history surrounding the Napoleonic Wars, invokes supernatural beings in ways reminiscent of Greek drama, and the drama opens with one of these, the Shade of the Earth, asking, "What of the Immanent Will and Its Designs?" Unlike the Immanent Will as depicted in "The Convergence of the Twain," though, this Immanent Will "works unconsciously":

> Eternal artistries in Circumstance,
> Whose patterns, wrought by rapt aesthetic rote,
> Seem in themselves Its single listless aim,
> And not their consequence.

In other words, the controlling Will listlessly prefers to watch artistic patterns emerge on Earth rather than to engage in the lives of Earth's inhabitants. This idea is hardly unusual in Hardy's work, nor is the idea that this Will is "automatic," a concept that *The Dynasts* shares with "Nature's Questioning." In a letter to his friend Edward Clodd, Hardy remarks that "Will" is not precisely the word he means, but he cannot find a better one. He explicitly notes that "Power" is not the correct word because "power can be suspended or withheld, and the forces of nature cannot."[3] He also notes, in a later letter to Clodd, that his unique theological contribution in *The Dynasts* is "the idea of the Unconscious Will becoming conscious with flux of time."[4] These two distinctions – between Will and Power, and between consciousness and unconsciousness – suggest a particular outlook on that divine being: the Will always exists and cannot be "suspended or withheld," but It can change from being unaware of Its actions to becoming aware of them.

Certainly "The Convergence of the Twain" challenges the conceptions of a human-centered creation and a benevolent or loving God, but it does so in a way that differs notably from the poems examined earlier in this chapter and in *The Dynasts* as well: it is utterly confident in its understanding of this "august event" and clear in its belief that "the Spinner of the Years / Said, 'Now!'" While the theology of this poem is no cheerier than the theologies of the other poems, it has a level of comfort that the others lack, and that lies in its certainty. "The Convergence of the Twain" lacks the profound doubt of the other poems in this chapter and instead offers readers some small comfort in knowing that someone – or, more accurately, some*thing* – knows how the world works. The randomness that exists in the world of some of Hardy's other poems is absent here, and that absence alone is reassuring, if only in the poem's surety that bad things will happen, definitely and inevitably, and that humans will not know when to expect them and so should expect them always. Unlike "Hap," which explores and then confidently dismisses the possibility that the world might be ordered, "The Convergence of the Twain" presents a highly ordered and divinely controlled world, but one in which that divine control consistently undermines human efforts.

Comparative Discussion

Perhaps one of the most important points to note in our comparative discussion is that these poems do not present a consistent worldview on Hardy's part. Because all of his poems are, in their own ways, bleak and deterministic, readers might initially assume that all of the poems offer a single, considered view of the world. On the contrary, they experiment with a variety of positions and therefore show us that Hardy is, as Evelyn Hardy (no relation) asserts, not a philosopher but an artist. His ideas do not remain consistent from one poem to the next and, as we see in "The Convergence of the Twain," even those ideas that seem most closely held – that the best humans can do is wonder whether God exists – are not always present in Hardy's poems. The only consistencies we can determine across these poems are that people continue to hope for clarity and that the world involves suffering and pain, but whence that suffering comes – whether it is necessary and intentional or a mere by-product of happenstance – changes from one poem to the next.

Concluding Discussion

The poems that focus on nature and life's meaning present a world in which God may or may not have a role, and the primary tension within these poems is a desire to feel God's presence comingling with a strong suspicion that there is no such presence or, alleviated slightly, that God exists but without purpose or intention. We can see this tension through the many terms that Hardy uses to refer to God, some of which are respectful and some of which indicate disgust with God, or with whatever power controls human life. Hardy's speakers both want to believe in something benevolent and find themselves unable to believe, except in the case of "On a Fine Morning," which allows the speaker to live happily only by consciously and articulately denying reality.

In all of these poems, the observed world interferes with the ideally imagined world, and faith in goodness is made impossible by what one observes. In each case, though, the final determination of how the world works differs: in "Hap," the world is definitely controlled by "Crass Casualty" despite the speaker's wish for meaning; in "The Darkling Thrush," the speaker has no concrete answer but holds on to a possibility of greater meaning and of a logic just beyond his grasp; in "Nature's Questioning," the speaker shares nature's confusion, and the poem ends with no clear answer, not even a leaning in one direction or another; in "On a Fine Morning," the world is doomed and dark, but that problem is surmounted by denying reality; in "To an Unborn Pauper Child," the world is similarly miserable but reality cannot so easily be denied; and, finally, in "The Convergence of the Twain," the worldview opposes that of "Hap" and is, instead, fully controlled and ordered, but by a being that metes out pain and suffering rather than joy.

As we see especially in "The Darkling Thrush," "Nature's Questioning," and "On a Fine Morning," Hardy continues to describe the same brutal, misery-filled world, but the way one perceives the world can lead to a greater sense of hope. When perceiving the world through the anticipated life of an unborn child, the speaker can see nothing but disaster. However, when the speaker hears the singing of the thrush, he is able to grasp at the possibility that the world has meaning, and when Nature questions its own existence, the speaker is able to feel some connection to the natural world and, therefore, some comfort. And, perhaps most uniquely, in "On a Fine Morning," the speaker is able to create his own alternative to reality by looking only at the margins of the world, a technique that allows him to live with comfort despite the real misery around him. Each of these poems is, ultimately, not about how the world really works but about how humans perceive it, and each one offers a different perception that leads to the philosophical differences among the poems. Of course, humans can possess no truth outside of their own perceptions, an entrapment in one's senses that apparently frustrates and baffles Hardy. Despite the anti-anthropocentric view of "The Convergence of the Twain," Hardy recognizes that humans have no option but to see the world from their own perspective, and therefore he offers, across his work, different ways that humans might see the world, sometimes finding hints of meaning and sometimes lacking the ability to find it. In those latter cases, though, the lack is not merely a shortcoming on the part of the humans but a limitation of the world itself.

Despite all this bleakness, the aesthetics of the poems often stand in stark contrast to the misery and ugliness described therein, and so the poems embody an essential irony about Hardy's worldview (not to mention his career choice). At the same time that he seems to believe beautification is impossible, he uses language constantly to beautify. The poems are not simply jeremiads lamenting the world's problems but works of art, and Hardy's attention to sound, imagery, form, rhyme, rhythm, shape, and pattern highlight the fact that these laments do more than just protest. Even in their use of jarring irregularity in line and stanza length, they create certain satisfying patterns and thus they delight and comfort, not only in their meanings but in their artistry. The poems may possess a fundamental irony, in that they are created by man and do not, ultimately, have their efforts thwarted. We can see this irony particularly in a poem like "To an Unborn Pauper Child," which mourns the fact that the child cannot hear the speaker, but also knows that someone *does* hear and that the poem does indeed have an audience, even if it is not, literally, the audience that the poem claims to address.[5] In other words, however lonely and miserable this speaker seems to be, he shares his work with an audience, and that fact alone eases some of the poems' misery. Along the same lines, although, according to the poems themselves, the kind of work enacted in these poems is almost certainly futile, readers persist in reading them as Hardy persists in writing them. The mere fact of writing here shows that Hardy is not as despairing as he often presents his speakers being; that depth of despair does not lend itself to the kind of aesthetic endeavor in which Hardy so regularly engages.

While Hardy's poems might easily be considered blasphemous because of their frequent doubts in both God's existence and His goodness, they are also deeply engaged in their efforts to understand Him, to know Him, and to believe. That wish to believe is one thing that connects these poems, from the most skeptical to the most traditionally spiritual. In each case, even when the speaker feels angriest and most in doubt of God's existence, he wants desperately to believe. That attitude in itself indicates a kind of devotion that might not be evident on the surface of the poems.

A frequent question posed about Hardy's work is whether he is essentially a Victorian or a Modern writer, as will be discussed further in Chapter 6. A more important influence than either of these, though, may be the Romantic influence. Although Hardy is chronologically connected to Victorian and Modern writers, we see, especially in the poems about God and the natural world, that Hardy seems to be wrestling with Wordsworth's legacy. On one hand, Hardy echoes Wordsworth's themes and settings while adhering to the Romantic exhortation to write poetry "in the language of the common man." On the other hand, he makes explicit his efforts to confront and confound Wordsworth's satisfaction with the natural world as well as Wordsworth's firm belief in a human-focused God, a benevolent natural world, and an overall sense of rightness and order.

Finally, as we see throughout these poems, questions are always more important than answers to Hardy, and prescience is a constant theme. The human's primary job seems to be to question, and to avoid questioning is antithetical to human existence. But the questions are also painful, particularly when, as is so often the case, no answers are forthcoming. Hardy's speakers want to trust their own senses and, at the same time, they want to know that what their senses perceive is false. They are constantly frustrated by their inability to know things with certainty or to understand the workings of the world.

As a professional writer, Hardy manages to control the worlds in which his characters operate, and so his writing makes sense as a way to order and control something that may feel to him painfully out of control. He also constantly questions, though: What might we have known that we did not yet know? What do we know that others do not yet know? How does our current knowledge color our hindsight? These questions are central to understanding Hardy's worldview and connect to his near-obsession with the passage of time, which we will examine in greater depth in Chapter 5.

Methods of Analysis

In these poems, we have examined not only Hardy's philosophical themes but also the way that form might shape and influence those themes. Our examination of rhyme in these poems shows how patterns of rhyme, in conjunction with rhythm, can affect one's reading of the poems. While tone is primarily affected by diction, rhyme influences tone as well. For instance, we have considered how certain patterns of rhyme might indicate cynicism or mocking while others lend themselves to more serious and straightforward readings. We have also examined how line length and a variety of metrical choices can complement and reinforce poems' meanings.

In addition, we have used comparative methodology to examine not only the beliefs expressed within individual poems but the ways that those beliefs extend across Hardy's body of work. Doing so helps us to recognize that Hardy does not necessarily aim to present a single, unified philosophy but a series of possible worldviews, each of which is based in certain presumptions but none of which necessarily speaks perfectly of Hardy's personal view. As Hardy himself famously wrote, each poem expresses a momentary view or vision that strikes him as true at the moment of its writing rather than as a comprehensive life philosophy.[6] Nonetheless, by comparing the poems with similar philosophical themes, we are able to consider the few ways that Hardy's philosophy remains unchanged throughout his poetic career and the many ways in which each poem allows him to consider and reconsider, to uphold and to change various philosophical positions.

Suggested Work

Study "Neutral Tones" (*CP* 12) and "Overlooking the River Stour" (*CP* 482) as nature poems with two different gazes. In "Neutral Tones," the speaker views nature through the lens of his human love and, like the Romantic poets, sees nature in concert with his feelings. Here Hardy combines two themes – human love and the natural world – and suggests that they work together, so that, as his love is doomed by "tedious riddles," nature echoes love's deception in "the God-curst sun, and a tree, / And a pond edged with grayish leaves." In "Overlooking the River Stour," on the other hand, Hardy focuses exclusively on nature, which is so profoundly beautiful that he laments having missed something while enchanted by beauty. In each case, perhaps not surprisingly, there is lament, but in one the speaker feels communion with another human being while in the other he feels communion with nature itself. Compare how these two poems are composed, paying attention to their difference in forms, especially the use of entire repeated lines in "Overlooking the River Stour."

Read "The Cave of the Unborn" (286), which depicts a visit to the dwelling-place of the unborn and the speaker's anguish at knowing the truth about the world into which the innocents will be born. Compare this poem with "To an Unborn Pauper Child." In "The Cave of the Unborn," the speaker addresses a reader or observer rather than the unborn themselves. How does that different audience affect your interpretation of the poem? And how does the fact that there are numerous unborn children in this poem alter its feeling and tone from a poem in which there is a single unborn child? Notice, also, that the unborn in "The Cave of the Unborn" are given voice in a way that the unborn pauper child explicitly is not. How does their ability to speak affect the speaker's perception of their eventual place in the world and the pathos of his address?

4

War and Its Casualties

Hardy's war poems are among his anthologized works, but, with few exceptions, they focus not on the fighting itself but on individuals and society in a time of war. In these poems, Hardy confounds expectations – as he so often does – but in these poems he does so by taking a subject that most people associate with death and focusing instead, with just a few exceptions, on the living. In the same way that Hardy often uses poems about love to meditate on death, he uses the subject of war to meditate on life, marriage, human relationships, religion, and writing, among other things.

When we compare Hardy's war poems not with his own non-war works but with the war poems of his poetic contemporaries, we find Hardy addressing a far different set of concerns from his fellow war poets. Early twentieth-century British poets have a strong tradition of war writings, especially among the poet-soldiers of World War I, including Edward Thomas, Isaac Rosenberg, Rupert Brooke, Siegfried Sassoon, Wilfred Owen, Robert Graves, Ivor Gurney, and Charles Sorley. Their poems employ extreme sarcasm, graphic imagery, and emotionally wrenching narrative to demonstrate the futility, horror, and pointlessness of war, and they emphasize the irony of brutality committed in the name of patriotism. Some of the more famous poems from this group include Isaac Rosenberg's "Break of Day in the Trenches," which explores the irony of humans pitted against each other despite their fundamental sameness; Siegfried Sassoon's "How to Die," which both celebrates the individual soldier and speaks with bitterness and cynicism about those who support, but do not fight in, the war; and Wilfred Owen's "Dulce et Decorum Est," which argues explicitly against propagandist patriotism on the home front. Here is Owen's description of a mustard gas attack:

> If in some smothering dreams you too could pace
> Behind the wagon that we flung him in,
> And watch the white eyes writhing in his face,
> His hanging face, like a devil's sick of sin;
> If you could hear, at every jolt, the blood
> Come gargling from the froth-corrupted lungs,
> Obscene as cancer, bitter as the cud
> Of vile, incurable sores on innocent tongues . . .

These graphic images illustrate not only the horrors of war and its uniqueness among all human experience but also the specific horrors of a specific war. It means to drive home the experience of fighting as it conflicts with the jingoism of the World War I home front. For Hardy, though, even as momentous a war as World War I serves mostly to illustrate a point of view he held long before the war began: that life is brutal, haphazardly ordered, and oriented toward human suffering. War does not alter this worldview for Hardy so much as it proves the point he had long made about the futility, horror, and pointlessness of life generally.[1]

"I Looked Up from My Writing" (*CP* 551)

"I Looked Up from My Writing," probably written in 1916, highlights Hardy's creative and unusual use of perspective in war poetry, a subgenre of poetry from which readers often believe they know what to expect.

> I looked up from my writing,
>   And gave a start to see,
> As if rapt in my indicting,
>   The moon's full gaze on me.
>
> Her meditative misty head
>   Was spectral in its air,

And I involuntarily said,
   "What are you doing there?"

"Oh, I've been scanning pond and hole
   And waterway hereabout
For the body of one with a sunken soul
   Who has put his life-light out.

"Did you hear his frenzied tattle?
   It was sorrow for his son
Who is slain in brutish battle,
   Though he has injured none.

"And now I am curious to look
   Into the blinkered mind
Of one who wants to write a book
   In a world of such a kind."

Her temper overwrought me,
   And I edged to shun her view,
For I felt assured she thought me
   One who should drown him too.

The regular rhythms for which Hardy is well known are slightly upset here, as the iambic lines, like "Of **one** who **wants** to **write** a **book**," are interspersed with occasional anapests (three syllable feet in the pattern unstressed-unstressed-stressed) whose irregularity lends a slight disjointedness to the rhythm: "For the **bo**dy of **one** with a **sunk**en **soul**." While readers cannot know how many of the rhythmic anomalies Hardy chose for their rhythms and how many he chose because they best expressed his meaning, at least the irregularity in the final line seems intentional. "**One** who should **drown** him **too**" not only draws attention to the first syllable of the line, the subject of which – the speaker of the poem – really is the poem's subject, but also forces a pause before "too," where readers might expect a repeated pattern. Thus, the poem ends with a thud as well as an accusation: who else is included in this "too"?

Rather than the typical soldier's voice that readers might expect in a war poem, here Hardy writes from the perspective of a writer

considering the effects of war. The poem actually contains four characters: a soldier son, a suicide father, the writer/speaker, and the
moon. The dialogue occurs between the first-person writer and the
moon, which is personified as a woman who questions the writer's
motivations. This feminine moon tells the writer about a young
soldier killed in battle and his mourning father, who drowns himself in sorrow. The moon then informs the writer that she searches
"pond and hole / And waterway hereabout" for the father's body.
The writer feels tremendous guilt at focusing on his writing during
a time of war: "I felt assured she [the moon] thought me / One who
should drown him too." In other words, the speaker believes that the
moon perceives him (and, by implication, all of us) as an antagonist
for the soldier, who "has injured none," and his miserable father.

The war here occupies the core of the poem, but one of the things
that the poem demonstrates is the many ways in which war – or any
crisis, really – ripples outward, encompassing more and more people
and, eventually, even the natural world. In this case, the core situation's effects include not only the death of the soldier's father but
the moon's accusatory searching and, eventually, the writer's self-
doubt. The moon articulates a concern about the violence of war but
ultimately seems more concerned with what war teaches her about
the world and, consequently, about writing. Her analysis reflects
the writer's worries about his own complicity in war and its effects.
The poem's premise might strike readers as far-fetched, but one can
imagine that, for Hardy, thinking about his own role in a world that
includes such brutality, and its concurrent sadness, is an absolute
necessity. This poem suggests that writing's inherent productivity –
its hopefulness, even – wrongly contrasts with the war-torn world
and, therefore, that one should not behave in this forward-looking,
aesthetically-focused way while people suffer and die. "Art" in this
poem is presented not as a solution to or an assuaging of suffering but as a kind of willful oblivion. In its insularity, art prevents
its practitioners from fully caring, so absorbed are they in their own
creations.

Within the world of the poem, the moon is more aware of this
speaker/writer's hypocrisy than the writer himself is, and he requires
the moon to point out his shortcomings. Hardy, unlike the speaker

of "I Looked Up from My Writing," is painfully aware of the potential hypocrisy of the poet in a time of war, an awareness that becomes especially clear through his creation of the moon's condemning voice. If, indeed, Hardy feels so acutely his own hypocrisy about the endeavor of writing during a time of misery, we can better understand the tension in his poems generally, which depict a blighted world but also a need to continue writing. Here, the moon's comments obviously reflect and expand upon the writer's own uncertainties, as he is forced to wonder how he can write "in a world of such a kind."

Of the two characters farthest from war in this poem, the writer and the moon, the writer feels certain that the moon is more sympathetic towards war's casualties than he is. He reads the moon's sympathy as an indictment, in that the moon searches for the drowned man while the writer keeps his head down, maintaining an inward focus and a reverie that is interrupted only by the forceful, accusatory moon. The moon's open, searching face is notably contrasted with the speaker's lowered head, his face hidden from sight. While the moon does not say so explicitly, the writer supposes that she thinks of him as "one who should drown [the father] too." The writer feels shame at his own selfish behavior, especially when he compares it with nature's compassionate efforts, which makes him re-envision himself as an accomplice to the father's suffering; while the writer did not cause the father's death, the moon – and consequently the poem – suggests that in his indifference he is complicit.

The title and first line, too, emphasize the difficulty of the writer's situation, which requires an insularity and inward focus. Writing entails introspection and solitude, but since the writer had to be jarred to "look up from his writing" and, having been surprised, "gave a start to see" the moon, this implies that the writer is insufficiently engaged with the world around him. Unlike the moon, which represents nature more generally, especially its feminine and nurturing side, the writer does not see what happens around him, while the moon possesses a "full gaze." As in so many of his poems, Hardy here emphasizes seeing as a necessary quality and shows how the writer (both this particular writer and, perhaps, "the writer" more generally), for all his insight, lacks the clarity of vision that nature possesses. In fact, the moon sees so well that she can see both the soldier's missing father and the writer's deep insecurities; her gaze is so strong that, in the final stanza, the writer becomes overwhelmed and "edged to shun her view," trying to move out of her line of vision but knowing, nonetheless, that she can see through him and recognize his worst qualities.

As we can see from this poem, Hardy's approach to war is not simply that war is terrible but that war's effects touch people in every way. The soldier's death leads to suicide, accusation, guilt, and shame, all of which cause doubt over the power and value of creation. War, Hardy posits, is hardly the only terrible thing in the world but acts, instead, as an illustration of one sort of terrible thing, a spark of awfulness that ignites other terrible flames. The father's death, caused by despair, is lamented as much as the death of the soldier, who "has injured none." Hardy's emphasis on the death of the father highlights the fact that war does not only affect its soldiers, a point frequently (and understandably) overlooked by the soldier-poets of World War I, and the poem raises larger questions about what it means for *anyone* to live in a world that can be blighted by war, by war's peripheral casualties, and ultimately by artistic indifference to those casualties. At the same time, Hardy highlights the irony of his continued poetic creation: by pointing out artistic indifference in verse, he undercuts the very notion of artistic indifference.

"The Going of the Battery" (*CP* 88) and "A Wife in London" (*CP* 91)

These two poems, written in 1899 in response to the Second Boer War (1899–1902) rather than World War I, underscore Hardy's interest in those peripheral casualties and in the effects of war on the home front, not merely to accuse civilians of misplaced patriotism or hypocrisy – as is often the point of the young World War I soldiers' poems – but to consider deeply the humanity of people touched by war in various ways. The Boer Wars took place far from England, but Hardy would have been well aware of the many debates concerning British imperial policy in Africa; nonetheless, his poems explore the human tragedies of war rather than specific political realities. Hardy's fundamental interest lies in human suffering, particularly that suffering which goes unnoticed or is marginalized by more obvious suffering. These two poems acknowledge and explore the pain that is experienced not only by the fighters themselves but by the people who surround them.

"The Going of the Battery," subtitled "Wives' Lament," presents the song-like lament of women left behind in England as their husbands fight the war.

I
O it was sad enough, weak enough, mad enough –
Light in their loving as soldiers can be –
First to risk choosing them, leave alone losing them
Now, in far battle, beyond the South Sea! . . .

II
– Rain came down drenchingly; but we unblenchingly
Trudged on beside them through mirk and through mire,
They stepping steadily – only too readily! –
Scarce as if stepping brought parting-time nigher.

III
Great guns were gleaming there, living things seeming there,
Cloaked in their tar-cloths, upmouthed to the night;
Wheels wet and yellow from axle to felloe,
Throats blank of sound, but prophetic to sight.

IV
Gas-glimmers drearily, blearily, eerily
Lit our pale faces outstretched for one kiss,
While we stood prest to them, with a last quest to them
Not to court perils that honour could miss.

V
Sharp were those sighs of ours, blinded these eyes of ours,
When at last moved away under the arch
All we loved. Aid for them each woman prayed for them,
Treading back slowly the track of their march.

VI

Some one said: "Nevermore will they come: evermore
Are they now lost to us." O it was wrong!
Though may be hard their ways, some Hand will guard their ways,
Bear them through safely, in brief time or long.

VII

— Yet, voices haunting us, daunting us, taunting us,
Hint in the night-time when life beats are low
Other and graver things. . . . Hold we to braver things,
Wait we, in trust, what Time's fulness shall show.

The poem recounts the husbands' departure and the painful emotions of the wives who remain, but the tone remains hopeful to the end, despite the sadness of the circumstance, as "someone" said that the soldier-husbands will never return and the wives steadfastly proclaim their belief in a higher power that will bring their men home.

The theme of this poem is fairly straightforward: the soldiers are being wrenched away from their families and homes in order to fulfill a larger duty to country, and the wives worry about them and attempt to convince themselves that their husbands will return safely. But despite the well-worn subject, Hardy's approach is both novel and enlightening. First, he writes in a communal voice, which is shared among all the wives (as the subtitle indicates), a technique that differs from his usual personal approach to poetic narration. The wives all speak with one voice, which both strengthens their lament and its concurrent faith and also depersonalizes it. Because all of these wives seem to feel identically and speak as one, readers feel distanced from any individual wife as a character and have less of a sense that these wives are real people than we do in many of Hardy's other poems, in which characterization has primacy. At the same time, though, the wives' unity of emotion and expression points to universal truths about suffering, loss, and self-delusion. As a group, they trust that God will guard their husbands, and the faith of the collective bolsters any individual doubts they might harbor. This group voice, unusual in Modern poetics, resembles the female choruses of Greek drama and alludes to the war tragedies of both Euripides and Sophocles.

In addition to the characters' solidarity and common voice, formal elements in the poem highlight Hardy's interest in the peripheral sufferings of war. The characters' emotions are expressed not only through their words but also through the sounds, setting, and patterns of the poem, which heavily emphasizes imagery and rhyme as a way to show the wives' sympathetic feelings for their husbands' circumstances. Readers may encounter many poems that discuss soldiers' seemingly endless marches through bad weather, but here that action is performed not only by the soldiers but by their wives as well. The wives, of course, are simply marching their husbands off to war, but the imagery suggests that they, too, submit themselves to the conditions that the soldiers experience. Immediately after the depiction of marching through mud, the poem offers imagery of weaponry. Hardy almost never employs this sort of battle imagery to describe literal scenes of battle but applies it instead to the figurative war being fought on the home front. Readers can understand why these guns might literally be present as the soldiers depart, but their presence and the way in which they are depicted suggests that the wives experience war almost as their husbands do, an approach to the fighting that Hardy borrows from Homer, whose presentation of Penelope prefigures the dedication of these loyal Boer War wives.

Those deep emotions, and the wives' awkward march alongside their husbands, are emphasized in the poem's repeated use of dactylic feet. The dactyl expands the traditional distance from one stressed syllable to the next and therefore, in conjunction with the images of the poem, underscores the sense of a slow and difficult march. A strict and formal march would use a pattern of trochaic syllables, with the sharp downbeat on the odd syllables of each line, or an iambic line, which also suggests the two-step march. Longfellow's *The Song of Hiawatha* employs a trochaic pattern, as in these lines:

> Ye who love a nation's legends,
> Love the ballads of a people,
> That like voices from afar off
> Call to us to pause and listen,
> Speak in tones so plain and childlike,
> Scarcely can the ear distinguish
> Whether they are sung or spoken; —

These lines enact the alternating stresses of a march, and such trochees are also used in the echoing military cadence drills conducted by the American army: "I don't know but I've been told, Navy wings are made of gold. Sound off, one, two, three, four." Another logical choice, the iambic foot, can be seen in Alfred Lord Tennyson's *In Memoriam*, among many other places:

> And what I am beheld again
>> What is, and no man understands;
>> And out of darkness came the hands
> That reach thro' nature, moulding men.

This rhythm suggests not only natural, fluent speech but also the heart-beat and, of course, the human gait. On the other hand, the dactyls of "The Going of the Battery" represent an extremely unusual choice for a poem about marching off to war. They accentuate the difficulty of this coupled march, the ways in which the participants hesitate and stumble, and, perhaps, the strange waltz – a three-beat musical form – between husbands and wives as they walk together towards their separation.

The wives become deeply sympathetic characters here because of their suffering alongside their husbands, but their suffering will occur a distance from the battlefield. More pointedly, the wives will suffer from an ignorance of their husbands' well-being that can be balanced only by faith. Readers can imagine the women's nightly worrying and the pain it causes, and the wives earn readers' respect by forcing themselves, through no small effort, to focus on their own bravery and waiting rather than on their deep fears of loss and pain. Readers may also feel some of that sense of time passing because of the almost tedious repetition and the heavy internal rhyme in the first and third lines of each verse, which pulls the lines with a kind of viscosity that reminds readers of their own waiting within the confines of the poem. Hardy uses form and style to create empathy for the wives and to highlight the pain of their often overlooked situation. Like the soldiers, the wives are heroic in their forbearance and sacrifice. In their nobility, perhaps the misery of war is alleviated slightly, but only to the extent that the wives believe in the surety of the husbands' safe return, a confidence that Hardy questions in the poem even if he does not state his doubt explicitly.

Hardy's interest in soldiers' wives continues in "A Wife in London," which approaches the same war from a similar perspective, of a wife left behind by her husband who is fighting in the Boer War, a location readers learn from the language of the poem. The wife here is presented as an individual rather than as part of a group, and her individuality is stressed by the poem's specific narrative. In this poem, any sense of hope this wife feels is destroyed in the second stanza of the poem, when we learn that her husband has been killed:

I
She sits in the tawny vapour
   That the Thames-side lanes have uprolled,
   Behind whose webby fold on fold
Like a waning taper
   The street-lamp glimmers cold.

A messenger's knock cracks smartly,
   Flashed news is in her hand
   Of meaning it dazes to understand
Though shaped so shortly:
   He – has fallen – in the far South Land. . . .

II
'Tis the morrow; the fog hangs thicker,
   The postman nears and goes:
   A letter is brought whose lines disclose
By the firelight flicker
   His hand, whom the worm now knows:

Fresh – firm – penned in highest feather –
   Page-full of his hoped return,
   And of home-planned jaunts by brake and burn
In the summer weather,
   And of new love that they would learn.

If she, like the women in "The Going of the Battery," maintained her faith that her husband would return home safely, she was quickly disabused of that notion. Hardy increases the pathos of the first half by adding the second section, which depicts the woman receiving a letter from her now deceased husband. While the wife is ostensibly the focus of the poem, or so the title indicates, the entire second half belongs to the voice of the dead soldier, who writes optimistically of their future together.

The two distinct sections here illustrate the isolation of people from one another, but, more significantly, they demonstrate the inability of people to see or know what is happening with one another. In some editions, the sections include subtitles: "I – The Tragedy" and "II – The Irony," making even more evident for readers the division between tone and knowledge in the two halves of the poem. "A Wife in London" provides the wife with more information than the soldier had because she is aware of both his plans for the future and his true fate, but while she waits to hear about him, she remains ignorant about his death, and when she learns of his fate, he has by that time entered the ultimate state of ignorance. Hardy expresses tremendous empathy for the wife, as he does in "The Going of the Battery," and he attunes readers to the suffering of the wife alongside the suffering of her fallen husband. But he also points out that this kind of suffering is not unique to war but to the ignorance from which all mortals must necessarily suffer.

Throughout these war poems, and in many of Hardy's other poems as well, he both laments and mocks human ignorance, but it is worth noting that he addresses two distinct kinds of ignorance here. The sort of ignorance demonstrated by the "Wife in London" is more common in Hardy's world: her ignorance is not by choice and instead is a result of her situation and the nature of human life; had she the opportunity to know more about her husband, she would certainly have elected knowledge, but, as Hardy frequently points out, humans lack the capacity to fully know, and therefore they live in perpetual and unintentional ignorance. The other type of ignorance is that demonstrated by the writer in "I Looked Up from My Writing" – a kind of willful ignorance, or a choosing not to know, which is more morally problematic for Hardy. Those people who wish to understand the world but are prevented by the world itself – or by the Immanent Will – from doing so are presented as victims of their circumstance, while those who could open themselves to greater knowledge but elect to remain in ignorance for their own comfort are treated with far less sympathy.

The objective of "A Wife in London" seems to be, as with so many of Hardy's poems, to observe that human plans are often foiled by a larger power that wants to remind us constantly of its control over the workings of the world. In this case, though, that power is not named or even referenced, so Hardy seems instead to emphasize the general irony of hindsight and of time's vagaries. The fact that the wife does not appear in the second section of the poem suggests that readers should imagine her reaction rather than read it explicitly. All readers know of her reaction to the announcement of his death, that she is "dazed," which was mentioned in the first half of the poem, but readers can, perhaps, envision her receiving his letter the very next day, written in "His hand, whom the worm now knows." The irony of his letter's optimism in the face of the wife's newfound knowledge shows both how time's passage inevitably creates misery and how tortured Hardy is by notions of foresight and hindsight, retrospective knowledge and imposed ignorance.

Of course, the soldier who writes letters home in this poem is also, at least in one sense, a writer who is ignorant in the face of his reader's greater awareness, a theme that could easily be applied to Hardy and his relationship with his readers. As we saw in "I Looked Up from My Writing," Hardy is concerned not only with the effects of war but also with writing in a time of war. In "A Wife in London," the writer is also a soldier, unlike the writer in "I Looked Up from My Writing," but the ideas that the writer is missing some important piece of information, that what he writes will soon and inevitably become obsolete, and that later readers will always be more knowledgeable than current writers seems to plague Hardy. The idea that a writer – in this case a letter-writer, but it could apply to a writer more generally – could serve as a seer and, at the same time, be so entirely ignorant of the workings of the world and of what the future will bring is both troubling and ironic. Writers should, at least in the broadly influential Romantic tradition, possess unique insight, but Hardy's war poems suggest the opposite: writers fail to have that vision while distanced readers are far more capable of seeing the full truth. Even then, though, readers lack necessary knowledge and, ultimately, no mortal can know what one needs in order to have a full picture of any circumstance. The passing of time offers some greater vantage point, but Hardy is only too aware of the lack of time any individual is allotted, a looming truth that serves to heighten his belief in insurmountable human limitations.

"In Time of 'The Breaking of Nations'" (*CP* 543)

Only a man harrowing clods
In a slow silent walk
With an old horse that stumbles and nods
Half asleep as they stalk.

Only thin smoke without flame
From the heaps of couch-grass;
Yet this will go onward the same
Though Dynasties pass.

Yonder a maid and her wight
Come whispering by:
War's annals will cloud into night
Ere their story die.

Seventeen years later, during World War I, Hardy revisits his concern with what humans can know and in what areas they must remain ignorant. This poem depicts domestic scenes in a time of war, just as the previous poems do. Again, Hardy does not provide images of battlefields, trenches, or bombings, but instead focuses on the home front as a way to depict war, a kind of distanced and syllogistic approach. Its rhythms immediately suggest a slowing down of time, with the juxtaposition of trochees and iambs leading to noticeable pauses in the reading. Just in the first two lines, Hardy inserts two long pauses: "**On**ly a **man har**rowing **clods** / In a **slow si**lent **walk** . . ." The first foot, "only," is a trochee, and the second, "a man," is an iamb; the next, "harrow," is a trochee again, and the next, "ing clods," is an iamb. This alternation necessarily creates a pause between "man" and "harrow" as readers prepare for the adjacent stresses. In the second line, readers again are forced to pause between "slow" and silent" because of the contiguous stressed syllables. Although the poem is quite short, its rhythms stretch it and give it a sense of suspension in time, a feeling that very much accompanies its imagery and philosophies.

The poem presents two images of people who do not fight the war but are part of it nonetheless: a man ploughs with his sleepy horse, and a young couple whisper together. Around these miniature scenes, Hardy offers philosophical musings on the war: certain images will always remain, regardless of changing politics, and war will fade away while love stays.[2] This hushed approach differs fairly significantly from many of Hardy's other poems, but, as in his previous war poems, he realigns readers from focusing solely on the soldier's individual experience to something both more personal to the civilian experience and more broadly philosophical.

J. O. Bailey quotes Hardy as having said that he actually observed the scenes he describes here in 1870, but did not use them in a poem until 1916,[3] and that the chronological distance, during which Britain fought in more than one war, may help to explain Hardy's sense that wars come and go while labor, love, and the natural world remain. That concept, while far more positive than the ideas in many of Hardy's poems, is still tinged with darkness. The images are not of joyous, bright work and irrepressible love but of slow, colorless, stumbling work and whispered love. That is, the "regular" life that happens in times of war is, like the regular life that happens at other times, muted and bleak. The ways that work and love are presented in this poem suggest that war is temporary and fleeting but that "thin smoke without flame" is lasting. As a whole, the poem implies that "there is nothing new under the sun," but rather than quoting from Ecclesiastes, Hardy here chooses Jeremiah to express a more appropriately war-based idea.

The passage Hardy cites, Jeremiah 51:20, is this: "Thou art my battle-axe and weapons of war: and with thee will I break in pieces the nations; and with thee will I destroy kingdoms." His choice of biblical references, though, points to an irony in the title: the nations in this poem seem not be particularly broken, and the violence and upheaval implied by the title are not borne out in the poem, which shows scenes of domestic placidity, if not exactly harmony. This disconnection between the images of Jeremiah and of the poem enables Hardy further to emphasize the cyclical nature of war and the fact that wars occurred long ago just as they do in the modern world. He does not attempt to offer any hope that after this "Great War," war will cease to exist, but he does privilege the small details of daily existence above the major historical events that people often use to shape their thinking about human affairs. For Hardy, the truth of Jeremiah's prophecy is a universal truth rather than a specific historical truth; the biblical prophecy seems to be as true in 1916 as it was 2500 years earlier. While many interpretations of this poem emphasize Hardy's supposed opposition to World War I, the poem itself hardly shows that opposition; instead, it presents a resigned acceptance of the simultaneous existence of peace and war.

The second-person voice in the passage from Jeremiah 51 implicates humans, specifically the people "in the Portion of Jacob," or Israel's descendants, as the tools of God's destruction. "With thee I will destroy," the chapter states repeatedly. God's vengeance against humans is highlighted throughout the chapter, and while certain people are exempted from the destruction, they are used as a medium through which God can show His anger. The direct address to the people by God personalizes their role in the war between Israel and Babylon, and it includes all people in war, either as the destroyers or the destroyed. Hardy's poem, on the other hand, maintains its distanced third-person description of people who are only peripherally affected by the war in their muted expressions and quiet existences. Yet these ordinary people could exist in any age, suggesting that as war rages cyclically, people continue to live their regular lives, neither "utterly broken" like Babylon nor, like Jacob's descendants, used by God to "break in pieces man and woman," as Jeremiah states: "with thee [the Israelites] will I break in pieces old and young; and with thee will I break in pieces the young man and the maid; I will also break in pieces with thee the shepherd and his flock; and with thee I will break in pieces the husbandman and his yoke of oxen." In this poem, we see all of these characters, neither broken nor breaking, but just plodding along, as though their very existence disproves the prophecy. In the times when such worldly upheavals occur, then as now, people just live.

"In Time of 'The Breaking of Nations'" highlights how Hardy's allusion to both the Bible and to a particular war can lead him not to particularism but to generalization. His microcosmic view here is less about these specific figures than about the fundamental humanity of their actions and emotions. By depicting the microcosm of daily life and allowing that to make larger statements about life and meaning, Hardy separates himself from the particulars of his time and aims instead to present a worldview. Such an approach differs from traditional World War I poetry, and it is distinct from the war poems of the young soldiers like Owen and Rosenberg, but it also proves that there are multiple ways to think about war, and the experience of the soldier is — contrary to what a poet like Siegfried Sassoon might believe — not the only relevant or reliable narrative. Instead, Hardy seems to say, the experience of the wife, of the writer, or, in this case, of the common farmer or maid is equally valid and meaningful.

Hardy's use of the word "only" at the beginning of each of the first two stanzas suggests that these scenes look simple, unimportant, and commonplace to the speaker just as they might to the reader. But the colon halfway through the last stanza negates the "only" of the poem by showing that even these simple scenes hold significance. These scenes initially seem so easily reduced to "only" images of farm labor and young love, and yet, according to the poem, they will outlast Dynasties and war. Such a perspective may be surprising to readers but also demonstrates Hardy's interest in the tiny moments of life and what they might potentially teach readers about big, earth-shaking events that loom large in popular imagination. While Hardy may seem to be blindly inward-facing in so many of his poems, this poem and many of his other war works instead accuse others of solipsism in their belief that *this* war is somehow greater or more significant than all previous wars. The nations are no more broken now than they were in Jeremiah's time, which is not to say that life is, or was then, rosy and pleasant but that it is, and was then, a series of small moments in which people tried to survive and find small happinesses; in other words, it is and was always broken and continually breaking, and still, simultaneously, carrying on.

One final note about "In Time of 'The Breaking of Nations,'" is that the order of the information in this small poem defies convention. One might imagine that Hardy would choose to place together the images of human scenes — the farmer and the lovers — and then move on to his philosophical points in the latter half or last third of the poem. Instead, he chooses to organize the poem by each sentence's opening word rather than by images. The first sentence (which is also the first stanza) begins with "Only," and the second stanza repeats that opening. In the second stanza, though, the image is not of human action, which will outlive war, but of the thin smoke rising from heaps of grass. The smoke imagery here echoes imagined images of war's destruction – the smoldering without flame – but it translates that potential war image to a rural, peaceful scene. Halfway through the second stanza (and, therefore, halfway through the poem), the line begins with "yet," which represents the poem's turn. That "yet" sentence presents the first philosophical statement of the poem, that these small scenes will outlast even Dynasties. Clearly what Hardy means here is not that this precise farmer will outlive Dynasties but that farming – not this man but this type, this movement – will outlast them. The attitude is one of both resignation to the futility of mortals' efforts to effect change and admiration for those who live honest, dull, quiet lives even in the face of GLOBAL upheaval.

In the final stanza, one might expect a continuation of the poem's philosophical approach, which would provide the poem with a logical split between the first and second halves, with "yet" serving as a pivot from illustrations to philosophies. Instead, though, after moving towards a more general statement of faith in the ability of daily labor to outlive dynasties, Hardy returns to another small image, that of "a maid and her wight." Their apparently insignificant story leads into the speaker's observation that "War's annals will cloud into night / Ere their story die." By choosing to organize the poem in this back-and-forth manner, with a shift from small, individual illustrations to larger, more general observations and then back again, Hardy emphasizes the ways in which the little moments add up to larger, more significant movements. Each small moment helps him (or his speaker) to notice the larger meaning of what might appear, initially, to be meaningless scenes of daily life. Hardy shows readers how daily life is part of a GLOBAL order just as much as war is and how a war in the background of civilians' daily lives serves to remind readers that no single war changes the small worlds of work, leisure and love. The characters might be accused of the very willful ignorance of which Hardy accused the writer in "I Looked Up from My Writing," and yet "In Time of 'The Breaking of Nations'" offers no such sense of condemnation of these characters; if anything, they are presented as stoic examples of endurance in the face of larger world events.

"The Man He Killed" (*CP* 287)

"Had he and I but met
By some old ancient inn,
We should have set us down to wet
Right many a nipperkin!

But ranged as infantry,
And staring face to face,
I shot at him as he at me,
And killed him in his place.

I shot him dead because –
Because he was my foe,
Just so: my foe of course he was;
That's clear enough; although

He thought he'd 'list, perhaps,
Off-hand like – just as I –
Was out of work – had sold his traps –
No other reason why.

Yes; quaint and curious war is!
You shoot a fellow down
You'd treat if met where any bar is,
Or help to half-a-crown."

As we have seen, Hardy frequently uses war as a setting or environment in which to explore other aspects of humanity. But he also writes about soldiers' battlefield experiences in various ways. "The Man He Killed," published in 1902, features a veteran who discusses, after the fact, his experiences in war. He does so in much more regular rhythmic patterns than "In Time of 'The Breaking of Nations,'" with almost perfect iambs throughout. The speaker talks about having killed an opposing fighter in the war and explores his lingering feelings of guilt as he recognizes that his opponent was very much like himself. Like "The Ruin'd Maid," this poem adopts the voice of a character who is distinct from the poet, which is made clear by Hardy's use of quotation marks that surround this entire poem. Also like "The Ruin'd Maid," this poem is tinged with humor, especially in its irony. Here, though, the speaker is well aware of the irony and presents it explicitly, while in "The Ruin'd Maid," readers are asked to pick up on the irony of the two characters' different situations despite the fact that the characters themselves seem not to notice the ironic qualities of their divergent situations.

"The Man He Killed" emphasizes the fundamental humanity of all fighting men. Later World War I poets also explore this theme, like Isaac Rosenberg in "Break of Day in the Trenches," which addresses a rat that can easily run back and forth between the British and German fronts, not distinguishing between the two types of soldiers. Siegfried Sassoon, too, humanizes the enemy in his poem "Glory of Women," when he writes of the "German mother dreaming by the fire" who is "knitting socks to send your son." And Wilfred Owen elides the distinction between friend and enemy in "Strange Meeting," where he writes from the perspective of a fallen soldier, who, chillingly, ends the poem with these lines:

> "I am the enemy you killed, my friend.
> I knew you in this dark; for so you frowned
> Yesterday through me as you jabbed and killed.
> I parried; but my hands were loath and cold.
>   Let us sleep now . . . "

Certainly war poets have seldom overlooked the fact that the men against whom they fight are also men, with families and dreams. In "The Man He Killed," though, Hardy makes that premise the entire theme of his poem by creating a character who reflects intently on his relationship to his enemy. Hardy's poem points out war's "quaint and curious" way of depersonalizing the enemy fighter, but this poem works hard to reanimate and make individual that often mysterious figure of "the enemy."

The veteran in Hardy's poem discusses "the man he killed" by observing that he and the enemy fighter shot at each other despite their many potential similarities. Of course, the speaker admits, "he was my foe . . ." But as the poem develops and the speaker considers their relationship more, he compares the fallen soldier more and more to himself, speculating that perhaps the enemy, just like the speaker himself, decided offhandedly to enlist because he needed the money. Once the speaker begins to establish that the man he killed is probably, more than anyone else, like himself, the poem's expression of war's arbitrariness becomes clearer. While the speaker's tone is eventually one of resignation to the way the world works, tinged with guilt and puzzlement, the reader's reaction is probably meant to be much stronger. By observing the uncomfortable position into which the speaker has been placed, readers may empathize with a surviving soldier's feelings of guilt and confusion.

The speaker points out, finally, that only the situations into which people are placed determine their relationships. If he and his enemy had met in a bar, they might have loaned each other money and bought each other drinks, but having met in battle, they shot at each other. In this, too, they are perfectly alike, and the speaker notes that "I shot at him as he at me," highlighting their mirroring of one another. In this case, their only difference is that the speaker survived and the enemy was killed. But, of course, the speaker could as easily have been killed, and the enemy could now be musing on war's curiousness.

Hardy's word choices highlight the speaker's confusion over his situation as well as his willingness to accede to circumstances. In the middle stanza, the speaker explains – as much to himself as to the readers or his listener – that he understands why he killed the man:

> I shot him dead because –
> Because he was my foe,
> Just so: my foe of course he was;
> That's clear enough; although

Hardy's repetition of the word "because" here implies the speaker's hesitancy at acknowledging the reason for his action, and the pause after the first "because" shows the speaker considering how he might address his own concern. He has to think for a moment before he can begin to explain – to himself or his listener – why he "shot him dead." The phrase "just so" at the beginning of line three shows readers how deeply the speaker feels the need to convince himself of the rightness of his actions. That sense is reinforced by the "of course" later in that line and the "that's clear enough" in the fourth line. Almost the entire stanza demonstrates the speaker's sense of inner conflict over his actions and his attempts to justify his behavior. For the most part, the speaker seems to succeed in this stanza, becoming more and more convinced of his righteousness and increasingly confident in his self-justification.

And then, poignantly, in the stanza's final word, he shows his tenuous grasp of confidence in his actions and again begins to question himself. The stanza is nearly done, but with the final semi-colon and that slight "although . . ." followed by an enjambment into the next paragraph, Hardy demonstrates for readers that the speaker will never truly feel assured again. He will always continue to doubt his actions, and the similarities he then imagines between himself and the man he killed only exacerbate his concerns. Thus the form of the poem implies that, no matter how great his efforts at legitimizing and justifying his behavior, all of his self-assuredness, forever, will be followed by an "although."

The speaker's efforts to distance himself from his own actions become clearer in the final stanza, where his earlier first-person voice is replaced by a more generalizing second-person voice. That switch to second person both separates the speaker from his brutality and serves to implicate the readers, telling them that they would have behaved just as he did because "you" – anyone, really – act that way in war. This is true enough, but it has the added psychological dimension of a speaker conflicted and troubled by his actions who attempts to comfort himself not only through logical justifications in the third stanza but through the psychological displacement in the last stanza.

In addition to the first-person voice of the opening stanzas and the second-person voice of the final stanza, this poem also includes an interesting and perhaps surprising use of third-person voice, in the title. The title of this poem is the only place in which we see a narrative voice, since the entire poem exists within quotation marks.

The title, though, exists outside of the speaker's voice, and because it differs so significantly from the voice of the poem, it prompts readers to ask whether it has any greater significance. The obvious meaning of "The Man He Killed" is that this is a poem about the man who was literally killed in war by the speaker. Clearly the speaker is shaken in this poem, and his lost confidence suggests that he was also changed. But the unique voice of the title, as well as its focus on the dead man rather than the living one, hint at another possibility: that "the man he killed" may be the speaker himself as much as it is his enemy. The speaker and enemy were, as the poem's doppelganger imagery quite evidently presents, parallel characters, and so the speaker may have been so altered by his experience of war that the carefree man he once was has also been, at least metaphorically, destroyed.

The poem's structure reinforces its conversational tone and the sense of the speaker as idealized in his childlike simplicity and untainted approach to the world. The lines are very short, and three of the four lines in each stanza have only three feet. (The third line of each stanza has one additional foot, giving each stanza a slight lopsidedness.) This trimeter structure is reminiscent of a nursery rhyme ("Ring Around the Rosy," for instance, has three stresses in each line) and suggests that the speaker's thoughts are a bit simple and undeveloped. Nonetheless, he seems to possess greater insight than many people who applaud war or who believe genuinely in the stark differences between the two fighters. The speaker's childlike simplicity, in this case, represents a childlike wisdom as well, and a willingness to acknowledge common humanity that more mature, adult speakers lack.

Ultimately, this poem possesses a deceptive simplicity. Its language and rhythms are straightforward, as are its characterization and its themes. But its psychology and use of perspective are complex. Hardy often misleads us with such simplicity, asking readers to delve deeper into poems and find more in a poem than what they experience on its surface. In the case of "The Man He Killed," readers may find some dark humor in the speaker's simplicity and the basic ironies he outlines, but more reading shows not only the lack of humor in the poem but also the depth of human emotions and the complicated, troubling, and subtle ways in which we justify our own brutalities, question our motivations, and manage somehow to go on living with ourselves.

"Channel Firing" (*CP* 305)

"Channel Firing" is probably the Hardy poem that most resembles the poems of the World War I poets who so poignantly depicted the plight of soldiers in battle. Particularly on first reading the poem, one imagines that the speakers are soldiers themselves, lamenting their situation and complaining to an uncaring God. Perhaps because we are so accustomed to those war poems that speak to readers from the trenches, we imagine that these soldiers lie in trenches that are likened to coffins. Too soon, though, we realize that this poem has more of Hardy's unique touches than we might first have realized, as the speakers are, in one of Hardy's favorite turns, ghosts themselves, conveying to us their laments from beyond the grave.

> That night your great guns, unawares,
> Shook all our coffins as we lay,
> And broke the chancel window-squares,
> We thought it was the Judgment-day
>
> And sat upright. While drearisome
> Arose the howl of wakened hounds:
> The mouse let fall the altar-crumb,
> The worms drew back into the mounds,
>
> The glebe cow drooled. Till God called, "No;
> It's gunnery practice out at sea
> Just as before you went below;
> The world is as it used to be:
>
> "All nations striving strong to make
> Red war yet redder. Mad as hatters
> They do no more for Christés sake
> Than you who are helpless in such matters.
>
> "That this is not the judgment-hour
> For some of them's a blessed thing,
> For if it were they'd have to scour
> Hell's floor for so much threatening. . . .

"Ha, ha. It will be warmer when
I blow the trumpet (if indeed
I ever do; for you are men,
And rest eternal sorely need)."

So down we lay again. "I wonder,
Will the world ever saner be,"
Said one, "than when He sent us under
In our indifferent century!"

And many a skeleton shook his head.
"Instead of preaching forty year,"
My neighbour Parson Thirdly said,
"I wish I had stuck to pipes and beer."

Again the guns disturbed the hour,
Roaring their readiness to avenge,
As far inland as Stourton Tower,
And Camelot, and starlit Stonehenge.

As is often true of Hardy's ghosts, these dead have greater insight than
the living and are able to take a long view of history and a wide view of
the world. Also in typical Hardy style, the poem includes several voices,
whose distinctions must be deciphered by the reader. At the beginning of
the poem, a "we" addresses a "you." The "we" turn out to be dead men,
some of whom may have been soldiers, but that identification is never
made entirely clear. The "you" are living fighters who, at this moment,
are engaging in gunnery practice over the English Channel. The sounds
of the guns, even absent immediate battle, are so loud as to wake the
dead, in Hardy's reinterpretation of the cliché. Once awakened, the
ghosts stay up awhile to converse with one another and with God.

Before the dead begin to speak, they observe that animals around
them have had similarly strong reactions to the guns' sounds. This
connection to nature is another of Hardy's hallmarks, and it usually demonstrates on which side of a debate righteousness lies. As
we observed in "The Darkling Thrush," animals for Hardy are like
ghosts, in that they possess unique insight into the world and are
particularly attuned to truth. The darkling thrush may know of some
hope of which the speaker is unaware; the fish in "The Convergence
of the Twain" recognize the ship's vaingloriousness; and the many
animals in "Afterwards" are perfectly attuned to the workings of the

world, as we will see in the next chapter. Here, in "Channel Firing," the animals recognize that the gunnery practice disrupts the structure of the world, forcing all of nature's creatures out of their routines and into hiding.

God's voice creates a pause in this natural upheaval, as He lets these risen dead know that they are hearing merely practice rather than real war. Nonetheless, He says disaffectedly, the world is the same as it has always been. Just because this momentary noise is not caused by fighting, war certainly has not ceased. And, further, God points out, the living are no better than the useless dead at serving Jesus or improving the world. As God continues to speak to the dead, his tone changes; he remains glib throughout, but he adds a tone of misplaced levity when he says that people should be grateful that this is not, in fact, Judgment Day. When God eventually says, at the beginning of the sixth stanza, "Ha, ha" and jokes about hell's heat, readers can see that this God may not be the kind and loving God of salvation people often envision. As He obliquely threatens that perhaps Judgment Day will never come and that the dead will simply rest forever, we see that this God is petty, disconnected, and impervious to human suffering. God's indifference and lack of responsibility are highlighted by the poem's setting, in a cemetery beside a church. As readers envision the church setting, Hardy inverts any pious thoughts of the holiness of the place by creating a God who takes human suffering far less seriously than the humans took God, or Jesus' suffering, in their lifetimes.

After God's three stanzas, in which His character is pretty well established as mean-spirited, childishly vengeful, and lacking control over human behavior and human suffering, the poem returns to the voices of the dead. "So down we lay again," the speaker tells us, and then his compatriots have a chance to air their thoughts. One of them wonders whether the world will "ever saner be," but the ghosts seem to agree that this chance is slight: "many a skeleton shook his head." Another of the ghosts, a parson, then expresses an explicitly anti-religious desire, to have lived his life hedonistically rather than having wasted it serving God. For forty years, he preached God's word, but, knowing the God of this poem, he wishes he had "stuck to pipes and beer." This character, Parson Thirdly, whose name invokes the trinity, also represents Moses; for forty years he tried to lead people through a modern wilderness. In the poem, he realizes posthumously, with the insight only possessed by Hardy's ghosts, that this was not a God worth representing on Earth, and he might as well have served his own purely physical interests. To have sacrificed oneself for *this* God was not a sacrifice worth making.

Finally, a narrative voice speaks, and while the voice of the last stanza might again be the ghost who spoke in the first stanza, the more distanced third-person voice suggests that Hardy or his narrator here takes over the poem, hearing the distant guns again, "roaring their readiness to avenge." The poem's list of places where this revenge might occur includes places both ancient and fictional, demonstrating that human history and human imagination are so filled with war that any other way of living is essentially unthinkable. The whole of the country echoes with the sounds of war, as it always has and, presumably, always will. The deep hopelessness of this poem reflects many of the ideas throughout Hardy's war poetry, which largely sees war as the default status for humans, with brief and anomalous periods of peace. This sense of war as never ending separates Hardy from the other war poets, who highlight the particular horrors of *their* war. For Hardy, though, each war has the same horrors, and this poem reinforces the cyclical nature of human conflict: people are always at war; they are powerless to improve the world; only the dead and animals can recognize the futility of human efforts to improve the world; and God is a farce.

The structure of "Channel Firing" emphasizes God's irrelevance in the world, since His conversational insertion into the middle of the poem has neither the weight of the biblical God speaking to his people nor the sense that this God has something of particular value to say. Instead, the poem ends with human voices, who reclaim rationality and who have the "final say" in their analysis of the world. God as a character in this poem can converse casually with the dead and also serves as a careless, arbitrary authority. In many ways, this conversational God character encourages the disobedience that Parson Thirdly articulates, and the Parson here is presented as perfectly reasonable in his recognition that smoking and drinking would have been at least as valuable as the preaching to which he had devoted himself. The fact that the Parson is allowed to speak last in the poem, following God's word and receiving no

further response, except from a distanced narrator, highlights the
sense that this God has no insight to add to the Parson's posthumous wisdom.

"Channel Firing" expressly counters the political rhetoric of the
First World War, the "war to end all wars," by nonchalantly stating that war always goes on. As in "In Time of 'The Breaking of
Nations,'" this poem expresses absolutely no hope that war will
ever end, seeing it instead as an eternal truth of human existence.
It also, of course, counters the religious rhetoric of the time, which,
as Sassoon and others so sarcastically demonstrated, proclaimed
England to be on the side of God. When God appears in this
poem, however, He turns out not to be a god worth fighting for,
and England's wars are apparently no more just or important than
any others. Thus, the primary angers in this poem are directed not
at the politicians or religious leaders, as they are in Sassoon's work,
but at the stupid people who continue to fight with one another
while placing their hope in a powerless, callous god, and at that
god who laughs derisively at humans' misplaced hopes in their own
ability to escape from entrapments with that same uncaring god's
help.

Concluding Discussion

Hardy's interest in war is less with war itself than with the peripheries
of war: the wives and parents left behind, the civilians who observe
war from a distance, the animals that suffer for man's violence, and
the sympathetic moon that detests man's egotism. For Hardy, the
most interesting characters in war are those whose voices are less often
heard; rather than the soldiers engaged in battle, he focuses on the
wives who stay home or the civilians who are affected by war in less
direct ways. As is the case in his poems on other themes, Hardy foregrounds silenced voices and gives them a space in which to speak. The
disenfranchised become the central figures, and their questions and
concerns become the reader's. Even when he does focus on soldiers, as
in "The Man He Killed," they are not soldiers currently in battle but
those who have returned home to civilian life and who can retrospec-
tively reflect on war experiences. For most of Hardy's war poems, the

soldiers' sacrifices and suffering are not diminished, but they are placed in less prominent positions than one might expect; Hardy's subjects are the various kinds of common people whose lives are touched by war in less obvious ways.

In keeping with his shifted focus away from the soldiers themselves, Hardy often takes a broad view of war, seeing it in a larger historical context or as one of an ongoing series of violent events, an approach that fits with his view of history and human experience more generally. His poems present war less as an aberration or interruption of peace than as part of a long continuum of suffering. War seems, for Hardy, not to represent some change in human behavior but to stand as a perfect example of all human activity. In other words, these poems are less a distinct category of poems for Hardy than they are a continuation of the themes that exist in all of his other poems, with a focus on war, which is representative of all human existence but not different in kind from other aspects of life. As we have seen in the poems in this chapter, even God emphasizes the fact that people will never change their violent ways. Similarly, Hardy's use of the phrase from Jeremiah illustrates his belief that the same warnings people required thousands of years ago continue to apply today.

This is not to suggest that the war poems are upbeat or optimistic in any way, nor that they ignore death, but instead that they treat death not as a shocking anomaly or an unusual horror but as a part of the natural order that is merely heightened by war rather than fundamentally changed by it. Because the poems often have a long view of the world and a broad perspective, they use death as a subtext but seldom as a poem's primary subject. W. H. Auden, who claims Hardy as one of his favorite poets and earliest literary influences, writes, "What I valued most in Hardy, then, as I still do, was his hawk's vision, his way of looking at life from a very great height . . . To see the individual life related not only to the local social life of its time, but to the whole of human history, life on earth, the stars, gives one both humility and self-confidence."[4] Auden's assessment may be nowhere truer than in the war poetry, where Hardy is often able to step outside of the experiences and emotions of individual characters to see how they fit into a GLOBAL or even universal scheme.

The poems largely remain neutral on the subject of war's right-ness or justification. Rather than taking a political stance, Hardy presents other perspectives on war, highlighting its ironies and illogic and empathizing with loss, but not going so far as to proclaim war generally (or any specific war) wrong or unjustified. Such political stances seem not to be his interest or objective. Instead, his lament is for human dysfunction, insufficient empathy, and fundamental human nature that cannot escape its basest tendencies. In addition, of course, he laments a God who is either too absent from human affairs or, perhaps, involved in the wrong way, with malice or mock-ing or utter indifference to human suffering.

The question of how Hardy feels about World War I is prob-ably simply the wrong question, for it is not the question that he addresses in his poems even though it is one that readers often wish answered. In fact, one of the reasons that the poems of the Boer War and those of World War I can be discussed together is that the poems approach war philosophically rather than politically. For many of these poems, readers would have difficulty determin-ing about which war they were written, and if readers were unfa-miliar with Hardy, they might equally guess that these poems are about other wars entirely. Unlike the other World War I poets, who emphasize the particular horrors of the First World War – the trenches, Flanders Field, the massive numbers of European casual-ties, poppies, mustard gas, specific weaponry – Hardy's images are almost entirely of the human faces of military and civilian life, and those humans are both timeless and universal.

Some of Hardy's poems have been read as politically-motivated patriotism, particularly the 1914 poem "Men Who March Away." However, as James Whitehead effectively demonstrates, even that poem, which rehearses jingoistic rhetoric, merely presents the thoughts of young men forced into battle rather than an unmediated narrative patriotism.[5] When the young men intone "In our heart of hearts believing / Victory crowns the just, / And that braggarts must / Surely bite the dust," the poem resembles the wives' lament in "The Going of the Battery" and illustrates the ways in which young soldiers explain and justify their actions. While it might be read as Hardy's patriotic view, his speaking through others, as he so often does, suggests an interest in others' perspectives of war rather than a declaration of the writer's feelings.

The poems that feel most personal and most closely tied to Hardy's own views are those that consider the role of the writer as part of the story of war. He seems to question his own motives as a writer during wartime, wondering how he can justify his documentation of horror and, conversely, how he can write about anything else when horror is occurring. This theme is most stark in "I Looked Up from My Writing," which serves as a kind of condemnation of writing as a response to atrocity and shows the insularity of writers, their separation from the "real world." But, although the theme is most overt in that poem, it exists in others as well, notably "A Wife in London," which addresses issues of writerly ignorance and the impossibility of a writer and reader fully connecting, despite all the best intentions.

Methods of Analysis

As we have done in previous chapters, we looked here at Hardy's use of voices and metrical structures, and we also considered overall poetic structures to see how Hardy attempts to influence readers. This chapter features poems on a similar theme, which allowed us to make some generalizations about Hardy's interest in war and his unique approaches to war poetry. We also performed two kinds of comparative work: we compared Hardy's war poems with those of other poets in the same era who wrote about the same theme, to see how Hardy differs from them in his philosophy and approach; and we compared Hardy's war-themed poems with his other poems to see how he addresses similar concerns regardless of his ostensible subject.

In addition, we considered the allusions that Hardy employs, particularly in "In Time of 'The Breaking of Nations.'" Because the poet includes an explicit reference to another text, we consulted that outside text to see how it informed and deepened our understanding of the poem. Poets choose allusions for the resonances they create and the connection they provide to other works and contexts, so learning more about an author's allusive texts can help us to understand the author's work.

Suggested Work

Hardy has a number of other war poems well worth consideration. Two of them, "The Sick Battle-God" (*CP* 97) and "Drummer Hodge" (*CP* 90), were written during the Boer War and demonstrate many of the same characteristics we have seen in this chapter but with slightly different angles. "Drummer Hodge" presents the story of another soldier, fallen in war, who perhaps resembles the fallen soldier in "A Wife in London." Consider how Hardy presents the soldier in "Drummer Hodge" as well as how he uses the voice of the speaker. Notice, too, the geographical distance Hardy creates as the poem moves from a narrow to a wide angle. Not only does the poem move geographically from the narrow "kopje crest" to "the broad Karoo," it also expands from geographic locations to universal "foreign constellations" and "strange stars."

"The Sick Battle-God" presents a kind of distance too, but in this case it is historical rather than geographical distance. Notice how stanzas are used here to create that growing sense of historical perspective. Consider what Hardy says in this poem about war, and notice again how he uses war as a way to reflect upon the writer's task (as in the "penman's pleading"). Does his sense of war in history differ in this poem from his presentation of war in "Channel Firing" or "In Time of 'The Breaking of Nations'"? Is the poem more hopeful about the possibilities for human improvement than those others? Analyze the tone of each stanza as you move through the poem.

5

The Self and Time

The concept of time manifests itself in two ways in Hardy's poetry: in form and in content. His formal layering of time periods, incorporating several distinct moments in a single poem, lends richness and scope to his poems, even very short ones, and deepens their narratives by presenting the same scene from multiple perspectives. This formal inclusion of time is often coupled with an explicit theme of time as he discusses, laments, ponders, and rails against time's passage in a variety of ways.

As we have seen in a number of poems already, Hardy makes time's passage a subject even in poems ostensibly about something else. For instance, "A Wife in London" moves between time periods to highlight the ironies of distance, death, war, and ignorance. Although the poem focuses overtly on the pain caused by war, Hardy's obvious playing with chronology as a formal technique causes time to become an additional subject of the poem. Similarly, in "The Convergence of the Twain," his regular movement between images of past hopes for the *Titanic* and its current sunken state foregrounds time's passage as a lens through which to view the disaster. In these poems, readers see three of Hardy's uses of time: as a formal technique, as a way of considering divinity, and as an imprisoning inevitability in human existence.

Arguably the most unique quality of Hardy's time poetry is what Dennis Taylor describes as its intimating present reality. Often the main character of a poem will see a location where past events occurred and feel immediately and uncontrollably transported back into those moments. These memory poems show how the past haunts the present as an inescapable, enticing, and constantly looming alternate reality. However, the present also haunts the past with its retrojection of futility, absurdity, and finitude. Otherwise pleasant memories are marred by the present awareness of their ephemeral and naïve quality. Being neither at peace with the past nor able to live fully in the present, the speakers of Hardy's time poems reflect a profound discontent coupled with a pained hope that time may be merely illusory.

"Afterwards" (*CP* 553)

The Hardy poem that most resembles other English poems in its attention to time is "Afterwards," which engages in the futile but common act of imagining the world after one's death. Here Hardy's speaker articulates the legacy he hopes to leave for "them," the nameless people who may consider what he did while alive. In this way, the poem very much resembles the work of earlier poets, from Shakespeare to Wordsworth, considering the timelessness of the poet's work and its ability to outlast him.[1]

> When the Present has latched its postern behind my tremulous stay,
> And the May month flaps its glad green leaves like wings,
> Delicate-filmed as new-spun silk, will the neighbours say,
> "He was a man who used to notice such things"?
>
> If it be in the dusk when, like an eyelid's soundless blink,
> The dewfall-hawk comes crossing the shades to alight
> Upon the wind-warped upland thorn, a gazer may think,
> "To him this must have been a familiar sight."
>
> If I pass during some nocturnal blackness, mothy and warm,
> When the hedgehog travels furtively over the lawn,
> One may say, "He strove that such innocent creatures should come to
>   no harm,
> But he could do little for them; and now he is gone."
>
> If, when hearing that I have been stilled at last, they stand at the door,
> Watching the full-starred heavens that winter sees,

Will this thought rise on those who will meet my face no more,
"He was one who had an eye for such mysteries"?

And will any say when my bell of quittance is heard in the gloom
And a crossing breeze cuts a pause in its outrollings,
Till they rise again, as they were a new bell's boom,
"He hears it not now, but used to notice such things"?

This poem, like many before it, questions the quality of the speaker's life and suggests that his role as an observer does indeed constitute a worthwhile existence. The language of the descriptive passages is so beautiful and so finely wrought, and the meter so fluid and conversational within the poem's elongated lines, that the question of whether the speaker, through mere observation, had done enough with his life seems to be answered implicitly in the affirmative. The passages describing nature illustrate some of Hardy's best poetic abilities, in their use of metaphor, personification, alliteration, density of imagery, and in their ability to "paint a picture" with words. The poem suggests that if this level of "noticing things" is not sufficient to prove that close observation – Hardy's or anyone's – has value, then nothing could.

In this chapter's other poems, though, and in the vast majority of Hardy's work, the relative clarity and satisfaction offered in "Afterwards" is replaced by a more typically Hardian tortured resistance to time's passage. His apparent unwillingness to accept the truth of time's movement generally distinguishes his work from others' because he equates time to a God-like force deliberately or arbitrarily undoing the lives and works of all humans. In that way Hardy's view of God, his understanding of the human experience, and his characterization of time are, as we will explore in the rest of this chapter, deeply interconnected.

"During Wind and Rain" (*CP* 495)

They sing their dearest songs –
He, she, all of them – yea,
Treble and tenor and bass,
And one to play;
With the candles mooning each face. . . .

Ah, no; the years O!
How the sick leaves reel down in throngs!

They clear the creeping moss –
Elders and juniors – aye,
Making the pathways neat
And the garden gay;
And they build a shady seat. . . .
Ah, no; the years, the years;
See, the white storm-birds wing across!

They are blithely breakfasting all –
Men and maidens – yea,
Under the summer tree,
With a glimpse of the bay,
While pet fowl come to the knee. . . .
Ah, no; the years O!
And the rotten rose is ript from the wall.

They change to a high new house,
He, she, all of them – aye,
Clocks and carpets and chairs
On the lawn all day,
And brightest things that are theirs. . . .
Ah, no; the years, the years;
Down their carved names the raindrop ploughs.

"During Wind and Rain" seems to depict a joyful gathering of people, but the final lines of each stanza illustrate the poem's actual subject: "Ah, no; the years, O!" This poem primarily uses time as a theme, but the theme takes over the poem so completely that time becomes part of the form as well. The poem begins quite happily, describing a party filled with people and music. People have gathered together to celebrate, sing, and play. They eat and enjoy one another's company as well as the lovely setting. What readers realize before the end of the first stanza, though, is that Hardy focuses on what happens after, or well after, the party; the final two lines remind readers that feelings of joy and celebration are unexpectedly fleeting.

Each subsequent stanza then follows an identical pattern: the first five lines reflect happiness and festivity, an ellipse symbolizes the speaker's almost mythical transportation to an emptier future, a repeated line emphasizes the passing of the years, and a final line employs images of decay. In each case, the final line of decay relies upon images of nature – flowers, birds, rain – to highlight the passage of time as a natural process. The inevitable connection between nature and destruction does not seem to comfort Hardy's speaker, but he does acknowledge, through natural imagery, that such eventual destruction is ordinary, not the result of some cataclysm but of the daily workings of the natural world.

The mood and vision of this poem move back and forth four times, once per stanza. While this technique works very well formally, emphasizing the poem's lyrical qualities and highlighting the stanzaic pattern, it also demonstrates the pull towards inevitable rot for Hardy and his speakers. The body of the poem is written in the present tense, and so a reader might assume that the speaker is currently at the party, looking toward a gloomy future. The title, though, suggest that the party is long past, and the speaker recalls it during a later, darker time. One might expect that the joyous event should distract the speaker from his visions of time's destroying power, but the regular repetition of "the years, the years" demonstrates how impossible Hardy's speakers find it to live contentedly in the moment. Even as the speaker gazes at the party-goers "blithely breakfasting" and "making the pathways neat / And the gardens gay," he is constantly reminded, in his mind's eye, of their temporality.

That pull among past, present and future is impossible for Hardy's speaker to avoid because any intimation of happiness implies, for him, an end to that happiness. At the same time, though, entrapment in that hyper-awareness means that the desire to enjoy happier moments, even those that may occur only in imagination or memory, cannot fully be ignored. Thus, as we see in this poem, there remains a constant back and forth from joyous moments, tinged with sadness at their fleetingness, to the painful absence of such joy. In each stanza, the sixth line begins with "Ah, no!" which illustrates the speaker's resistance to the problem of time's passage. He feels traumatized by it, and, despite his willingness to acknowledge time's presence and to force that recognition on his readers, he nonetheless resists it.

Hardy is, in some ways, a miserably failed hedonist. He wishes to live in the moment, feeling the beauty and cheer of his present experiences, and to indulge himself fully in sensual pleasures, but his constant awareness of time's passage prevents him from doing so. Every happy moment is inevitably colored by Hardy's knowledge that sadder times are coming, that happy moments pass, and that everyone's eventual end is death and decay. So while the characters in "During Wind and Rain" seem oblivious to "the years, the years," their observer is acutely aware of what will become of them.

Of course, the very idea of an "observer" here is fraught since the poem subtly suggests that the speaker who observes might be one of the characters of whom he speaks. That is, the "He, she, all of them" of the poem may include the speaker himself, who looks upon these revelers in a kind of "out of body experience," recognizing that they are oblivious to time's passage while he is not. If that is the case, then the poem is not only about the depressive preoccupations of the speaker but also a kind of morality tale for the reader: be aware that your joy is always tinged with the reality of joy's passing. Something about the characters "blithely breakfasting" suggests that that naïveté is problematic and that they should be more fully aware. By removing his speaker from the frivolous scene and focus on existential concerns, Hardy seems to suggest that daily life is utterly futile, almost ridiculous in its apparent importance but actual insignificance, and also that humans are inevitably made fools by caring so much about its individual moments and petty details.[2]

The speaker here expresses some terror about the passage of time despite his apparent recognition that time's passage is simply the natural way of the world. The natural sense of decay in the poem is belied by the way that the decay presents itself, not as a slow and gradual process but as something violent, sudden and painful: "The rotten rose is ript from the wall"; "How the sick leaves reel down in throngs!" "Down their carved names the rain-drop ploughs." Ordinarily we might ascribe to raindrops such movements as dripping, sliding, even cascading. But to "plough" down the wall suggests a level of violence and proactivity that seems not to describe the innocuous raindrop. In this case, of course, the raindrop is hardly innocent, as it viciously erases names that had been carved in joy and with a sense of their permanence. The raindrop, for Hardy, does not simply coincidentally erase those names but does so with malice and intentionality. Similarly, the leaves "reel down in throngs," with a kind of passion and aggression seldom associated with falling leaves. Thus nature, while obviously "natural" in its definitional sense, is far from the innocent, purifying nature of Wordsworth's poems; instead, it is cruel and spiteful, doing its "natural" thing by undermining any potential pleasure that humans might manage to eke out for themselves.

Although the poem seems primarily to express the speaker's solitary devastation at seeing these happy times ended, even the first halves of each stanza express some sense of time's passage. This is particularly true in the last stanza, where the players who earlier sang and ate now "change to a high new house." The meaning of their action is not entirely clear. In the plainest sense, they have simply moved the location of the party, but the image of a "high new house" also suggests an existential change, especially when the objects associated with this new location include "clocks"; even during the apparent celebration, the primary symbol of time's passage is present, "on the lawn all day." The first stanza, too, has a slight sense of ominousness in its description of the people's singing faces, "with the candles mooning each face." That ghostly imagery suggests that, even in the moment of happiness, there is a hint of the partiers' mortality. Thus the chronological changes throughout this poem highlight a supernatural sense: who can see the future? What does it mean for the speaker to feel an abiding sense of ultimate oblivion in the face of others' momentary oblivion?

Finally, the fact that the poem's title reflects dark weather rather than the summer of the party demonstrates not only that the speaker is forever reminded of time's passage but also that the state of inclement weather reminds him powerfully of the absolute eventual end of happiness. The poem reminds the speaker of wind and rain despite the fact that most of its action occurs explicitly in bright sunlight. The title may also allude to the Fool's song at the end of *Twelfth Night*, which begins "When that I was and a little tiny boy" and concludes with "A great while ago the world begun." Among stanzas that detail development from childhood to adulthood within the context of the creation of the world, the Fool repeats "Hey Ho the wind and the rain" and "For the rain it raineth every day." In

Shakespeare, as in Hardy, the steadiness of the weather is connected to the passage of time and the steady movement of a life, a work of art, and the world. While even the objects on the lawn contain sunniness – "And brightest things that are theirs" – the poem ends with that ploughing raindrop and is contained within a title that implies not only storminess but also nature's means of eroding the past: wind and rain dissolve the memories of what once was. Thus the title's reminder of destructive weather undermines the happy images the poem describes.

"The Self-Unseeing" (*CP* 166) and "At Castle Boterel" (*CP* 351)

Both "At Castle Boterel" and "The Self Unseeing" play with similar ideas to those presented in "During Wind and Rain," but they approach the idea of the deep pain associated with time's passage from different perspectives. Like "During Wind and Rain," these two poems are about time and also incorporate time into their forms. Each of them affirms a sense of the speaker outside of himself, as an observer of his own life, and each considers the past from a more painful present moment. In each case, the physical place triggers the speaker's memories of the lives that used to inhabit that space. In addition to noticing the ways in which the place reminds him of long-past events, the speakers in both of these poems highlight the ignorance of the people who participated in those events, including each speaker's younger self. The vivacity of the speaker's memories creates a sense of temporal movement in the poems as the speaker wavers between images of past and present.

    The touching and simple poem "The Self-Unseeing" encompasses both the innocence of youth and, perhaps to a slightly lesser extent, its willful blindness.

> Here is the ancient floor,
> Footworn and hollowed and thin,
> Here was the former door
> Where the dead feet walked in.

She sat here in her chair,
Smiling into the fire;
He who played stood there,
Bowing it higher and higher.

Childlike, I danced in a dream;
Blessings emblazoned that day;
Everything glowed with a gleam;
Yet we were looking away!

The rhythm of this poem is unusual in that each line both begins and ends with a stressed syllable, a technique that increases the choppiness of the poem. Rather than fully transporting readers to a time of music and dancing, it remains haltingly in the present, only recollecting those times to observe that they have passed forever. The speaker's observation of the now-empty room prompts him to reflect on the feet – now dead – that once stepped there. Next, he notes "her chair" and the place where "he" stood and played an instrument for her. And, finally, he remembers his own dancing in the room. The memory here is of a very precise situation, and rather than being transported to that time, as often happens in Hardy's poems, in "The Self-Unseeing" the speaker remains decidedly in the bare present, and the scene he pictures remains firmly in his memory.

The last stanza is most effective in demonstrating Hardy's oft-expressed philosophies of time's ironies. In the first line, the speaker notes his own dancing as though it was "in a dream." Of course, it exists in a memory rather than a dream, but, for Hardy's speakers, memory is often dreamlike because of time's transitory nature and because it is apparently hard to believe that something that exists only in memory was ever real, just as a dream seemed real at the time but lives on only in the mind. For Hardy's speakers, the past seems to have that same quality: it seems once to have been real, but it is so distant that this speaker can hardly believe his own mental image of the past. In addition, everything that happened in the past seems to have been vastly better than the present, and he is pained by the fact that he was not aware at the time of the pain that was to come and, perhaps simultaneously, grateful to have had those moments of blissful ignorance and despondent to be more fully aware now. As he writes in the second line of the last stanza, "blessings emblazoned that day," but he seems to attribute that sense of abundant blessing both to the dreamlike state of the memory and to his immaturity at the time. Having been childlike, he sensed blessing; the implication is that now, in his older years, he recognizes both that he was naïve in his innocence and that the blessings that seemed to exist may have been dreamed just as the events seem to have been.

The third line of the final stanza reminisces about the gleam and glowing that seemed to exist at the time: "everything glowed with a gleam." As you may recall, Hardy uses the term "gleam" in another poem, "On a Fine Morning," in which he encourages others to look at the margins of the world, to escape from worldly suffering by "cleaving to the Dream / and in gazing at the gleam / Whereby gray things golden seem." That poem suggests that the only effective way to live happily is to purposefully ignore misery by "gazing at the gleam" at the edges of the world. The "gray things" at the center of the world seem, in "On a Fine Morning," to be elements of present reality, and so the "gleam" is an escape from reality to a level of comfortable ignorance. In "The Self-Unseeing," the gleam also seems to be a sort of ignorance, suggesting that people who live in "the gleam" are unaware of what they have, a kind of obliviousness that leads to joy.

In "On a Fine Morning," the speaker presents "gazing at the gleam" as advice, but in "The Self-Unseeing," the speaker simply points out that this gleaming world exists only for the young, who are so accustomed to it that they neglect to notice it and can therefore live in a carefree world, removed from gray reality. As an adult looking back, though, he is no longer able to see the gleam when confronted with the empty room and its powerful memories, except to the extent that he realizes it was once there and is no longer. His remembrance of the glowing and gleam is wistful and yearning, but he is also pained by the fact that, as he says in the last line, "we were looking away." That is, he might have been able to see that glow directly because he was still young and lacking in worldly knowledge, but rather than appreciating it as he might have, he looked away, finding something else worthy of attention. In hindsight, though, nothing else would have been as valuable or worth noting.

This poem, like so many of Hardy's others, emphasizes the small but powerful ironies of aging: that the things an old man wishes he had appreciated are now gone; that the knowledge gained through age might better have been used in youth; that youth and ignorance are necessarily paired; and that, once insight is gained, it can no longer be forgotten, and so the innocence of youth can never be recaptured. Just as we noted the tensions between Hardy's hope and his despair – the unending and unresolved pull between those two poles, neither of which Hardy is willing to abandon – so too these poems about time and the self demonstrate a powerful tension. Hardy fixates on this primary trap in which time catches people: age might exist without wisdom, but youth cannot exist without ignorance. The speaker's self existed in his youth, but it was "unseeing"; now, by contrast, the self has gained vision, but what it sees is desolate and empty.

"At Castle Boterel" similarly approaches the tension between joyful past experience and the sadder, emptier present, and it again does so through the revisiting of a physical place that remains the same, as the lives around it have changed, inevitably for the worse. Again, the explicit theme of time's passage becomes embedded in the poem's form as remembered figures become mystically corporeal through the power of memory.

> As I drive to the junction of lane and highway,
>   And the drizzle bedrenches the waggonette,
> I look behind at the fading byway,
>   And see on its slope, now glistening wet,
>   Distinctly yet
>
> Myself and a girlish form benighted
>   In dry March weather. We climb the road
> Beside a chaise. We had just alighted
>   To ease the sturdy pony's load
>   When he sighed and slowed.
>
> What we did as we climbed, and what we talked of
>   Matters not much, nor to what it led, –
> Something that life will not be balked of
>   Without rude reason till hope is dead,
>   And feeling fled.

It filled but a minute. But was there ever
    A time of such quality, since or before,
In that hill's story? To one mind never,
    Though it has been climbed, foot-swift, foot-sore,
      By thousands more.

Primaeval rocks form the road's steep border,
    And much have they faced there, first and last,
Of the transitory in Earth's long order;
    But what they record in colour and cast
      Is – that we two passed.

And to me, though Time's unflinching rigour,
    In mindless rote, has ruled from sight
The substance now, one phantom figure
    Remains on the slope, as when that night
      Saw us alight.

I look and see it there, shrinking, shrinking,
    I look back at it amid the rain
For the very last time; for my sand is sinking,
    And I shall traverse old love's domain
      Never again.

In this poem, the speaker remembers "Myself and a girlish form benighted / In dry March weather." Of course, the rainy weather as he observes this remembered place suggests bleakness, but the memory is of a more pleasant time; as is often the case for Hardy, the weather reflects human emotions, and memories of a sunny past are replaced by the truth of a rainy present. In "At Castle Boterel," Hardy briefly outlines the two characters' actions together, climbing the same road the speaker sees now years later.

Immediately after providing these precise details, the speaker pauses to remark that his actions had little worldly import. After having established where the speaker is now, what happened then, and what about it did not matter, he moves on to explore what did matter: "was there ever / A time of such quality, since or before, / In that hill's story?" Hardy is seldom content to choose a single perspective, though, and in this case he perceives the world not only from the present and the past but also from the human and natural angles. Hardy acknowledges that the vast importance of the place exists only for him since "it has been climbed . . . by thousands more." The event that holds such significance for him happened on the hill, but it is important only to him and not to the hill; his deep feelings for this place are entirely unreciprocated. The very nature of time's passage necessitates that an event that holds great significance to a person holds almost no significance for the natural world, whose span is so much greater than that of a human life.

In the last two stanzas, he moves on to a relationship even more significant than the one between the hill and the humans, and that is the one between his previous self and his current self. Only one "phantom figure" is left: not his lost love but his lost self. No longer youthful or in love, the speaker looks back at this lost self and sees it "shrinking, shrinking . . . for my sand is sinking." He sees his current self disappearing into the landscape, soon to be absorbed completely by the earth. While most people do realize this truth, even if they choose not to fixate on it as Hardy does, they may not visualize their former, happier selves as fully separate beings from their current selves, nor do they envision themselves gradually and imminently nearing their full absorption into oblivion. Hardy, however, palpably connects to his youthful self and sees him as a separate being whose presence he can see gradually disappearing.

At the same time that Hardy's speaker considers the relationship between human couple and physical landscape, he emphasizes the relationship between his two selves, a juxtaposition that helps him to consider the different lifespans of man and earth. Even as the hill remains utterly unchanged, already only one of the two human figures survives, and the speaker recognizes his own mortality and impending end. The hill, on the other hand, is bounded by "primeval rocks." Sand and rock, which are essentially the same, are contrasted by rock's steadiness, in the form of the hill, and sand's shifting nature, evoking an hourglass as well as the unsteady ground on which the young speaker stands. There is no sense of absolute permanence in this poem, but the comparatively significant length of the Earth's life, and the hill's, reinforces the fleetingness and brevity of human life. In the penultimate stanza, Hardy's speaker fully articulates the thrust of his reflections: it is "Time's unflinching rigour" that has mindlessly closed off possibilities for this couple's happy continuation. Instead, only one figure – the speaker's own – remains on the hill, and, as the final stanza recognizes, that figure is "shrinking, shrinking," and will soon be gone too.

In the final lines of the poem, Hardy's speaker seems to lament not just his impending death but also that fact that "I shall traverse old love's domain / Never again." That is, the loss of love pains him as much as, or even more than, the loss of life. And that sense of loss is heightened not only by the loss of the female figure who once walked beside him but by the human juxtaposition with nature, which remains, on and on, in the face of human transition. "At Castle Boterel" ultimately has both a positive and a negative implication: the Earth's near-permanence is a kind of comfort in the face of Time's endless march, but the tininess of human life when compared with the lifespan of nature makes humans feel even smaller.

Both "At Castle Boterel" and "The Self-Unseeing," like "During Wind and Rain," emphasize the distances from which every scene is viewed and the profound ways in which that perspective changes perception, understanding, and emotional reaction. They also demonstrate how a discussion of time transforms itself into a movement through time. Hardy thus covers the wide view of geologic history, the narrower view of a single village or home or room, and the immensely focused view of an individual existence. Every individual's reactions to his life and its transience are couched in terms of perspective: How old was I when I experienced this? How do I experience it differently now? How do I wish I had experienced it then? How does nature see what I see, and how does nature's perspective differ from mine? In each case, Hardy seems troubled by the fact that there is no real truth to any experience but only a series of incomplete perspectives that are limited – both physically and chronologically – by where and how the individual is positioned, whether by his own choice, through his ignorance, or by random chance.

"The House of Hospitalities" (*CP* 206)

Here we broached the Christmas barrel,
Pushed up the charred log-ends;
Here we sang the Christmas carol,
And called in friends.

Time has tired me since we met here
When the folk now dead were young,
Since the viands were outset here
And quaint songs sung.

And the worm has bored the viol
That used to lead the tune,
Rust eaten out the dial
That struck night's noon.

Now no Christmas brings in neighbours,
And the New Year comes unlit;
Where we sang the mole now labours,
And spiders knit.

Yet at midnight if here walking,
When the moon sheets wall and tree,
I see forms of old time talking,
Who smile on me.

The form of each stanza, three lines of tetrameter and a final line of dimeter, leads to an abruptness as each quatrain ends. Two "missing" feet at the end of every stanza highlight emptiness in the missing beats. That curtailed final line not only forces a significant pause between stanzas but also hints at the poem's theme of something cut short or ended too soon; at the same time, the regularity of the rhythmic pattern suggests a certain level of comfort and ease.

The scene, set almost entirely in the speaker's imagination, again highlights one of Hardy's favorite techniques for emphasizing the passage of time: he describes an empty space and imagines it filled with people, life and joy. As in other poems, its ostensible subject is human interaction, but its profound subtext is time's passage. In this case, the events are associated with Christmas, and the first stanza highlights the various ways in which a celebration of Christmas was pleasant and carefree. The physical locations, empty now, prompt the speaker to recall human relationships and activities, and chronology becomes integral to the poem's form, not merely to its theme.

The "we" of the first stanza is notable in its difference from Hardy's usual pensive, solitary voice, and three of the poem's four stanzas attend primarily to the communal nature of the Christmas celebrations. Immediately thereafter, though, the speaker acknowledges that those events can occur no longer and that the "we" becomes the more conventional "me" of Hardy's other memory poems. The "we" remains in the text, posited against the tired, older "me," but the "we," while present in memory, are dead in the speaker's current world. The next two stanzas articulate the ways in which time's passage has altered the human landscape: the instruments that used to accompany the carolers have been eaten by worms, the clock – again, a clock – has rusted, the neighbors are dead or gone, and the room itself has been taken over by spiders and moles. Nonetheless, for segments of the poem, at least, Hardy's speaker can still invoke the "we" of his memories, and the solitary "I" who has outlasted his colleagues; he shifts rather comfortably between the plural and singular visions of himself. Unlike in "During Wind and Rain," which invokes the partygoers in a distanced third-person voice, the plural pronouns of "The House of Hospitalities" include the speaker and integrate him into the happy actions he describes.

"The House of Hospitalities," like "At Castle Boterel," imagines the human lifespan against the lifespan of the world. In this poem, the role of nature that was played in "At Castle Boterel" by the hill is played by animals. Animals, unlike the hill, are indeed affected by the passage of time, usually at an even faster pace than humans, but Hardy treats them not as individuals but as a collective representation of the natural world. The worms, moles, and spiders that gradually take over and destroy human homes and accoutrements outlive and triumph over humans, who remain, in Hardy's conception, as fragilely mortal individuals. The "folk" die, but worms and moles continue on, incrementally replacing human existences with their own. Rust plays a role here as well, and is a further example of nature's ability to destroy both man and his possessions, even those that feel impenetrable.

The last stanza of the poem suggests that, despite the dreariness of the setting, the speaker is not entirely unhappy; perhaps he is not unhappy at all. The ghostliness of the scene is emphasized by the speaker's final, not displeased observation that, despite the death and destruction in the house, when he walks there at midnight, he still sees "forms of old time talking, / Who smile on me." What those "forms of old time" are is open to debate. Most likely, though, they are the shadowy, ghostly figures that the speaker recalls with such precision. They accompany him in his imagination despite the fact that the reality of his location is desolate and still disintegrating. The overall tone of this poem is less desperate than some of the others that deal with time's passage, and the "yet" that begins the last stanza encourages readers to find some hope in the speaker's observations even though they feel fairly hopeless. Of course, it is not "old Time" that smiles on the speaker; that would be far too benevolent for per- sonified Time as Hardy generally invokes it. But "forms of old time" may be those happy human figures who once celebrated Christmas by his side, and they remain somehow present.

What accounts for these hints of hope in an otherwise bleak poem? Perhaps it is the Christmas theme, which is one of the sig- nificant ways in which this poem differs from others that focus simi- larly on time's passage. While the poem is hardly theological in its approach to Christmas and instead emphasizes the cultural aspects of the holiday – the songs, the food, and the fireplace rather than the birth of a savior – the holiday does seem to lend some optimism to the speaker, who appears in this poem not to fear death but sim- ply to recognize its coming. In addition, those "forms of old time" smile on him, an action which suggests that he has nothing to fear from death, to which his friends have already succumbed, apparently without horror or misery. He feels death approaching, as it already has taken his former acquaintances, but he does not express dread. Instead, the hospitality of this decrepit house may mirror the hospi- tality of impending death.

The poem's title similarly acts as a kind of comfort. "The House of Hospitalities" obviously had one meaning years earlier, when the house truly served as a place of warmth and welcome for neighbors and friends. Now, of course, "Christmas brings no neighbors," and the friends who once sang are dead, but the house remains hospitable nonetheless, this time occupied by spirits and memories, which serve a welcoming function for the speaker. While many (perhaps most) of us would consider a house filled with spiders, moles, worms, and human ghosts somewhat less than hospitable, Hardy's view, as is so often the case, contradicts preconceived notions. Instead, something about the natural order of things, and perhaps about the memories of Christmases spent in this place, reinforces the speaker's comfort in this environment rather than his desire to flee.

"The Going" (*CP* 338)

Why did you give no hint that night
That quickly after the morrow's dawn,
And calmly, as if indifferent quite,
You would close your term here, up and be gone
 Where I could not follow
 With wing of swallow
To gain one glimpse of you ever anon!

 Never to bid good-bye,
 Or lip me the softest call,
Or utter a wish for a word, while I
Saw morning harden upon the wall,
 Unmoved, unknowing
 That your great going
Had place that moment, and altered all.

Why do you make me leave the house
And think for a breath it is you
I see At the end of the alley of bending boughs
Where so often at dusk you used to be;
 Till in darkening dankness
 The yawning blankness
Of the perspective sickens me!

 You were she who abode
 By those red-veined rocks far West,

You were the swan-necked one who rode
Along the beetling Beeny Crest,
   And, reining nigh me,
   Would muse and eye me,
While Life unrolled us its very best.

Why, then, latterly did we not speak,
Did we not think of those days long dead,
And ere your vanishing strive to seek
That time's renewal? We might have said,
   "In this bright spring weather
   We'll visit together
Those places that once we visited."

   Well, well! All's past amend,
   Unchangeable. It must go.
I seem but a dead man held on end
To sink down soon. . . .
   O you could not know
   That such swift fleeing No soul foreseeing –
Not even I – would undo me so!

"The Going," published in Hardy's *Poems of 1912–13*, is widely regarded as among his best and most moving poetry, but it also demonstrates a series of complex philosophies about time, as well as formal movements through time, that deserve greater attention. Unlike some of the other poems that detail time's passage and its accompanying losses, the poems in *Poems of 1912–13* frequently address an absent person – almost always explicitly a woman – rather than speaking in a more general third-person voice. The *Poems of 1912–13* also tend to emphasize the absent woman, rather than an empty physical location, as the speaker's motivation for his musings. "The Going" has both of these characteristics, addressing the departed woman directly and also mentioning locations but not making them the focus of the poem; instead, the woman's absence is the focus. In keeping with Hardy's poems of other years and collections, though, he continues to be nearly obsessed by the passage of time and the painful ironies of hindsight's clarity. In addition, it is worth noting that this is one of Hardy's most beautifully crafted and deeply felt poems, and its aesthetics in some ways overwhelm its themes rather than the other way around.[3]

The speaker of the poem sounds positively shocked by the woman's death and, initially at least, even angry at her for not having given him any warning that she would "leave" him. Of course, readers eventually recognize that his anger is actually at time itself – or at the power that created time and enforces its passage and ravaging effects – rather than at the woman, but because he addresses her and asks why she would leave him this way, he seems to accuse her of foreknowledge that she neglected to share with him. The speaker continues to accuse the woman of negligence or disregard when he blames her for the tricks his eyes play on him, as though his illusions and misperceptions are her fault. The poem is tinged throughout with regret, as the speaker laments the things he should have known and should have done but about which he remained unaware. As in "During Wind and Rain," the speaker seems angry that he did not better recognize his own joy when it existed and, even more importantly, that he did not sufficiently prepare for his current sadness.

Like many of Hardy's poems, "The Going" offers a distinction between "then" and "now," moving back and forth between the times of ignorance and times of knowledge, a dichotomy that Hardy frequently presents as synonymous to his conception of "before and after." The speaker remembers his blissful times with the woman, and he laments his current existence, in which he has visions of his lost love and regret at not having said good-bye. The speaker recognizes that his greater despair lies in his simultaneously holding multiple views of their relationship, and he cries out, "The yawning blankness / Of the perspective sickens me!" It is, indeed, perspective itself that causes his pain, and if his perspective were different, he might be less tormented. As in poems we have already examined in this chapter, the speaker seems positively plagued by the facts that someone may have known something that he did not know and, furthermore, that he should have known it. The idea that the dead woman may have had some premonition of her death before it occurred but that she neglected to share it with him causes him tremendous pain, but now that she is gone, he can only question her hypothetically. The speaker likely recognizes the illogic of this accusation, but his pain causes him to cast around for others to blame.

This "before and after" dichotomy exists in many of Hardy's poems, but "The Going" actually includes two other time periods as well: the cold and silent recent past and a looming, desolate future. While the first three stanzas literally address the woman's "going," noting how abruptly and permanently her departure has "altered all," and the fourth stanza recollects the loving times that the couple shared, long ago, the fifth stanza questions "Why, then, latterly did we not speak . . . ?" This question about the couple's more recent past is filled with his regret and guilt at not having tried harder to retain the loving glances and shared experiences of those early years. Instead, the speaker implores his lost love in the fifth stanza to consider why they made no effort to recreate those happy times and chose to live in a bitterer present. Hardy thus complicates the notion of the past as inevitably better than the present and demonstrates a more nuanced and realistic view of this couple's relationship, which had once been sublime but more recently lacked any connection between the two lovers.

The future, perhaps not surprisingly, also holds no prospect of happiness or joy as the speaker anticipates his own death, using imagery similar to that in "Castle Boterel": "I seem but a dead man held on end / To sink down soon . . . ." But he seems frankly less upset by the prospect of his own approaching end than by his not having labored to make the recent past as pleasant as the distant past and not having, during either of those past times, anticipated the despairing present. Certainly this is a poem that deeply laments the loss of a love, but its even greater sadness seems to be in the speaker's own earlier blindness in predicting or anticipating the future. Here again, the speaker feels that life has made a fool of him; the power of hindsight and its dispelling of ignorance too late to effect any meaningful remedy injures the speaker, who is almost taunted by his imprisonment in time.

The poem's final stanza employs a masterly command of psychological insight to bring us closer to the speaker and his inner turmoil. His tone at the beginning of the stanza suggests resignation and acceptance: "Well, well! All's past amend, / Unchangeable. It must go." This brusque dismissal of his recent regret implies that the speaker is prepared to leave behind his lamentation and move on with his life. Furthermore, the conversational tone suggests that he is prepared to speak realistically both to himself and to his readers. But that stoicism and apparent self-control last only for those two lines. Immediately thereafter, the speaker looks vaguely to a not-too-distant future that includes his own "sinking," and then again pursues the themes that dogged this poem throughout: knowledge and ignorance. As the poem ends, the speaker distances himself from accusations that the woman might have predicted her own demise and instead acknowledges that she could not know "that such swift fleeing . . . would undo me so." In other words, perhaps she did recognize that her own death was near, but she could not possibly have known how deeply painful her loss would be to him. As a recognition of the impossibility of this kind of knowing, he admits that "No soul foreseeing – / Not even I –" could have anticipated the depth of his mourning for her.

This powerful statement presents readers, finally, with a new perspective on ignorance and knowledge, with "knowledge" meaning not prescience but a particular type of emotional self-knowledge. In other poems, we have seen Hardy regret his youthful ignorance, recognizing it as an inevitable aspect of youth. But in "The Going," uncharacteristically, the speaker acknowledges that there was simply no way of knowing the depth of his emotional response short of experiencing it himself. While he feels deep regret and a tremendous sense of loss, those emotions are reactions not exactly to a lack of knowing but to a lack of experience. His mourning allows for that experience, but he wishes, impossibly, for an ability to have anticipated his response so as to have alleviated it preemptively by having acted differently in his relationship while the woman was still living. Of course, to have done so would have neutralized his later regret, thus eliminating the need for him to have reflected on and altered his behavior. Hardy thus subtly presents characters so in thrall to their deep emotions that they continue to yearn for situations they simultaneously recognize as existentially unattainable.

The active title here supports the power of the final stanza, implying that the woman's "going" continues even after the moment of her actual death because of his continual awareness of what her "going" does to him. And, of course, "The Going," rather than "Your Going" or "Her Going," leaves open the possibility that this poem is about his own going, which may or may not mean death. It may, instead, mean a kind of emotional movement that surprises even himself. The speaker has "gone" from ignorance to knowledge, from complacency to activity, and from indifference to love. "The Going" also shows a movement through time, from a happy distant past to an unhappy recent past to a miserable present to a bleak future. Just as time is going, happiness and hope are going, all of which are reflected in the woman having gone. The pathos of this poem reflects a general "going" of all people as well as the very specific going of the poem's subject; the speaker's attention to a variety of time periods also highlights time's "going" by using the term to demonstrate a connection between the ways that both time and people pass.

"I Look Into My Glass" (*CP* 81)

I look into my glass,
And view my wasting skin, And say,
"Would God it came to pass
My heart had shrunk as thin!"

For then, I, undistrest
By hearts grown cold to me,
Could lonely wait my endless rest
With equanimity.

But Time, to make me grieve,
Part steals, lets part abide;
And shakes this fragile frame at eve
With throbbings of noontide.

This is the rare Hardy poem that does not transport its speaker through time but laments time's passage without any shift in the speaker's temporal placement. It is a poem of an old man, although Hardy composed it a full thirty-eight years before his death; while very brief, it offers an exceptionally effective examination of the ironies of time and the ways in which the self is defined by time and defies time. The poem begins with the speaker looking in the mirror and seeing how time has ravaged him; immediately after making this observation, the speaker expresses a surprising wish, not that his body looked younger but "Would God it came to pass / My heart had shrunk as thin!" The speaker's dissatisfaction is not with his appearance but with the fact that his appearance does not accord with his feelings. As Hardy often does, he confounds readers' expectations, in this case by asking for a change not in his physical self but in his emotional and psychological state. While most people in a similar position might wish for a complete return to youth, Hardy's speaker simply wishes for accord, for consistency between mind and body, and for a diminution of desire.

The pain of time's passage strikes him again in the third stanza, where he presents personified Time not as random but as malicious. Time aims to "make me grieve" by making him externally old while leaving his inner youth intact. Thus, in his old age, he still possesses feelings that should belong to a younger man. In describing this tension as parts of a day, he engages in the long tradition of seeing a human life as the macrocosmic version of a single day. But he also emphasizes the way that time confounds him by leaving part of him at noon and forcing part of him into evening. This malice on Time's part, a desire for the speaker to suffer and grieve, presents an utterly antagonistic relationship between human existence and the passage of time.

Interestingly, this poem was written in the same year as Oscar Wilde's *The Picture of Dorian Gray*, a novella that deals with precisely the same theme as "I Look Into My Glass." For Dorian, though, the pain of aging results in a wish for external, physical youth (and, ultimately, in supernatural occurrences to retain that physical beauty), while Hardy's speaker would be content merely with a more complete and comprehensive aging. What troubles the speaker of this poem is not aging itself but the discord he feels when looking at his own physical being. Because he still *feels* young in certain ways, the reality of his physical body is that much more painful; he imagines that the pain would be lessened if only he felt like an old man too. If he felt old, he claims, then he would be content to anticipate death, but because he still possesses the passions and desires of youth, he cannot wait "with equanimity" for death and will, instead, fight it and feel distress at his physical deterioration.

This poem, though tiny, presents very well two questions with which Hardy often grapples in his poetry: does time merely pass blindly or does it act with malice? And can one, as one ages, ever feel satisfied with one's lot? The answer in both of these cases seems consistently to be the most pessimistic of the options. Time wishes for him to feel pain and misery, and he can never be satisfied. What he can sometimes envision, however, is a world in which satisfaction is possible, but that world exists only in his imagination or in memory. In nearly every one of Hardy's poems, we see some moment when the equanimity for which he wishes may have existed but the speaker didn't notice it at the time, or a situation in which that equanimity might exist if only this or that were different. But spiteful Time disallows the achievement of any actual present happiness, a fact that is demonstrated in "I Look Into My Glass" by the insurmountable disconnection between the speaker's physical being and his mental state, a juxtaposition that Hardy's speaker views not merely as unpleasant coincidence but as an illustration of Time's pointed intention to cause and then increase human suffering. The absence of a transporting time in this poem underscores the speaker's pain: unlike in other poems in this chapter, the speaker's memory or imagination does not lead to temporal relocation. The old man is truly trapped, not only in time's relentless forward march, but also in an attachment to present reality that prevents the short-term temporal escape of this chapter's other poems.

Comparative Discussion

Each of the poems in this chapter identifies a disjunction between a place now void of its inhabitants and the place as it once was, or between the speaker as he is now and as he once was. That constant juxtaposition of past and present, of the imagined and the real, and of the self as he might be and as he truly is, depicts a philosophy that, as Gillian Beer says, "makes the past anew, and yet declares that it cannot be retrieved as present happening."[4] As we have seen throughout these poems, Hardy finds the passage of time endlessly interesting, and he approaches it in different ways, considering what he could have known, what others might have known but did not tell him, and what others might know when he is gone and knows no more.

In each of these poems, time is presented as a cage in which humans are trapped. Perhaps Hardy's fascination with God, as we observed in Chapter 3, lies with God's unique ability to transcend the linear time from which people cannot escape. In each of these time-focused poems, the speaker recognizes that some event has passed that can never be recreated, a realization that troubles him, as does his concurrent awareness that the amount of knowledge one has changes with time but does not coincide with the moments when that knowledge might be most needed or best appreciated. The problem with time, for Hardy, is not so conventional as the fact that people age but that the aging traps people in a particular plan of which they may not be aware until it is too late, and the consequent absurdity of life in the face of such entrapment.

In some ways, these poems about time's passage resemble Hardy's war poems, not only because those, too, focus on the ironies of time but also because they seem to advise a move towards self-awareness. For instance, both "Afterwards" and "I Looked Up from My Writing" underscore the poet's qualities within his worldly context, and many other poems from among both the "time" and "war" poems point to the ignorance that exists alongside satisfaction and the eventual misery that exists alongside knowledge. To compare the war poems with the poems not explicitly about war only highlights the extent to which Hardy's concerns are not dictated by worldly circumstances: the ironies and pains he sees in the world exist in wartime, but no more so than they exist the rest of the time. While the war poems may suggest a particular outlook caused by war, the poems about time show that war is only tangential to Hardy's larger worldview, as we saw from the non-war poems of this chapter.

Concluding Discussion

The poems examined in this chapter do not just inhabit the past but show how the past constantly haunts and informs the present. At the same time, while the past serves as an unvarying motif throughout these poems, their weight rests on the knowledge and realization of the present and on the looming reality of the approaching future. These poems also attempt to decipher how a living person functions in a world of the dead and gone and how to live with constant echoes of the past and eternal haunting. Memory is an alternate reality, as Hardy writes in "Rome: On the Palatine": "And blended pulsing life with lives long done, / Till Time seemed fiction, Past and Present one." Because the speakers of so many of Hardy's poems possess such minutely detailed memories of the past, which can be combined with the wisdom that comes with age, the speakers are tormented by their inability to reinhabit the happy scenes of their memories or to recreate the innocence that existed at that time.

The poems' speakers envision time as an inescapable prison to which one's own body and mind, others' bodies and minds, objects, and places are inevitably subject, but rather than placidly accept this fact as implicit in human existence, the speakers lament and rail against it. They see their humanity as so inescapably subject to time that nothing else really matters. Any realization they make will be destroyed by time's passage, any beauty they see will be ruined, and any knowledge they gain will disappear. To come to terms with this reality is something with which these speakers constantly struggle.

As part of his discussion of time's painful passage, Hardy often uses images of ghosts to make observations about the world of the living, and that technique is especially noticeable in the poems about time. In some ways, though, the most prominent ghost in these poems is not a lost love but the speaker himself. The present self, the poems seem to argue, is also a ghost, transitory and perhaps only imagined. In almost all of these poems, even as the speaker considers the deaths of friends or loves, it is his death – and, perhaps most importantly, the death of his prior self – that is most poignantly mourned. He frequently sees himself slipping out of life, and so his own ghostliness becomes the focus of the poem. "Afterwards" deals, in its entirety, with this concept, but many of the other poems also bring in the speaker's eventual death, including "The Going," "I Look Into My Glass," and "At Castle Boterel." In each case, his remembering, his self-awareness, and his recognition of other ghosts prompt the speaker to see himself as a ghost.

Temporality is a complex and multilayered concept, and, in Hardy's poems, speakers are trapped in time but use their memories and imaginations to escape the bounds of fixed chronology, and thus the poems also escape linearity. Chronology therefore becomes malleable in the mind, at least for brief moments, and both the present and the past (and, in certain cases, the future) coexist in the speaker's – and the reader's – mind. Despite these brief respites from time's oppression, the poems' characters yearn for complete escape from Time's bounds and feel nonetheless compelled to live in the present reality; they are magnetically pulled towards the present even though they are occasionally successful in locating themselves temporally elsewhere. While these poems endeavor to relocate their speakers in time by remembering or imaging the past, the poems generally vacillate unendingly rather than settling in one chronological location. Thus, happier scenes are unavoidably tinged with the sadder reality of the present, and the imaginative work of the speaker almost necessarily results in the speaker being drawn to consider his own imminent demise.

Methods of Analysis

In addition to the methodologies used in other chapters, in this chapter we considered pairs of poems to see how poems read in conjunction with one another might alter their individual interpretations. In addition, we considered the ways in which textual absences may speak as loudly as what exists in a text. For instance, how does the absence of gender designations in "Your Last Drive" open its interpretive possibilities, and why might a poet choose such an absence?

We also continued to consider the interaction of form and content, exploring the ways that perspective and theme can complement each other, and how, particularly in poems about time, Hardy's experimentation with various presentations of past, present, and future affect the poems' content. By creating movement through time within the poems, their themes of time and time's passage are underscored as well as complicated.

Suggested Work

We can find themes of time and time's passage throughout Hardy's work, but it might also be interesting to see how other poets, especially those who are nearly Hardy's contemporaries, explore similar issues. Look at Dylan Thomas' "Fern Hill," for instance, to see how Thomas remembers his happy childhood and recognizes now, as an adult, how bound he was to time's passage. Consider how Hardy might have approached these same memories differently. Would Hardy have said, "Time held me, green and dying, / Though I sang in my chains like the sea"? How does that line resemble Hardy's work, and in what ways does it move away from Hardy's ideas about time? Consider, too, Philip Larkin's "Aubade," whose speaker imagines his own death. Because Larkin does not believe in corporeal ghosts the way Hardy does, Larkin's view of his own death is both bleaker than Hardy's and more based in the present fears. In what ways does Larkin reflect some of the concerns Hardy raises, and how does he manage the entrapment in plodding time that both Hardy and Thomas also consider?

For more examples of looming time in Hardy's verse, you can look just about anywhere. A few that you might read closely are "Autumn in King's Hintock Park" (*CP* 215), "The Fiddler" (*CP* 248), "Rome: Building a New Street in the Ancient Quarter" (*CP* 103), and "Tolerance" (*CP* 333). What ideas about time that we have already discussed do you see reflected in those poems? Do any of them approach time in a new way?

In "The Going of the Battery," which we considered in the previous chapter, Hardy capitalizes "Time." Usually that capitalization indicates that Time is undermining human happiness or destroying human plans, but in that poem, written in the voices of army wives, "Time's fulness" is presented hopefully and with a sense of optimism. Do you think that Hardy adjusts his sense of Time's destructive power in that poem in deference to these devoted wives, or does he use Time there as foreshadowing the women's eventual, inevitable losses?

You may also find concrete objects evoking memories in many of Hardy's poems. One particularly interesting example to consider is

"The Garden Seat," which is, as poet Seamus Heaney argues, "about the ghost-life that hovers over some of the furniture of our lives."[4] This poem considers a particular couch, and the speaker's thinking about the seat and its former functionality brings him to thinking about the people who were once sitting there and who, at night, return to the seat but do not break it or freeze with it because now "they are light as upper air." Consider how the repetition in this poem affects your reading of it, and think about how Hardy uses an object to evoke past human lives.

PART 2

THE CONTEXT AND THE CRITICS

6

Hardy's Life and Works

A Biographical Outline

Thomas Hardy was born in 1840 in Dorset, trained in his youth as an architect, and moved to London in 1862 to work in architecture. After the publication of *Far From the Madding Crowd* in 1874, Hardy became sufficiently successful to focus full time on his writing, and he did not return to architecture thereafter. He married his first wife, Emma, whom he met in Cornwall on a business trip, in 1874 and moved with her to Max Gate, a home he designed in Dorset, in 1885. Although Hardy is most often associated with rural life, he did live for several years in London and then chose to return to his geographical roots. Hardy and Emma remained together until her death in 1912; two years later, he married his much younger secretary Florence Dugdale. During his years with Emma, he is thought to have had one or two chaste affairs with other women with whom he felt an intellectual kinship, and his eventual marriage to Florence grew out of their many years of professional and personal relationship during Hardy's marriage to Emma. He continued to write prolifically until his death, at the age of 87, in 1928.

Although the central details of Hardy's biography are fairly well documented, questions do arise concerning certain aspects of his life, including the nature of his friendships with women during his marriage to Emma and the socioeconomic class in which he was raised. Critics have long questioned whether Hardy had sexual relationships with his various female friends while married to Emma, including his cousin Tryphena Sparks and Florence Dugdale, who became his wife, but no definitive evidence has been produced either way. In addition, Hardy's intimate friendship with Florence Henniker, with whom he exchanged many letters over the course of almost three decades, has raised questions about the chastity of that relationship. Some critics, among them Claire Tomalin, believe that Hardy was indeed engaging in sexual affairs, while others believe that he "loved" various women but remained physically faithful to Emma.

The debate about class continues today as well, with a general perception that Hardy was relatively poor and uneducated and that he "exaggerated his family's social and economic status in order to conceal its actual poverty and obscurity."[1] Some scholars, though, argue that "Far from being self-taught (a term that for some traditional English critics simply means that he didn't go to Oxford or Cambridge), he received a better education than most of his compatriots do today. Like so many major nineteenth-century novelists, Hardy sprang neither from the people nor the patricians but from the lower middle class."[2] The difficulty of determining some of these biographical details is exacerbated by a rather tangled web around Hardy's willingness to control and shape his public perception, which will be discussed in more detail in "Further Reading."

Novelist to Others; Poet to Himself

Hardy was deeply invested in his public perception, and his desire to be known as a poet more than a novelist was no exception. He expressed on many occasions a wish to be regarded "as an English poet who had written some stories in prose," and W. L. Phelps wrote that Hardy was "'evidently pained' by the idea that his poetry was less good than his prose."[3] Hardy said that poetry "is the heart of literature" and once wrote that "a sense of the truth of poetry, of its supreme place in literature, had awakened itself in me."[4] Dennis Taylor writes that "Hardy continued to regard himself as first, if not last, a poet; and he continued to maintain his poetic ambitions through the novel-writing years, 1870–96. In 1874 his attitude was that 'he did not care much for a reputation as a novelist in lieu of being able to follow the pursuit of poetry – now for ever hindered, as it seemed.'"[5] "If Hardy had not been so prominent as a novelist, his stature as a poet would have come clear earlier."[6] In 1915 he advised that readers should "treat my verse . . . as my *essential* writings, & my prose as my *accidental*."[7] Again and again we see Hardy asserting his belief in the centrality of poetry and his desire to be regarded primarily as a poet rather than a novelist. Hardy was quite attuned to life's ironies, and perhaps one of those is that he continues to be more highly regarded and better known as a novelist than a poet despite his desires to the contrary.

Although many readers would consider the divide between poetry and prose rather conventionally, Jean Brooks argues that, even within the novels, Hardy's power is a "poetic power" to "make real those great commonplaces of heroic, though doomed, human nature."[8] Brooks finds in Hardy's work an overall poeticism that carries through his novels, his philosophy, and even his early career in architecture: "Hardy's emotionally charged poetic pattern integrates all his personal interests into a new artistic unity . . . The long passage on rural migration to the towns that begins Chapter LI of *Tess* falls into place as a re-creation in social terms of the central poetic image of purposeless mechanical process driving units of life in an unnatural direction . . . The passion of Hardy's total portrayal of the cosmic predicament . . . is the achievement of the poetic vision."[9]

Brooks may take the idea of "poetry" well outside the realm in which we generally define it, by approaching poetry as a kind of feeling, philosophy, or worldview rather than as a literary genre. Nonetheless, the overwhelming idea of "Hardy the Poet" suggests that while the poems are less frequently read and less well known than the novels, they are, in some way, more significant to understanding Hardy as a literary figure. Although we must be careful not to privilege Hardy's stated preferences above our readings of the works themselves, his repeated assertions about the greater value of poetry and about his own ambitions as a poet, as well as the fact that he composed poetry throughout his entire life, point to the possibility that while the novels are better known, the poems deserve as much or more attention.

A Man of Many Genres

Among the more interesting aspects of Hardy's publication history, as we have discussed briefly already, his life spans two distinct literary eras, and his writing falls primarily into at least four discrete genres: poems, novels, stories, and an epic drama. His career as a novelist fell firmly in the Victorian age: he was ten years old when Dickens published *David Copperfield* and thirty when George Eliot serialized *Middlemarch*. While he began writing novels in 1867, at the age of twenty-seven, his first significant success occurred seven years later, with *Far from the Madding Crowd*. Thereafter, he produced novels at a regular pace through the 1890s, with *The Return of the Native* in 1878, *The Mayor of Casterbridge* in 1886, *Tess of the D'Urbervilles* in 1891, and *Jude the Obscure* in 1895. Technically, he published an additional novel after *Jude* called *The Well-Beloved*, in 1897, but because this novel was a rewriting of his 1892 *The Pursuit of the Well-Beloved*, and neither of them is widely discussed, *Jude* is generally considered the last of his novelistic productions.

After having established himself as a successful novelist, though, Hardy began to publish in other genres. As he became more celebrated for his novels, he published a number of short stories, including *Wessex Tales* in 1888. He also wrote the enormous but relatively unpopular historical dramatic work *The Dynasts* in the 1900s, which is now beginning to garner more critical attention. Around that time, he began to publish poetry exclusively and achieved some measure of success and recognition with *Wessex Poems and Other Verses* in 1898. After the turn of the century, he published an additional eleven books of poems, including a *Collected Poems* in 1919. Although Hardy remains known primarily as a novelist, even had he not first written fourteen novels, he would nonetheless be among the most prolific and influential writers of the era.

During the second half of his career, from the 1890s until his death in 1928, he was exclusively a poet, leaving behind his novelistic career. Unlike many artists who compose in multiple genres, Hardy made a distinct break from novel writing, but his reputation as a novelist remains to this day. Many critics and biographers have speculated about Hardy's reasons for leaving behind his novels.

Robert Gittings, in *Thomas Hardy's Later Years*, offers three possibilities: one possibility is that Hardy was growing older and increasingly finding novel writing a burden, whereas "poetry needed far less weight of words."[10] "Secondly, the highly personal themes of his secret youth were now beginning to force themselves uncomfortably into his novels." Gittings speculates that poetry would allow Hardy to express personal emotions "but less of the biographical circumstances." And finally, Gittings suggests, Hardy was pushed to poetry by necessity because Emma, who had offered him significant help with his novel writing, was so alienated from him by the publication of *Jude the Obscure*, his most controversial and publicly criticized novel, that he could no longer return to the form without her constant support. Because he could no longer count on Emma as his copyist, he could not write novels, according to Gittings.[11] Keith Tuma settles on one portion of the third of Gittings' options as the central motivation for Hardy's genre switch: Hardy was prompted to "give up fiction" because of the "hostile reaction to *Tess of the D'Urbervilles* and *Jude the Obscure*."[12]

All of these are possibilities, but another is that Hardy genuinely valued poetry more than fiction – or, at least, so he claimed – and so his move towards that genre demonstrated that he had sufficiently established himself as a writer that he felt freer to pursue the genre that felt most important to him. According to Michael Millgate's Hardy biography, Hardy said that "his one literary ambition had been to 'have some poem or poems in a good anthology like the Golden Treasury.' "[13] Hardy's rationale for postponing writing *The Dynasts* may have followed a similar logic: perhaps expecting that the play would not be enormously popular, he composed it after his novels had garnered sufficient approbation to allow for his own greater experimentation. Hardy writes in his Preface to *The Dynasts*, that "When, as the first published result of these accidents, *The Trumpet Major* was printed, more than twenty years ago, I found myself in the tantalizing position of having touched the fringe of a vast international tragedy without being able, through limits of plan, knowledge, and opportunity, to enter further into its events; a restriction that prevailed for many years."[14]

Of course, what appears to be a straightforward switch from novels to poems reflects a more complicated truth: that Hardy had written poems well before he became known as a poet and that, as we explored in Chapter 1, his poems maintain many of the novelistic qualities that led to his initial literary successes. Millgate asserts that Hardy had long harbored poetic ambitions and that many of his first published poems "had been conceived during those decades of apparent blankness."[15] In other words, even as his literary production seemed to be slowing in various periods, he was composing poems in preparation for his eventual move to his "preferred" genre. So while he may have been a Victorian novelist, he was a poet of multiple eras and with discernible connections to at least three distinct poetic periods, as we shall see shortly.

Reading a Literary Life

One common temptation is to look for biographical details in Hardy's verse. From having read a number of Hardy poems, we now know that many of his poems feature obviously fictional characters while other poems' speakers seem to resemble Hardy in a variety of ways. Yet all the poems that could possibly be autobiographical are not inevitably so. Furthermore, as we will see, Hardy himself objected strenuously to an autobiographical reading of his verse; his stated interpretative preference is not a mandate, of course, but it should at least be considered.

In some obvious ways, an author's life can teach readers about his works: learning of Dickens' early experiences with poverty and child labor informs the novels' preoccupations with social justice and class inequalities; knowledge of Coleridge's opium addiction gives readers insight into his turmoil in "The Pains of Sleep"; and recognizing that Mary Shelley had recently been thinking about the scientific work of Erasmus Darwin and Luigi Galvani can help readers to see those scientists' influence on *Frankenstein*, as can an awareness of the Romantic poets' interest in the Promethean myth.

At the same time, using any individual facts from an author's life as the basis for textual interpretation can subtly or overtly encourage readers to find that detail in more of the writer's work than is actually warranted by the text. Biographical information can distract readers from what a text says. Because a whole life is complex and multi-faceted, and because readers may be most intrigued by the juiciest biographical details – child abuse, drug addiction, or marriage to a celebrity, for instance – readers should be careful about using particular details of any author's life to interpret his or her works. In Hardy's case, critics interestingly pick and choose among his works to decide which ones are "autobiographical" and which are not. Critics frequently find some of Hardy's later novels, particularly *Jude the Obscure*, autobiographical, and they assume that many, but not all, of the poems written in first-person voice must feature Hardy himself as a speaker.[16] At the same time, they recognize that certain first-person speakers must not be Hardy when they very evidently differ from him, whether in circumstances, gender, or location. Hardy was clearly capable of creating a first-person character who was not fully himself, but frequently critics prefer to find parallels between the poet's life and the poem's speaker.

In her introduction to *The Ashgate Companion to Thomas Hardy*, Rosemarie Morgan makes a point of emphasizing Hardy's longstanding desire to separate himself from the "I" of his works. Her principle in choosing articles for the volume relied on the idea that it should not ignore "the 'Aristotelian' dictum that art is not life – that a writer's fiction and poetry are not autobiographical unless otherwise indicated." She notes that "the conflation of art and life was a highly vexed issue for Hardy"[17] and quotes from a number of Hardy's personal writings to demonstrate his frustration with critics who "devoutly believe that everything written in the first person has been done personally."[18] As Hardy wrote to Vere Collins, "Fancy using the absolute fabrications of a novelist (which they were) and such erroneous inferences . . . as facts in the history of the writer."[19] Hardy's evident frustration may be at least partially disingenuous because significant segments of his writings must be based to some degree upon his own experiences. Such ambiguity is inherently part of artistic creation. The potential kernels of truth or historical accuracy notwithstanding, though, Hardy expresses his desire for readers to approach his works with the sense that they are truly fictional. As he wrote admiringly to one critic, "You appear not to have stumbled into the pitfall which has been the undoing of some previous critics – that of assuming [my] inventions to be real personifications of experiences of [my] own."[20]

Poems of 1912–13: How and Why We Read Poems

Hardy's impatience with critics who imagine that he is consistently the "I" of his poems can be understood by examining some relatively recent criticism of the *Poems of 1912–13*, Hardy's works most often read as purely autobiographical. In this series of poems, written shortly after Emma's death, Hardy creates a number of situations similar to his own and characters who resemble himself and Emma. Perhaps understandably, then, these poems are most often read as autobiography. I will suggest, though, that in any situation of textual interpretation, the poems might illuminate the life, or the life might illuminate the poems. Hardy's preference, according to his own writings, is for the latter, but many critics become preoccupied with the former. By examining some of the criticism of these poems, we can see the ways in which a search for truth about Hardy's life, rather than about Hardy's work, can mistakenly dominate critical readings.

The Hardy biographer Robert Gittings writes about Hardy's travels with his brother immediately after his first wife Emma's death. During those travels to Cornwall, Hardy wrote "Beeny Cliff," "The Phantom Horsewoman," "Under the Waterfall," and several other poems. Gittings explains that, in those poems, Hardy "was creating a myth of their [Hardy and Emma's] life and writing out of himself the nagging guilt of reality."[21] In other words, according to Gittings, these poems demonstrate Hardy's efforts to rewrite reality; essentially, because the details of the poems do not fully accord with what we know of Hardy's biography, the poems must, in Gittings' view, be a personal mythologizing. Rather than reading the poems as consciously created works of art, he approaches them as textual versions of grief therapy. Perhaps the poems do encompass both possibilities, and it is only natural to assume that Hardy's personal life informed and shaped his verse; but Hardy also quite obviously knew that he was writing poems, and, after a lifetime of creating compelling fictional characters, he must surely have taken into account more than the need to create a personal mythology in writing these works.

Along similar lines, Ross Murfin calls the *Poems of 1912–13* "Hardy's poetic response to the death of his wife" and goes on to explain that Hardy has taken reality and begun, perhaps unconsciously, to alter it through imagination or, as Gittings might say, to mythologize the reality:

> That Emma and he once rode horses along "beetling Beeny Crest" is, of course, an historical fact; that the reality of the past moment to which Hardy recurs has been acted upon by the imagination, however, seems equally indisputable. It is unclear whether the alteration of reality by the poetic mind was begun during the courtship described by the lines – in which case Hardy is now building upon a self-delusion that once led him toward the altar – or whether it was begun only after Emma's death.[22]

Murfin's assertion suggests that Hardy was probably unaware of the acting of imagination upon reality, a problematic argument about a man who devoted his life to the creation of imaginary worlds that resembled reality in their emotions, events, and even locations. And yet Murfin, like many critics of Hardy's poems, avoids envisioning a situation in which Hardy might take some details of his own biography and create artistic works that intentionally veer from historical or biographical events.

One might object to Murfin's rather narrow reading because it implies that poems are meaningful only to the extent that they reflect or diverge from biography and because interpretation is limited by beginning with biographical knowledge rather than with openness to the text itself. If the literature is sufficiently interesting to make people want to read it, they need not find the author in its every detail. To do so is to suggest that we read literature only, or perhaps primarily, to learn more about the individual who created it rather than about what the literature itself says. In the case of "Beeny Cliff," what Murfin calls an "alteration of reality" may instead be, more simply, a poem.

Jahan Ramazani, like many other readers of the *Poems of 1912–13*, also uses the poems to inform the life. He writes, for instance,

> Angry at his dead wife and angry with himself for having this anger, Hardy tries to flee from the tumult of their recent relationship by regressing to its earliest stages. From the poems, Emma seems during the courtship to have been the object of unambiguous love when she was little more than Hardy's narcissistic fantasies about her, and so Hardy tries to sew up the ragged sleeve of their marriage with the thread of his earliest feelings about her.[23]

This critique is based entirely on the poems themselves, and it assumes and imposes the identity of both the speaker and his subject: Ramazani sees the "I" of the poem as an accurate, unfictionalized version of Hardy, and the "she" of the poems, while not named, as a true representation of Emma. For Ramazani, as for Gittings, any poetic adjustments from pure biographical reality point to Hardy's unselfconscious efforts to redeem psychologically his failed relationship.

Linda Austin goes even farther with her reading of the *Poems of 1912–13*, indiscriminately plucking details from the biography and the poems to explore Hardy's mental state and ultimately using the poems to diagnose Hardy with clinical depression:

> Emma is the breathtaking girl of Cornwall, the affected and lame wife at Max Gate, the overbearing hostess in "Lament," the revenant that possesses him in "The Haunter" and "The Visitor," the creeping corpse in "I Found Her Out There." Images of Emma can be ghastly: the elegist imagines her buried in "Lament" and underground in "I Found Her Out There . . . " Indeed the various images of Emma as ghost or corpse reveal Hardy's uneasy sense that the spirit of the dead one is at large.[24]

Ignoring the fact that the poems never name Emma and that the many "errors" in historical detail must be variously explained away – as Hardy's overuse of memory, as his effort to remove himself from reality, and as his evidence of psychological distress – Austin and these others produce arguments that begin with the poems only to end with the life. Austin concludes her piece by stating that "it may be hard to read poems like Hardy's outside the paradigm of therapeutic psychology."[25]

As a reader of the poems myself, I do not find it difficult to read Hardy's poems outside the paradigm of therapeutic psychology. Instead, I try always to read Hardy's poems, as we have done in the previous chapters, as artistic creations rather than as psychological artifacts that can illuminate the author's biography: his self-delusions, failures, misrememberings, and psychoses. In addition, as a reader, I aim to place at the center of literary study the uncovering of truths about the poems rather than truths about the author. When plumbing the depths of the author's life becomes the sole or primary purpose of studying the poems, the poems are treated simply as biographical documents alongside letters, diaries, marginalia, interviews, and conversations. Unfortunately, for many readers, the fact of these poems' artistry – not to mention the potential artistry of letters and diaries and the like – is subsumed by the facts of Hardy's biography, and the poems become merely another tool for learning more about Hardy and the ways in which he represented and misrepresented the details of his life in verse. Why Hardy should be interesting at all, outside the fact of his artistic creations, is a question seldom broached, but I wonder why Hardy should matter as a person to anyone if readers are interested in his works primarily as a way to study his life. Other individuals likely had more interesting lives, and so it is worth recalling that Hardy's life is studied because of his literary works and not the reverse.

Perhaps obviously, I feel uncomfortable using any artist's life as the ultimate goal in examining that artist's creations even though many smart and well-respected scholars seem to feel that psychoanalyzing Hardy is a sufficient reason for studying his works. My assumptions – and every scholarly approach is indeed based upon some assumptions – are that Hardy was a thoughtful enough poet to write with self-awareness and artistry even as he mourned a loss, and that his poems, even those that feel most intimate, are poems nonetheless. That is, they are works of art that address specifically artistic concerns and not merely private diary entries written in verse form. Perhaps more importantly, I begin reading the poems with the assumption that they are capable of standing alone as artistic works and that they can speak to situations and realities outside of the author's immediate personal concerns. While I recognize that poems come from a specific time, place, and person, the poems most worth reading can transcend that time, place, and person to speak to broader audiences about more than just a single personal situation. As Morgan reminds us, the term "speaker" "permits acknowledgment, exploration and understanding of the art form in question and its innate truthfulness."[26] By considering all of Hardy's speakers in such terms, readers may be able to create a continuum of closeness to and divergence from Hardy's life, but they can remember that every speaker remains a creation of the poet.

Hardy's Place in Literary History

Classifying any writer by his affiliation with an era can be problematic in its oversimplifications, but it can also be useful in its ability to help readers categorize and evaluate the influences of history on writers as well as where those writers fit in among others. Hardy's poetry can meaningfully be compared with poems of the Romantic, Victorian, and Modern eras. We may be able better to understand aspects of his writings by finding similarities between his work and that of his contemporaries. Making such period generalizations is difficult because almost every writer both fits into and fights against his or her period. Some writers, like Wordsworth, may be practically synonymous with their own periods, at least in part because they created the very characteristics with which they are associated; that is, Wordsworth articulated the ideals of British Romanticism, and so he becomes practically inseparable from them. T. S. Eliot, as Larkin writes, created "a cunning merger between poet, literary critic and academic critic (three classes now notoriously indistinguishable)," and so Modernism and Eliot are, or were for a time, so closely aligned as to be indivisible.[27] But for the vast majority of writers, certain characteristics are shared with those era-defining figures while other characteristics diverge from them. For Hardy, who spanned eras, a series of similarities and divergences is unavoidable. His poetry shares formal techniques with his contemporary Victorian poets, including his use of metrics and stanzas accompanied by some experimentation with a variety of stanzaic forms and patterns, but it also draws profoundly from the Romantic poets and demonstrates notable characteristics of Modernism as well.

Hardy the Victorian

Perhaps the Victorian era is the most logical place to start thinking about Hardy's place in literary history, for reasons purely of chronology. He was born three years into Queen Victoria's reign, and his novels fit the pattern of Victorian novels in many ways, first and foremost in their production history. Like Dickens, Eliot, Trollope and others, Hardy first published his novels serially and eventually found success with the publication of non-serial novels. Much of his subject matter also echoes the themes and preoccupations of other Victorian novelists, most notably class distinctions, the workhouse, and the legal system (as Steve McCarty demonstrates in his article about legal cases in *Far from the Madding Crowd*).[28] Hardy, like Dickens and others, is also concerned with the mistreatment of the weak and vulnerable; for Dickens, these are primarily represented by children while for Hardy they are often women, but the principle is similar.

Hardy's fascination with post-Darwinian ideas of scientific truth and human reason also highlight concerns of the late Victorian era, as Jane Bownas demonstrates.[29] His interest in Darwin's theories and discoveries reflects the concerns of many Victorian novelists: "Hardy repositioned humans in nature, at a time when biology was being looked to to explain forms of social and sexual behavior."[30] Gillian Beer demonstrates extensive parallels between Hardy and Darwinian ideas, noting that "most commentators have emphasized the point of connection between Hardy and Darwin in terms of pessimism, a sense that the laws of life are themselves flawed," but also that Hardy, like other Victorian novelists, acts "within the language of the text as observer or experimenter rather than designer or god."[31] In other words, the writer resembles a scientist more than an omnipotent creator.

A general Victorian interest in scientific developments is especially evident in Hardy's novels, as Anna Henchman shows in "Hardy's Stargazers and the Astronomy of Other Minds," which emphasizes Hardy's interest in late-Victorian developments in the study of astronomy and optics: "For Hardy, the recognition that much of the stellar universe is formless, vast, and invisible to us set nineteenth-century astronomy apart from earlier studies of the solar system."[32] Kay Heath argues that Hardy manifests a particularly Victorian conception of the self and of aging in his novels, where she notes that Hardy, like other Victorian novelists, explores "how psychological aspects of aging were imagined in the nineteenth century" and also "how fiction instructed Victorians to think about age."[33] That is, we see in Hardy's fiction a concern with many of the same themes that captured the imaginations of other novelists of the time.

In considering Hardy as a Victorian poet, though, the case is slightly more difficult to make. Certainly many of the themes of Victorian novelists make their way into Hardy's poems; his interest in social inequality, class, power structures, scientific developments, and the place of God in the natural world are as present in his poems as they are in his novels. These issues, particularly the last, are also present in the works of many great Victorian poets, including Matthew Arnold and Alfred Lord Tennyson. Nonetheless, Tom Paulin dismisses most of Hardy's potential connections to Victorian poetry, writing that "Hardy does not follow Tennyson, who bases a sense of the supernatural upon the split between faith and sense-data."[34] Of the Victorian poets, Hardy most closely resembles Robert Browning, especially in his creation of distinctively-voiced characters and, as Paulin says, in his use of "infinite moments" that "are always won in despite of an ingrained, reductive pessimism." Hardy's similarities to Browning are notable, especially in his creation of memorable – and evidently fictional – first-person speakers. Browning's dramatic monologue, a style in which the reader "takes the part of the silent listener" and pieces together the situation based on the words of the speaker, closely resembles some of Hardy's poems, but Hardy adheres less consistently to the strictures of the style.[35]

For instance, in "My Last Duchess," Browning creates a head-strong duke who speaks, without quotation marks, to a visitor in his home. Readers become a secondary audience whose role is to decipher the present situation, the oblique history described by the duke, the unheard responses of the visitor, and the implications of the duke's language. The title of the poem is also written in the voice of the duke. Hardy uses a similar style in his adoption of others' voices, but he makes fewer demands on the reader in decoding the scenario; often because Hardy's titles are written in a voice different from that of the poem's speaker, his titles offer more explicit clues to the speakers' identities and situations. In addition, Hardy's poems more often include internal dialogue that helps to clarify the scene and identify the characters involved.

In *Time's Laughingstocks*, Hardy creates a variety of speakers in a range of scenarios. One poem begins, "I wanted to marry, but father said, 'No – / 'Tis weakness in women to give themselves so.'" The speaker here is clearly a woman, and her past situation is evident. But Hardy's title prepares readers for the situation and characters: "The Orphaned Old Maid." Readers learn from that title that the situation the female speaker describes is from the distant past, that her father is no longer alive, and that she now faces difficulties based on his earlier pronouncement. In another of *Time's Laughingstocks*, "The Dead Man Walking," the title again speaks outside the voice of the poem's speaker and acts as a descriptor rather than an additional line of the poem. The speaker is, again, a victim of circumstance rather than Browning's triumphant villain, and he more explicitly articulates his situation for readers than does Browning's duke. In both of these Hardy poems, the implied listener is not made clear as he is in Browning's poem. Whereas the duke says, "the Count your master," offering readers a clue to the identity of the poem's internal audience, Hardy's speakers' audiences may be the poem's readers themselves or may be unidentified, silent characters within the poem. The addressee is never identified or even hinted at. As it does in "My Last Duchess," the past plays a part in the current situation and is described within the poem in the voice of a fictionalized character; but Hardy's ideas are made more explicit than Browning's, and the speaker is, more often, the oppressed rather than the oppressor.

Despite these distinctions, we can see how Hardy's poems resemble Browning's, not only in their playing with time and in their pessimism, as Paulin points out, but also in their style, voice, and structure. David Miller argues in *With Poetry and Philosophy* that both Hardy's and Browning's poems can be read as poetic restatements of modern philosophical positions, and Dennis Taylor suggests that Hardy's *The Dynasts* may demonstrate the "post-Romantic disillusion of . . . Browning's *The Ring and the Book*."[36] Hardy does indeed echo and develop some aspects of Browning's poetic style, adding his own philosophical and empathetic twists to the characters and situations he creates; despite their differences, parallels between the eminent Victorian poet and Hardy abound.

In addition to drawing comparisons between Hardy and Browning, critics have considered Hardy's links to the *fin de siècle* writers of the 1890s. Norman Page writes that, although some of Hardy's work, "including two of his greatest novels and his first volume of verse, appeared in the 1890s, he was decidedly not *of* the nineties"[37] Those of us familiar with the work of the 1890s, the poems and plays of the Aesthetes, of Oscar Wilde and Aubrey Beardsley, for instance, certainly know what Page means. But, as Suzanne J. Flynn points out, the differences that appear on the surface between Hardy and Wilde may also exist in more subtle ways: "Having noted Hardy's perceived exclusion from avant-garde literary movements, Page and [Gillian] Beer go on to show that Hardy's work does indeed show marked affinities with both aesthetic and decadent principles."[38] Donald Davie and others argue that Hardy did look forward more than most of his contemporaries, so perhaps this affiliation is not surprising.

Hardy the Romantic

Although Hardy's formative years coincide most closely with the Victorian poets, he was raised on the poetry of the Romantics and, as we have seen already, employs a number of Romantic styles and paradigms in his work. Eric Christen calls Hardy the Romantics' "heir in more than one sense," and Hardy indeed builds on many of the hallmarks of Romanticism, including their individualism, their empathy for and interest in the "common man," their use of accessible language, their belief in the innocence and purity of youth, and their deep ties to the natural world.[39] Dennis Taylor notes the multiple comparisons of Hardy's work that can be made to Romantic poetry: "to the romantic meditative poem and traditions of reverie, to romantic aesthetics and its connections with the Gothic revival, to the romantic visionary sensibility and its relation to theories of the grotesque, to the romantic version of the pastoral ideal."[40] Among the Romantic poets, Shelley is most often compared with Hardy and seen as his most significant Romantic influence. Paulin notes that "Shelley's influence on Hardy's work was vast"[41] and lists complete phrases and philosophies from Shelley's work borrowed and reused by Hardy.

Hardy also "likened himself as a tale-teller to Coleridge's Ancient Mariner"[42] and often adopts a Wordsworthian voice as well. Taylor remarks that "Hardy's basic sense of what the poet does, his notion of himself as an observer and recorder of his 'unadjusted impressions' is fundamentally Wordsworthian" and, furthermore, "even where Hardy disagreed with Wordsworth, he did so in Wordsworthian terms."[43] Taylor also points out that "several Hardy poems seem to parody and reverse Wordsworth poems," a comparison we examined in Chapter 3 with Hardy's undermining of certain Wordsworthian tropes. John Paul Riquelme similarly discusses Hardy's reversal of Wordsworth and observes that Hardy "specifically rejects the consolation that Wordsworth's speaker experiences."[44] That *specific* rejection demonstrates that Hardy continues to grapple with the Romantic legacy and offer alternatives to the Romantic worldview, perhaps especially as it relates to nature and God, but that he does so in terms that adhere closely to the Romantic style and poetic philosophy.

For instance, Riquelme demonstrates how "Nature's Questioning" illustrates Hardy's difference from Wordsworth: "By choosing not to answer back or by being unable to do so, the 'I' cuts itself off or is cut off from the possibility of continued speaking as a sign of life and thought on both sides of a dialogue. The children speak, perhaps to him, but he does not address them as Wordsworth addresses the child in the 'Immortality Ode.' "[45] Indeed, much of the subject matter of Hardy's poetry – the innocence of youth, the individual's relationship with the natural world, God's role in nature and in human existence, the writer's place in society – resembles the subject matter of Wordsworth's work, but the ways in which those topics are broached and the answers each poet provides differ profoundly.

Hardy the Modernist

Ultimately, though, Riquelme believes that Hardy the poet belongs more to the Moderns than to any other group, arguing that he sees in Hardy's poems Beckett's language and Yeats' masks.[46] This echoes the arguments of quite a number of scholars, including Donald Davie and Samuel Hynes. As Mary Ann Gillies writes, Hardy is often pushed aside by American strains of Modernism, as manifested by Eliot and Pound, and the Celtic, manifested by Yeats. Hardy's particularly British brand of Modernism, that which touched Auden, Larkin, and Ted Hughes, among others, is a kind of Modernism that has fared poorly when compared with the loud proclamations of Eliot and Pound but that is Modern nonetheless: "Not all modernists sought their subject matter in the modern city; . . . Nor are modernists difficult or comprehensive; . . . Nor . . . do modernists always layer their poems with difficult or obscure allusions."[47] Furthermore (as Larkin also said), because Eliot "performed the dual role of critic and artist," he "articulated criteria which justify the type of poetry he wrote. Despite Eliot's pretense of objectivity, his assessments of other poets are an elaboration of his own artistic predilections."[48] "In fact," Gillies writes, "Hardy shared many of the same concerns as Eliot, though his articulation of them differed."[49] In other words, Hardy is absolutely a Modern poet, provided that readers are willing to broaden their definition of Modernism beyond that rather narrow variety promoted by Eliot and Pound.

Certainly we can see the concerns of the Moderns developed in Hardy's work, and although the Modernist conception of the "unreal city" might, in Hardy, be expanded to the "unreal country," Hardy's encompassing skepticism, pervasive sense of isolation, dread mingled with a desire for universal betterment, and existential pain resemble the works of his early twentieth-century contemporaries. He was decades older than the bulk of the Modernist writers, but that fact does not lessen his Modernist sensibility. His prosody, though, is both less linguistically experimental and more heavily patterned than Eliot's. Nonetheless, "by simultaneously employing and redefining traditional poetic forms and models, Hardy does carry out the modernist campaign to reappropriate tradition, redefine it, and 'make it new.' "[50]

A parallel principle exists across Hardy's stylistic, philosophical, and conceptual relationships with the poets of these three eras. For each of these three time periods, readers may note certain echoes, reflections, and influences in his work. At the same time, Hardy's work feels uniquely Hardian and consistent across the decades of his production. How both of these observations can be simultaneously true, and how we can determine of what value it is to make such observations, may be the more interesting and relevant questions. Perhaps these two simultaneous truths – of Hardy's firm attachment to the literatures of his times and of his own uniqueness among other writers – only prove that every writer contains multitudes, as another of Hardy's contemporaries said.[51] Perhaps they also demonstrate that Hardy was able to take themes, preoccupations, ideas, forms, sounds, and developments from the writers around him and fold them into a body of work that was, in its essence, uniquely his.

7

Critical Views

Critical and scholarly work on Hardy is probably 70% about the novels and 30% about the poems; within the body of work about the poems, a large portion of that – perhaps half – concerns the *Poems of 1912–13*. And yet much important work has been done on the poems more generally, so this chapter will offer some representative critical views of Hardy's verse, both from his time and more recently, culminating with studies of four contemporary Hardy scholars whose focus is primarily the poetry, especially the broad views of his poems.

During Hardy's lifetime, he received mixed responses to his poetry, and since then his reputation as a poet has undergone some brutal critiques as well as a more modern resurgence, especially among the next generation of poets, who have been among his greatest defenders. His poetry has especially been criticized for its "obviousness" and for what some critics have perceived as shortcomings in style and diction. It has also been belittled for its apparently antiquated patterns and language and for its depressiveness. On the other hand, those same qualities have drawn praise from many readers, who find the poems thought-provoking and innovative. By examining the specific ways in which Hardy has historically been praised and disparaged, we can gain a clearer understanding of the qualities of his verse that touch readers and the ways in which readers have reacted – and continue to react – to his rather polarizing poetry. Perhaps surprisingly, even Hardy's defenders frequently point out the defects in his verse, as we shall see in this chapter, but his strongest supporters inevitably find in the poems value and innovation that supersede whatever flaws may also exist.

Early Twentieth-Century Critical Views

Many critics, during Hardy's lifetime as now, focused on his extreme pessimism and the depth of despair presented in the poems. His reputation for darkness increased as his career continued, an attitude that divided readers' opinions; William Dean Howells, for one, approved wholeheartedly of that increasing misery, even if he did not perceive it in the world himself: "But even pessimism without a cause, if it results in poetry like Mr. Hardy's, is justifiable, and if it is his increased pessimism which has made 'Poems of the Past and Present' better than 'Wessex Poems,' one must wish it to abound more and more."[1] Alfred Noyes similarly found redemption in Hardy's pessimism, comparing him to the Hebrew prophets and writing that "If Hardy sees men as insects crawling over their little ball of dust, he is only able to do this because, as a poet, he himself can soar high enough." Noyes did not find Hardy's pessimism unique but in keeping with a long tradition of great writers: "From beginning to end the poetry of Thomas Hardy is the very voice of pessimism, but it is the pessimism of Shakespeare's tragedies, a pessimism so profound that it goes down to the depths where construction begins."[2]

Others found the pessimism to be a kind of willful disagreeableness. T. H. Warren complained in *The Spectator* that "Mr. Hardy seems to prefer the unpleasant to the pleasant, the ugly to the fair . . . He describes too seldom either charming maid or happy wife."[3] And a *Times Literary Supplement* review of *Satires of Circumstance* protested that all of Hardy's poems "give us merely a situation, an ugly situation, with all the emphasis of verse laid on the ugliness, as if he had a brief against life."[4] Some of these critics see Hardy's bleakness as a profound philosophy while others regard it as mere contrarianism.

In addition to the bleakness of his verse, a number of contemporary reviews commented on his apparently unwavering beliefs. As we have seen in this volume, his attitudes may have been less consistent than they sometimes seemed, but even so, an overall sense of his steadfastness of philosophy struck his contemporaries. Harriet Monroe approvingly noted that "One must take him or leave him as he is in all his austere sincerity, this poet who, in the teeth of the chill gray wind, utters the truth of life as he feels it in music whose discords make a bitter tune."[5] And Thomas Seccombe, while not necessarily endorsing Hardy's worldview, admired its consistency of perspective: "That Thomas Hardy is a true luminary is revealed, if in no other way, by the imperturbability of his flame."[6]

Critics also paid attention to the broadness of Hardy's view, sometimes remarking that he ranged too far from the individual experience by making unnecessarily large pronouncements about the universe. In 1926, Hervey Allen defended Hardy against these critics by emphasizing the value of this wide range: "Critics of a school, a place, or a time might complain that Mr. Hardy's poetry too often lacks ingenuity or the continuous glitter of dazzling lines, the 'magic' which this thrill loving generation cries for. The poet's weaving is on so vast a scale, however, that a charge like this is like complaining that the figures on a tapestry covering a whole castle hall are not embroidered with beads." A bit of a poet in his own right, Allen concludes that Hardy "is right in regarding the universe he has thus created as more important than one of its systems, [which] will become increasingly evident as the ever lengthening perspective of the future leaves the whole body of his work shining as a complete universe in the milky way of time." Allen's own "universal" approach to Hardy's work dismisses those critics who wish for a more localized focus.[7]

All of these qualities – his attachment to an unusually dark perspective, the vastness of his scale, and the stolidity of his lines – earned praise and critique alternately. The qualities of his poetry were largely agreed upon by his contemporaries, but the value of such characteristics was open to wide debate. Even these critics who praise Hardy, though, do so without accepting his worldview, which they seem to recognize as a darkness that occasionally exists in most people whereas in Hardy it is an apparently permanent state of being.

Many of Hardy's contemporaries who most staunchly defend him argue that he should be considered among the greatest twentieth-century poets, and lament the fact that he was not. Probably the most memorable of those arguments comes from this review by John Gould Fletcher, in considering Hardy's 1917 volume *Moments of Vision*:

> If one were to pick out at random a hundred readers of English poetry, and ask them the question: "Who is the greatest English poet to-day?" about ninety-eight would instantly reply, "Kipling." The remainder might be indecisive, or might cast their votes for Masefield, or for Yeats, forgetting that the latter is an Irishman. Nobody, probably, would remark, "Thomas Hardy." And yet there is no doubt that Mr. Hardy is the greatest English poet now living. No one among his contemporaries has been able to turn aside from verse-writing for twenty years, and to return to it with the selfsame powerful grip and mastery. No one has been able to construct a poem of the dynamic energy and epic caliber of *The Dynasts*, but he. No one, finally, but he, is able, at the patriarchal age of seventy-seven, to produce poems marked with the same poignant sincerity of accent that he displayed at thirty.[8]

Fletcher's support for Hardy lies not only in his dynamism as a poet but in his longevity and consistency. That Hardy remains both poignant and sincere, and that he has maintained those qualities for decades and with a twenty-year lapse in publication, impresses Fletcher as much as the qualities of the poems themselves. From a contemporary perspective, Hardy has certainly fared better than Kipling, whose enormous popularity in the early twentieth century has been supplanted by others, like Hardy, whose politics are more palatable to modern minds and whose attitude feels more congruent with modern life.

Despite these many supporters, in the years after Hardy's death, his reputation dipped a bit, as critics like F. R. Leavis expressed their admiration for more evidently "modern" and experimental prosody. Leavis was among the early critics who only backhandedly complimented Hardy, noting his "solidity" but also believing that such solidity was "archaic." Leavis, an early advocate of T. S. Eliot and his innovative style, categorized Hardy firmly as a "Victorian," a classification meant as a denigration. Leavis writes that "Hardy is a naive poet of simple attitudes and outlook . . . there was little in his technique that could be taken up by younger poets and developed in the solution of their own problems."[9] As we shall soon see, this is a statement with which those "younger poets" very much disagreed, but Leavis preferred poetry less familiar, in form and content, than that which Hardy provided.

Mid-century Criticism

In the decades during which High Modernism gained prominence, Hardy's poetry was treated even more harshly. In particular, some of the outspoken New Critics of the 1950s and 1960s found his "imperturbability" less compelling than their predecessors had found it. Among the most critical of the post-Hardy scholars was Irving Howe, who wrote, among other things,

> Hardy's faults are notorious, and generations of critics have declared themselves scandalized. His ear was uncertain: many of his lines drag and crumble, lending themselves neither to song nor fluent speech . . . Hardy's diction is queer, ill assorted and ill tuned: a strange mixture of the 'literary' and flat colloquial, of jargon and romantic poesy. Though he toyed a great deal with stanzaic patterns, Hardy's notions as to verse structure tended to be mechanical . . . What can easily be learned from Hardy is not worth the trouble, and what is very much worth the trouble can hardly be learned at all.[10]

Howe's recognition that something in Hardy's poetry is "very much worth the trouble" is negated by the apparent fact that that thing cannot be learned in any case. Howe argues that it is certainly not Hardy's manipulation of language that is "worth the trouble," nor is it his formalism. But, as Howe explains, neither is it Hardy's ideas. In fact, "Hardy held to a limited version of life, unskeptical of his skepticism and after a time, cozy in his doubt . . . the convictions to which he clings with naïve integrity keep him from engaging with the variousness of life and changes in thought; his poems tend to become vehicles for the rehearsal of settled views."[11] How true this statement may be of any poet is a question worth asking, but, in Hardy's case, it feels patently untrue, as later scholars have recognized. In fact, Hardy's skepticism grows and wanes and takes on multiple forms.

What Howe seems to object to, more even than Hardy's recitation of "settled views," is his divergence from Modernism as Howe regards it. "The scathing assaults upon untested convictions, the playfulness and deviousness of mind we have come to expect in modern poetry – these are not here, not here at all."[12] In fact, as we have seen in Hardy's theological poems, Hardy does almost nothing but apply scathing assaults to untested convictions, but the untested convictions to which Hardy applies himself seem less interesting to Howe than do the untested convictions of Eliot and Pound, and so Howe asserts that Hardy settles into a "cozy doubt." For most readers, though, "cozy" is hardly the word that comes to mind when reading Hardy's pained, searching poems. What Howe may reject but does not fully articulate here is that Hardy's forms and patterns reflect an older, more staid sensibility, even if his ideas do not. The externalities of Hardy's poems, which do indeed differ significantly from the boundary-pushing forms of Eliot and Pound, may have disguised for mid-century readers the degree to which Hardy moved beyond certain Victorian orthodoxies.

The backhanded compliment Howe offers when he acknowledges that some aspect of Hardy is "very much worth the trouble" resembles the critique of another mid-century literary critic, Mark van Doren, who writes, "There is no core of pieces, no inner set of classic or perfect poems, which would prove [Hardy's] rank. Perhaps no poem of Hardy's is perfect; indeed, there is no great poet in whom imperfection is easier to find. Yet he is a great poet . . ."[13] That "yet" at the end of van Doren's comment highlights a tone of resigned admiration common in Hardy criticism throughout the 1960s, which includes long litanies of Hardy's shortcomings followed by grudging recognition of some obscure, indefinable "greatness" in his work.

Richard Carpenter, in 1964, similarly recognized some "greatness" in Hardy but complained that "it can only be regretted that Hardy sank his few good poems in a sea of mediocrity, so that we have to dig them out from masses of silt and barnacles." Those good poems, like Howe's "what is very much worth the trouble," are counterbalanced in Carpenter's assessment by all the terrible poems that surround the few worthwhile ones. Moreover, Carpenter writes critically of Hardy's ideas: "Since the ideas of Hardy's philosophy are few and relatively simple, it is unfortunate that he should have taken himself seriously as a philosophical poet and that many of his readers should have gone along with him, often to find fault with either the philosophy or with his mode of employing it in literature."[14] Carpenter saves the bulk of his ire for *The Dynasts*, which he accuses of being too "monumental": "more imposing to look at than it is comfortable to live in." It is a work, he claims, that inclines readers not "to do more than genuflect and pass on."[15] Interestingly, these same observations are what attracted early critics to that epic work[16] and have drawn the attention of more recent critics as well, prompting a renewed interest in the work. As Harold Orel writes in 2010, "the degree of [Hardy's] success in executing his programme is extraordinary. *The Dynasts* is different in kind from anything he had ever attempted in prose, and it may well be even more than his crowning achievement as a poet."[17]

Poets on Hardy

Perhaps not surprisingly, poets, especially those in the generation following Hardy's, have been more complimentary about his poetry, and quite a number of poets have commented on his work's influence on their writings. Delmore Schwartz, for instance, argues that Hardy has a profound angle on truth and experience, noting that in many of his poems "Hardy says with the greatest emphasis: 'You see: this is what Life is.' And more than that, he says very often: 'You see: your old conception of what Life is has been shown to be wrong and foolish by this example'".[18] W. H. Auden is equally impressed by Hardy's verse, writing that Hardy has a unique perspective on life: "For from such a perspective the difference between the individual and society is so slight, since both are so insignificant, that the latter ceases to appear as a formidable god with absolute rights, but rather as an equal, subject to the same laws of growth and decay".[19]

Hardy was quite popular with the World War I poets as well, and Siegfried Sassoon wrote to him that "I have always liked your 'Men Who March Away' more than any other poem which the war has produced."[20] The poet Edward Thomas, in reviewing *Time's Laughingstocks*, praises Hardy for his boldness in forcing readers to acknowledge hard truths: "Mr. Hardy looks at things as they are, and what is still more notable he does not adopt the genial consolation that they might be worse, that in spite of them many are happy, and that the unhappy live on and will not die . . . He sees this and he makes us see it. The moan of his verse rouses an echo that is as brave as a trumpet."[21] The writer-soldier T. E. Lawrence wrote to poet Robert Graves that "There is an unbelievable dignity and ripeness about Hardy; he is waiting so tranquilly for death, without a desire or an ambition left in his spirit, as far as I can feel it: and yet he entertains so many illusions, and hopes for the world, things which I, in my disillusioned middle-age, feel to be illusory. They used to call this man a pessimist. While really he is full of fancy expectations." Lawrence sees past Hardy's pessimism or, at least, sees it as paired with hope and expectation, a tension for which he expresses his admiration.

The much-beloved Philip Larkin made significant strides towards redeeming and defending Hardy, frequently mentioning him in interviews and writing about him extensively. To the *Paris Review*, Larkin said that he learned from Hardy "not to be afraid of the obvious. All those wonderful *dicta* about poetry . . . Hardy knew what it was all about."[22] He wrote about "Mrs. Hardy's Memories" for a 1961 collection about Hardy and, more famously, wrote "Wanted: Good Hardy Critic" for Roy Morrell's 1965 collection of essays. In his contribution to the volume, Larkin praises Hardy by "trumpet[ing] the assurance that one reader at least would not wish Hardy's *Collected Poems* a single page shorter, and regards it as many times over the best body of poetic work this century so far has to show."[23] Larkin's main argument throughout his essay is that mid-century literary critics see as their primary responsibility only "to demonstrate that the author has said something other than he intended," a literary game that works more effectively for Eliot's and Pound's verse than for Hardy's. And yet, Larkin points out, Hardy's "books have continued to sell and to be read in schools, the principal post-Eliot poets (Auden, Betjeman, Dylan Thomas) have acknowledged his power, and there has been a continual ascent of tribute from what one might call the British Academy reservation." His critique, therefore, is not of Hardy but of the critics: "Eliot was hostile, Leavis patronizing, Wilson, Empson, Blackmur, Trilling – none has been other than neglectful."[24] Larkin's evident frustration with Hardy's treatment, in conjunction with the popular backlash against the complications and obfuscations of High Modernism, helped to prompt a reappraisal of Hardy's verse.

The hostility to which Larkin refers when discussing Eliot is clear in the underhanded compliment Eliot offers in 1933:

> the work of the late Thomas Hardy represents an interesting example of a powerful personality uncurbed by any institutional attachment or by submission to any objective beliefs; unhampered by any ideas, or even by what sometimes acts as a partial restraint upon inferior writers, the desire to please a large public. He seems to me to have written as nearly for the sake of "self-expression" as a man well can; and the self which he had to express does not strike me as a particularly wholesome or edifying matter of communication. He was indifferent even to the prescripts of good writing: he wrote sometimes overpoweringly well, but always very carelessly; at times his style touches sublimity without ever having passed through the stage of being good.[25]

Eliot's apparent wish for Hardy to submit "to an objective belief" rather than to explore a range of beliefs does not accord with Hardy's more investigative style, as we have seen. Like many mid-century critics, Eliot's halfhearted compliment about Hardy's sublimity comes across rather more like an insult. But, as a number of scholars have since pointed out, the difference between Hardy and Eliot does not lessen Hardy's modernism, nor does it reduce the worth of Hardy's verse. Eliot's criticism echoes the writings of many other critics, who find Hardy's work less innovative or pioneering than the work of the High Modernists, but, as Mary Ann Gillies has effectively demonstrated, Modernism encompasses many things, and Hardy's modernism differs in kind from Eliot's but does not differ in spirit.

Four Critics in Depth

The four critics at whom we will look in some depth all find value in Hardy's poetry and consider it as poetry that has passed the test of time, perhaps in a way that Kipling's has not, and that continues to speak to readers in the contemporary world. Each of them has quite a different approach to Hardy's work, though, and so their various methodologies and angles are worth examining more closely.

Samuel Hynes

Hardy's patterns are the focus of a number of important studies, and the first of those that we will consider is Samuel Hynes' 1961 volume, *The Pattern of Hardy's Poetry*. Hynes has edited a number of important editions of Hardy's work, including the Oxford *Selected Poetry* and *The Complete Poetical Works of Thomas Hardy*, and has completed scholarly volumes on a number of other authors. Hynes is also well known as a memoirist, having written about his experiences as a fighter pilot during World War II. He obliquely draws on that personal experience in his "Hardy and the Battle God," where he observes that, unlike the soldier-poets of World War I, Hardy never saw war himself and instead imagined a war in his mind, constructed from Greek tragedy, local history, newspapers, personal connections, and literature. For Hardy, Hynes posits, war was inherently "epic," not only because such a view fits with his theology and naturalism but also because his experience of war was literally in the form of epics rather than real-life experience.

In *The Pattern of Hardy's Poetry*, Hynes asserts that all poetry has a pattern and this is Hardy's: "the eternal conflict between irreconcilables, which was for Hardy the first principle, and indeed the only principle, of universal order."[26] Hynes' book explores Hardy's collected poems to demonstrate this tension "not only in the philosophical content . . . but also in their structure, diction, and imagery – it gives form to every aspect of substance and technique." One of Hynes' most interesting chapters, "The Search for a Form," considers the basis for Hardy's "anti-formalist aesthetic" and for his lifelong use of "personal and eccentric" poetic forms.[27]

Hynes notes the vast variety of stanzaic forms Hardy employs, "generally rather elaborate combinations of lines of various lengths, often rhymed in a complicated way." Hynes finds these forms particularly ineffective for narrative poems and notes that the forms "are not, in most cases, particularly appropriate to their subjects."[28] In the manner of most mid-century critics, Hynes finds significant fault with Hardy's verse, concluding that Hardy's "abundance [of verse forms] was not a sign of a rich, fruitful technical imagination. Rather, it was a sign of fundamental disability in Hardy . . . He never developed a characteristic form." Hynes speculates on the reasons for this "failure," and declares the *Collected Poems* "a scrapyard of ideas that did not work."[29]

Interestingly, about twenty years later, Hynes revisits the criticism he leveled against Hardy in the wonderfully titled "On Hardy's Badnesses." In that article, Hynes acknowledges the condemnation he faced following the publication of *The Pattern of Hardy's Poetry.* "I have been scolded ever since for my lack of positive critical thinking . . . Still, I am unrepentant. I do not doubt that Hardy was a great poet, but I also think that he was peculiarly prone to write bad poems, and I see nothing irreverent or wrong in saying so . . ."[30] Hynes goes on to examine the worst of the worst, as it were, categorizing their various badnesses and bolstering his assessments with reviews from critics who concur as well as with Hardy's self-praise, which Hynes demonstrates to be "exceptionally fallible" and "in general, usually wrong."[31] Among the problems Hynes notes in Hardy's bad poems are "a fundamental lack of humanity," lack of "metrical variety and interest," "an inability to find actions that would adequately express his sense of the world," "awkward or monotonous or mechanical" sound effects, and a "slightly strangulated quality." These condemning conclusions aside, though, in both pieces Hynes uncovers some fascinating aspects of Hardy's verse forms that can be very usefully applied to Hardy studies in today's more forgiving critical environment.

Hynes begins "The Search for a Form" by noting that "in Hardy's poems a relation between form and idea exists which is different from that which we assume in most contemporary poems . . . For Hardy, that is, the inseparability of form and content, which we set so much store by, simply did not exist."[32] Perhaps "simply did not exist" is too strong, and we have noted a number of poems throughout Chapters 1–5 where Hardy's forms do echo his poems' contents. Nonetheless, Hynes' point that, for Hardy, "metrical form was not something which grew up organically with the poem, but was rather a framework or mold" may seem to hold true for Hardy more than for many other poets. Indeed, because Hardy did not have a distinctive "Hardian" form and instead continued to experiment with stanzaic structures throughout his poetic career, it may be true that form functioned differently for Hardy than for other poets.

Hynes comments that Hardy "clearly regarded choosing a meter as a kind of contract, which, once entered into, was not to be broken," and he uses Hardy's revisions to demonstrate that Hardy frequently changed words and phrases but almost never deviated from his chosen forms, an idea that he states in both "The Search for a Form" and "On Hardy's Badnesses." Once selected, the stanzaic pattern was unalterably attached to that poem, and Hardy seemed, to Hynes, imprisoned by his selection of a form, arbitrary as it might be. Furthermore, within his vast stanzaic experimentation, Hardy "never ventured far from the iambic norm," a demonstration of the ways in which he was and was not open to new styles and sounds.

The most valuable contributions of both "The Search for a Form" and "On Hardy's Badnesses" lie in Hynes' tracing of the origins of Hardy's metrical patterns. Hynes effectively demonstrates that Hardy did not entirely draw on the English literary tradition, especially in his metrics. Far from establishing himself formally as Wordsworth or Browning did, by settling on an overarching style or personally distinctive form, Hardy "went on to the end of his life trying again" so that "scarcely two [of his poems] are in the same metrical form."[33] The reason for this, Hynes argues, is that English literary tradition is only one of three traditions from which Hardy's verse draws, the other two belonging to the overarching category of folk traditions: popular ballads as well as hymns and country songs. Given the nature of Hardy's subjects, his drawing on a folk tradition may not be surprising, yet few scholars have recognized the ways in which Hardy moves outside of the literary tradition by attaching himself to a different, but equally authentic, stylistic practice.

Hynes notes that "Hardy shared the ballad view of life – its violence, its fatality, and its indifference to man's desires" and argues that this "ballad-view" is evident throughout not only the poems but also the novels.[34] For the most part, Hynes believes that Hardy's indebtedness to popular ballads lies primarily in their "*dramatic* form and not *metrical* form," and that the popular ballad provides for Hardy a basis for creating poetic setting, action, and voice. But "if ballads gave Hardy a dramatic form, popular music (both religious and secular) gave him metrical form."[35] Hynes points out places in which Hardy referred to his own writing as "music," focusing particularly on Hardy's description of his poems as "lyric ecstasy inspired by music." While Hynes disagrees with Hardy's self-assessed "lyric ecstasy," he does find a number of ways in which the poems grow from popular secular music traditions, especially in *Time's Laughingstocks*, whose poems seem to "have drawn upon the rhythms of folk music" for their meters. The influence of religious music, especially hymns, is also pervasive throughout Hardy's novels and poems. Hynes lists poems, including "A Spot," "I Have Lived with Shades," and "Bereft," among others, that follow the metrical pattern of Psalm 148 as it was written in *A New Version of the Psalms*,[36] the standard Anglican edition with which Hardy would have been intimately familiar.

The formal patterns and influences Hynes articulates throughout "The Search for a Form" and "On Hardy's Badnesses" help to explain Hardy's self-described idiosyncrasies and the oddities of his forms and diction: if his poems' origins were in popular rather than "literary" traditions, much of the awkwardness and variety for which he was so often criticized can be reassessed to recognize a different sort of authenticity in Hardy's work. Hynes concludes "On Hardy's Badnesses" by stating that when Hardy tried to write within a literary tradition, his poetry felt imitative rather than authentic (or, in Hynes' balder language, "not just relatively unsuccessful, but awful"). But when he wrote "in an English tradition, . . . drawing on folk poetry and hymnology and the Bible," he was a great poet. His precursors in that tradition, according to Hynes, were "anon., Hodge, and God," not a bad group to be included among.[37]

As Hynes points out at the end of "On Hardy's Badnesses," both "halves" of Hardy may have been necessary: "Hardy would not be Hardy without his bad side." Rather than seeing his divergence from English literary tradition as a failure, it can be seen as the precise kind of success that has been valued more recently, as poetry has redefined itself well outside a narrow canon of privilege and inherited literary tradition. The very idea of a poetry that grows from the "folk" tradition prompts a reevaluation of Hardy's boundary-pushing and modernity. While Hynes, writing in 1961, used these insightful observations to reflect further on Hardy's failures as a poet, and in 1983 to defend his evaluation of Hardy's poems as falling into dichotomous categories of either "great" or "awful," they might be used today to come to quite different conclusions about Hardy's considerable successes as an artist, whose work should be judged using less staid, "literary" criteria.

Dennis Taylor

Taylor, one of the most prolific of the Hardy critics, focuses almost exclusively on Hardy's poetry and primarily performs what might best be called "textual criticism," looking closely at Hardy's marginalia and other writings to gain insight into Hardy's literary allusions. He also, though, addressed the issues raised by Hynes, not only by writing extensively about Hardy's poetry in more flattering ways but also by composing "The Patterns in Hardy's Poetry" in 1975 to "propose an alternative explanation" for Hardy's use of patterns. While Taylor directly addresses critiques by R. P. Blackmur rather than Hynes, his title's similarity to Hynes' title and his explicit efforts to redeem Hardy from criticism that emphasizes his various incompetences strongly suggests that he has Hynes' work in mind.

Blackmur expressly disapproved of Hardy's patterns as "rigid frames to limit experience," while Taylor argues that Hardy's poems show that the patterns of human experience become both outdated and vulnerable as life changes.[38] Taylor explains that "the abstract figure of a pattern underlies many concrete activities in Hardy's world from the smallest to the most embracing," and he identifies concentric circles of patterning in a person's life and in Hardy's poems: "a man meditates in a natural setting"; "a man has a romantic vision of a 'well-beloved'" that "grows in intensity until the beloved woman dies and reveals the tragic obsolescence of the dream pattern"; "a man's life develops . . . a set of assumptions, in short, a patterned character, which grows eventually old-fashioned until it is overwhelmed by the secret changes of the man's ageing body."[39] We have, of course, seen all of these patterns throughout our reading of Hardy's verse, and Taylor points to the significance and mastery of Hardy's use of patterns, arguing not that these patterns demonstrate Hardy's failings but that they emphasize his poetic power. He writes, "for myself, I experience exhilaration in following these patterns, partly because of their beauty and economy, partly because of the intimations of a larger life outside any one pattern of experience. Hardy makes us aware of the obsolescing patterns of our own consciousness."[40]

Beyond his overt efforts to refashion conventional views of Hardy's verse, Taylor has applied textual analysis to many volumes in Hardy's library, including his editions of Shakespeare, noting Hardy's allusions to *Hamlet* and *Othello* by focusing on the annotations in Hardy's copies of the plays. By examining the specific passages Hardy marked in those volumes, Taylor explores the ways in which those passages influenced Hardy and made their way into his writings. In "From Shakespeare to Casterbridge: The Influence of Shakespeare," Taylor discusses the plays Hardy saw (and the dates on which he saw them) as well as the Shakespearean phrases he entered into his notebook entitled *Studies, Specimens &c*. In "Hardy's Copy of Shakespeare's *Othello*," he analyzes Hardy's annotations to determine the specific nature of the play's influence on Hardy's writings.

Taylor performs a similar analysis of Hardy's first copy of Palgrave's *Golden Treasury*, an examination that helps to bolster his comparisons of Hardy to both William Wordsworth and Thomas Gray.[41] About Hardy and Gray, Taylor notes that they are seldom compared and that Gray's influence on Hardy deserves additional attention. Although they differ in social class and poetic manner, Gray's graceful, sophisticated pessimism touches Hardy's less polished pessimism.[42] Taylor's writings on Wordsworth and Hardy are more extensive, and Taylor argues that Hardy's poetry "can represent a third great stage of the English meditative lyric, a Victorian resolution. At the same time, it is so consistent with Wordsworth's premises that it seems their natural development." To prove this point, Taylor presents specific parallels between Hardy's "Darkling Thrush" and Wordsworth's "To a Skylark" as well as Hardy's "At Castle Boterel" and Wordsworth's "Tintern Abbey." Ultimately, Taylor uses his analysis of the poems as well as of the extant archival materials to prove that "Hardy was extremely responsive to Wordsworth and extremely critical of him."[43] He also explores Hardy's use of Tennyson's *In Memoriam*, using similar methodology.[44]

In addition to this careful textual criticism, Taylor has been the primary scholar responsible for dating Hardy's poems and for drawing attention to the importance of those dates. He performed an impressively comprehensive analysis of Hardy's chronology, published in *Victorian Poetry* (1999), and published three parts of his chronological studies in *Thomas Hardy Review* in 2001 and 2002. Again, by examining Hardy's letters, private writings, drafts, and marginal notes, Taylor reconstructs Hardy's composition dates in ways that had not been done before. These chronologies include not only explanations of Taylor's methodologies but lists of poems, arranged by date and with evidence for that dating. Although his primary attention is to the verse, he also articulated the chronology of Hardy's novel *Jude the Obscure* using similar techniques.

Taylor has also written substantial studies of Hardy's poetry and, especially, its connections to Romanticism and Victorianism. In particular, he examines Hardy's connections to Romantic, Gothic, and Victorian traditions in *Hardy's Poetry 1860–1928* (1981); to Victorian poetic forms in *Hardy's Metres and Victorian Prosody* (1988); and to Victorian uses of language in *Hardy's Literary Language and Victorian Philology* (1993). In the most recent of these studies, Taylor examines the linguistic awkwardness that has often been criticized in Hardy's poetry and argues that his sometimes questionable diction grows from Hardy's deliberate efforts to integrate English history into his work, a topic Taylor also explores in "*Jude the Obscure* and English National Identity."

Hardy's Literary Language and Victorian Philology draws powerful connections between Hardy's poetry and the development of the *Oxford English Dictionary* (*OED*), a fascinating expansion of textual and archival approach to the study of Hardy's verse. Taylor writes that "Hardy's use of the OED was to draw on its historical inclusiveness, and at the same time to undermine, in his own poetry, the 'prison-house' of idiomatic phrases and the blind authority of a standard norm."[45] Taylor argues that the compilation of the

1879–1880 *OED*, for which the editors requested that the English public submit entries of all obsolete or unusual words, prompted Hardy's linguistic self-consciousness and his desire to preserve a less standardized English. Taylor also writes that Hardy intentionally chose unusual or dialectic words – often the very choices with which his critics found the greatest fault – when he felt that they conveyed ideas that would be less evocative in Standard English.

Norman Page

Like Taylor, Norman Page also notes the awkwardness of Hardy's diction and also considers Hardy's verse in conjunction with the writings of other periods, especially the Romantics. His emphases, though, fall primarily on aesthetics and on the ways in which Hardy pushes boundaries rather than conforming to them. Page has written about an enormous range of authors, and Hardy is merely one of nearly twenty about whom Page has published or whose works he has edited. His work on Hardy spans decades, and he served as editor of both the *Thomas Hardy Annual* and *Thomas Hardy Journal*. He edited the *Oxford Reader's Companion to Hardy* (2000) and *Thomas Hardy: The Novels* in this *Analysing Texts* series.

Much of Page's work on Hardy, in addition to the editing of five of his novels and the substantial Oxford reference work, involves visual imagery in Hardy's writing, including Hardy's "forgotten illustrators"[46] and "visual techniques" in the novels.[47] His 1977 volume *Thomas Hardy* explores Hardy's unique style, to which Page frequently applies the word "idiosyncratic," a word Hardy himself used to describe his art. Page's primary arguments in this volume focus on the uniquely "personal" nature of Hardy's poetry; his intentional breaking from a Romantic literary tradition, in both form and content; and his ability to use poetic technique to enhance reader response. Page's chapter "Art and Aesthetics" in the *Cambridge Companion to Thomas Hardy* explores the ways in which beauty – a subjective measure, to be sure – is enhanced in Hardy's work by a "highly, even eccentrically personal vision."[48]

By focusing on Hardy's non-conformity, Page distinguishes Hardy from other poets in his "constructed sponteneity" and use of personal associations as the basis for determining beauty. In addition, Page discusses Hardy's jarring diction, arguing that a close study of Hardy's revisions illustrates the poet's consciously choosing awkward phrasings for effect and "in defiance of poetic orthodoxy."[49] Thus, as Page argues in "Art and Aesthetics," rather than idealizing ugliness, Hardy simply finds beauty in what others might consider ugly. Page quotes Hardy having written that "The beauty of association is entirely superior to the beauty of aspect, and a beloved relative's old battered tankard to the finest Greek vase" because, as Page posits, the former possesses a human connection while the latter exists in the purely aesthetic but emotionally disconnected realm of Romanticism, a tradition from which Hardy distances himself.

One of Page's most entertaining studies is "Opening Time: Hardy's Poetic Thresholds," in which he explores the openings of Hardy's poems to see what they say about Hardy as a poet. Page describes the openings of Hardy's novels as "traditional and conservative" while the poems' openings are "original, innovative, and . . . idiosyncratic," a function, Page claims, of Hardy's being "a Victorian novelist and a modern poet."[50] Early in the chapter, Page notes the colloquialism that opens many of Hardy's poems, especially the uses of "Well," in a conversational manner, and "yes" and "no" as opening words that place the reader *in medias res*, picking up a conversation or observation in the middle of the action. As Page writes, "the effect produced . . . is to suggest that the poem is in the nature of a fragment rather than a complete entity, and that the reader has, so to speak, entered a discourse already in progress. This is of course very different from the effect produced by the opening of *The Mayor of Casterbridge*, where there is a strong sense of the opening as an opening."[51]

For most of the chapter, though, Page focuses on Hardy's use of pronouns at the beginnings of his poems. Certainly we have noted already the many pronouns Hardy uses, from the most obvious "I," which occurs nearly everywhere in his verse, to the common "she" and "they" and even the occasional "you." Page quantifies this pronoun usage, focusing on its occurrence in the first word of a poem, and determining that 92 of Hardy's poems begin with a second- or third-person pronoun and an additional 162 begin with "I." Page compares this high number with the number of Wordsworth's poems beginning with the first-person pronoun, and finds that Hardy comes out way ahead; Wordsworth has only 11 poems structured this way.

Page comes to a number of interesting conclusions about this observation, first among them that "there is a sense in which his collected poems constitute an extended, albeit fragmentary, autobiography, covering his long life from infancy through the pains of early love, and the friendships and infatuations of a lifetime, to the death of Emma and old age. The favorite "I," therefore, can be seen as the natural mode of the autobiographer." Of course, as I have argued throughout this volume, the "I" might also be seen as the natural mode of the storyteller, and Page does make note of a fictional "I" in "a few ballads and narrative poems, and others where the speaker is plainly not the poet himself."[52] Overall, however, Page finds that the poems as a whole tell the story of Hardy's life.[53]

Page's conclusions based on his intriguing observation are twofold: first, Hardy's pronouns produce "a sense that the reader is not being directly addressed but is overhearing something very private and confidential," and second, that Hardy's privacy makes his use of "pronoun-openings . . . an apt counterpart and vehicle" for his observations of the world. As Page had earlier asserted in "Art and Aesthetics," Hardy makes valiant attempts to persuade his readers that "the first-person lyrics should be 'regarded, in the main, as dramatic monologues by different characters'" and that Hardy wishes to "depersonalize his own intensely personal work, and to encourage the reader in the direction of certain kinds of reading while inhibiting other kinds."[54] In particular, Page compares Hardy to Tennyson and the *Poems of 1912–13* to *In Memoriam* to demonstrate the ways in which Tennyson's published identification of his poetic subject differs from Hardy's obfuscation of his subject through the use of pronouns. Page does not question the received truth that the *Poems of 1912–13* are absolutely about Emma, but "still, the fact – and I believe it is a revealing one – remains that Hardy bypasses the identification of his subject."[55] For Page, the reasons for Hardy's disguising Emma in these poems have to do with Hardy's privacy-seeking personality and his desired relationship with his readers rather than because the woman therein might not be fully identifiable as Emma. Nonetheless, his conclusions about pronouns positioning readers as voyeurs and contrasting with both the Romantic and Victorian poetic traditions prompt a number of worthwhile considerations, not least of which is that a close study of diction can elicit the emergence of telling patterns in a poet's work, as we have already seen discussed by both Hynes and Taylor.

Susan M. Miller

Susan M. Miller, while far less prolific than any of the other scholars we have examined here, wrote the frequently-cited "Thomas Hardy and the Impersonal Lyric," one of the most insightful and valuable studies of Hardy's poems in recent years. In this article, Miller argues that Hardy develops a uniquely impersonal form of the lyric that maintains his belief in emotion as poetry's core but that also removes emotion from immediate personal experience. For Miller, the distinction Hardy enacts between philosophy and emotion is "a carefully managed lyric devise." To demonstrate the profound, and often misread, balance that Hardy achieves between personal emotion and experiential distance, Miller reexamines Hardy's well-known statement that "his poems should be understood as feelings, 'mere impressions of the moment' rather than as 'convictions or arguments.'"[56] She believes that Hardy intended, with that statement, to encourage readers to avoid looking in his works for a single consistent philosophy but that the statement was not intended to mean that the moment is Hardy's "primary unity of experience." In other words, Hardy generalizeson the basis of a series of experiences rather than finding richness or meaning in any individual experience or reflection.

According to Miller, though, Hardy seemed to some of his contemporaries to have "reduced ambitions for the genre of poetry itself," the fine line between emotion and philosophy on which Hardy balances himself creates an utterly new poetry of "neither feeling nor philosophy, but the impersonal emotional weight of an idea that has been abstracted from the current of lived experience."[57] Miller acknowledges both the philosophical and novelistic leanings in Hardy's work, but posits that "the extent to which Hardy's poetry veers towards the philosophical on the one hand and towards the novelistic on the other is the extent to which he resists a poetry of direct personal experience and emotion."[58]

Miller's argument is primarily couched in terms of Romanticism and, like Taylor, Miller finds that Hardy both engages with and rejects Wordsworth's use of personal experience. The Romantic poets, especially Wordsworth, validate personal experience "as a source of understanding or personal enrichment" and see reflection or hindsight as potentially problematic; Hardy reverses these, placing primary importance on later, removed reflection. Like Wordsworth, Hardy tries to separate emotion from meaning to see how they work in conjunction, but Hardy's perspective "exchanges immediacy for scope."[59] Put another way, Hardy borrows a Romantic poetic technique without borrowing its accompanying outlook. For Wordsworth, both experience and recollection are "rich with meaning," but in Hardy's poems, both are "strangely empty."[60] As we have noted many times in this volume, for Hardy "hindsight offers very little benefit . . . Wisdom won through retrospection is less often a gift than a torment."[61] Miller thus argues that Hardy's poetry isolates moments to show how they do not fulfill their "revelatory promise."[62]

Ultimately, Miller writes, "Hardy's critique of the intense momentary insight reveals a sensibility tortured by the awareness that lived experience is always discredited by the changes that will come. A person has to stand outside himself to a certain degree to have his awareness."[63] That quality, which many critics have recognized and which we have observed throughout this volume, Miller describes as a "split consciousness, an agonized awareness of two perspectives that don't quite match." One of those perspectives is more knowing than the other, and the two together create a third: only as an experiment of the imagination." That is, as Hardy's speakers view (in their memories) an ignorant but happy past, and (in reality) a knowing but miserable present, they create (in their imaginations) a knowing but happy existence; the very act of bringing together joy and knowledge in imagination, though, clarifies for those speakers the impossibility of happiness and knowledge existing simultaneously, which leads to what Miller calls "epistemological pain . . . the suffering felt when the intellectual sphere comes together with the emotional without the promise of any credible fusion."[64]

Miller also helpfully points out that the *Poems of 1912–13*, which we have discussed at some length, differ in kind from Hardy's other volumes. These poems, unlike almost all of his others, "do not insist upon being read as dramatic projections – even though Hardy would probably say that they should be." In other words, it is possible and often easier, as we saw in Chapter 6, to read the *Poems of 1912–13* as lyrics in the deeply personal Romantic mode, relying on primary experiences and their accompanying emotions, with a secondary emphasis on recollection and reflection. Miller acknowledges that Hardy would likely prefer them not to be read that way, which underscores the likelihood that these apparently personal poems are only approached as Romantic emotional projections because, unlike some of Hardy's other poems, they *can* be. Their ability to be read in this more conventional way, though, does not mean that they must be nor did Hardy see them as different in kind from his other poems. The difference that Miller notes between *Poems of 1912–13* and Hardy's others may explain why they are more widely considered, why they feel more comfortable to readers, and why they seem to hearken back to more familiar poetic tropes. At the same time, Miller's more challenging approach to Hardy's poems generally can also meaningfully be applied to the *Poems of 1912–13*, an approach which creates a consistency among his poems and demonstrates the ways in which that one volume may be less different from the others than it seems.

Finally, Miller argues that Hardy is indeed a precursor of Modernism despite the fact that he is often thought to have opposed it. His poetry is connected to the "puppeteer's manipulation of circumstance and emotion, and the modernist poetics of impersonality suggested in the collage-aesthetics of poems like *The Waste Land* and *The Cantos* . . . "[65] She observes that Hardy's forms often prevent readers from noticing his modernist aesthetic but also that, although he never adopted the "radically impersonal style that modernism ushered in," he moves in that direction with his impersonal lyric.[66] Like the High Modernists, Hardy maintains a consistent philosophy, but not in the way that many readers expect: his poems "know what they know, and they insist especially on certain patterns of disappointment with a relentlessness that hints at conviction."[67] Hardy's Modernism, then, lies not in formal experimentation, linguistic game playing, or genre boundary-crossing, but in the overriding conviction of his poems that resembles and prefigures the poetic concerns of Modernism: "a longing for a total picture."[68]

An examination of these four critics may help to give readers a fuller picture of the many ways in which Hardy's poetry can be approached and the variety of conclusions that can be drawn from readings of the same poems. These are merely representative samples, though, and there is still so much more to read and learn. With each additional analysis you read, you may be able to construct a more complete picture of Hardy's poetry and, most importantly, develop the analysis that is most true to your experience of the poems. By studying these critics, you may also notice some trends in criticism over the years: older critics tend to be more interested in creating lists of "good" and "bad" poets and "great" and "insignificant" poems in a way that contemporary critics are less interested in doing. You might consider why that change in approach has taken place and which style of criticism you prefer. By reading some of the additional suggestions you'll find on the following pages, you may be able to create a fuller picture of how critics approach poetry and your own style of literary criticism.

Further Reading

Over the years, anthologists have chosen certain poems of Hardy that they feel deserve to be studied and have republished them in schoolbooks and anthologies. Reading these poems is often a wonderful practice, but a similarly valuable experience is to open up the *Collected Poems* to any page and read what you find there. Having someone else choose the "best" poems for you may be a good way to begin your acquaintance with Hardy's works, but anthologists are frequently influenced by one another, and so their choices are often self-perpetuating. Hardy's work is so rich and various, though, that you may find wonderful poems by exploring his entire collection rather than an edition that has already made selections for you. You may be surprised by the discoveries you can make in poems that are infrequently or never anthologized, and you may question the choices made in well-known anthologies.

When you do read the poems, whether those you find in anthologies or those you have chosen from the *Collected Poems*, consider reading them aloud or with a friend. Reading has become either a solitary or a classroom experience in the modern world, but reading for pleasure together with others can add to both your enjoyment and your understanding. I never cease to be amazed at how much more I find in poems when I read them with another person. Merely the experience of trying to explain my own interpretation opens and clarifies my reading for me.

Works by Hardy

If you are interested in Hardy at all, of course you should read his novels. *Tess of the D'Urbervilles* is a good place to start because its story is accessible, and you will recognize many of its characters, settings, and themes from Hardy's poems. Almost all of the novels are available in many, many editions, but be careful to choose unabridged editions because some versions are shortened or altered in significant ways. For a more comprehensive experience of the novels, consider the Norton Critical editions of *Tess of the D'Urbervilles* (ed. Scott Elledge, 1990), *The Mayor of Casterbridge* (ed. Phillip Mallett, 2000), *Jude the Obscure* (ed. Norman Page, 1999), *The Return of the Native* (ed. Phillip Mallett, 2006), and *Far from the Madding Crowd* (ed. Robert Schweik, 1986). These editions enhance the reading experience by providing context for each novel and following the novel's full text with critical responses from Hardy's time as well as from a representative sample of contemporary critics.

You might also try your hand at *The Dynasts*, but be warned that this work is very long and can be tough going at times. Still, it is worth at least a cursory glance and, for history buffs, it can offer a new and poetic angle on the Napoleanic Wars. If you do not wish to invest in a hard copy of this work, which is available from Clarendon Press edited by Samuel Hynes, you may find a full-text edition online at Project Gutenberg. Hardy's short stories, especially the *Wessex Tales* (Oxford World Classics, ed. Katherine King, 2009), are far more approachable and offer the reader an experience somewhere between the experience of reading the poems and reading the novels. Again, some of these will feel familiar to you because of your experience with the poems, and you will see some of the same themes and philosophies we have discussed in the poems but with different stylistic concerns.

Finally, a number of important primary materials are available, including Hardy's eight-volume set of letters (eds Michael Millgate, Richard Purdy, and Keith Wilson, Oxford University Press) and a number of his notebooks, in various editions edited by Michael Millgate, Pamela Dalziel, and William Greenslade, among others. While these primary texts are too comprehensive for the casual reader, they do contain some quite interesting moments and statements. In any case, reading the personal writings of an author whose public works you already know may offer additional insights into your understandings of his art.

Reading around the Poems

If you want to know more about how Hardy's poetry fits into other poetic traditions, you should read a lot of other British poetry, especially Wordsworth, Shelley, Tennyson, Browning, Larkin, and Eliot. Wordsworth's and Coleridge's 1798 *Lyrical Ballads* and especially Wordsworth's seminal "Preface" to that Collection offer insight into the prominent poetic philosophies during Hardy's early years. The 2008 Broadview edition (eds Dahlia Porter and Michael Garner) includes the 1798 and 1800 *Lyrical Ballads* along with contextual materials. Tennyson's *In Memoriam* (Norton Critical Edition, ed. Robert H. Ross, 1974; also available online at the University of Virginia's e-text site) and Browning's *Selected Poems* (Penguin Classics, 2001) can be compared with Hardy's work. And to see the kind of poetry being written alongside Hardy's in the 1910s and 1920s, read Eliot's *The Waste Land* and "The Love Song of J. Alfred Prufrock" (both in *The Collected Poems of T. S. Eliot*, Harcourt Brace Jovanovich, 1991). Reading an anthology of the British World War I poems may also demonstrate the ways in which Hardy's war poems resemble and differ from theirs. The two best editions of these are Dover's *World War I British Poets* (ed. Candace Ward, 1997) and *The Penguin Book of First World War Poetry* (ed. George Walter, 2007).

Reading some of the works about which Hardy was thinking is also a valuable approach to better understanding his work. Probably the most important of these is Charles Darwin's *Origin of Species* (Signet Classics, 2003), but Darwin's other writings also played a part in Hardy's thinking.

To see how Hardy's verse affected others, certainly read the poems of Philip Larkin (*The Collected Poems*, ed. Anthony Thwaite, 2004) and of W. H. Auden (Vintage, ed. Edward Mendelson, 1991). Larkin's *Required Writing* also offers some valuable insights into his views of Hardy and the ways in which he defended Hardy from his many critics (University of Michigan, 1999). Many other poets have claimed Hardy as their predecessor, including Delmore Schwartz, and traces of his style and voice can be found in the work of the American "Confessional" poets, including Robert Lowell, John Berryman, and W. D. Snodgrass.

Biographies (and Their Difficulties)

Reading a biography of Hardy may be more complicated than one would expect. The biography *The Life of Thomas Hardy*, originally published in two volumes, *The Early Life (1840–1891)* and *The Later Years (1892–1928)*, was ostensibly written by Hardy's second wife Florence with the assistance of a few close friends, foremost among them the playwright J. M. Barrie, of *Peter Pan* fame, and published immediately after Hardy's death in 1928. The volumes were treated as an authorized biography for decades, and even the volumes' earliest readers knew that Hardy had contributed significantly to their content. But until Richard Purdy studied the manuscripts of the *The Life of Thomas Hardy*, no one realized that Hardy himself had been the volumes' primary author.

The work of Purdy and, later, Michael Millgate demonstrated how Hardy had composed the *Life* in third-person voice, given the pages to Florence for revision, destroyed his original copies, made changes to Florence's typescripts, and then performed two more levels of revision to Florence's work before the biography was published posthumously. Because of these discoveries, Millgate examined the biography's manuscripts and delineated which pieces had been composed by Hardy and which had been added or amended by Florence or Barrie. Based on this extensive research, Millgate then published a one-volume version, called *The Life and Work of Thomas Hardy*, in 1984, which aimed to excise Florence and Barrie's work to leave behind a more purely Hardian text. (*Life and Work* is an original title Hardy himself had used for notes on an autobiographical manuscript.) Millgate's goal in his 1984 edition was to identify "Mrs. Hardy's independent additions and deletions" so as to clarify the text's "shared or at any rate successive authorship" (*Life and*

Work, p. xxx). Millgate's volume is, for the most part, considered Hardy's definitive account of himself because this excised version of Florence's biography is most often read as Hardy's own work and self-portrait. References to "Hardy's autobiography" generally mean the Millgate version.

The considerable and well-founded confusion about biographical authorship described here can be extended to encompass ongoing confusion about the many extant Hardy biographies. To clarify, *The Life of Thomas Hardy* is the title given to the combined edition of two texts: *The Early Life of Thomas Hardy* (published in 1928) and *The Later Years of Thomas Hardy* (published in 1930), both of which were published under Florence Hardy's name. This volume is often referred to in books and articles as the *Life*. Millgate's 1984 excised volume is generally referred to as *The Life and Work* and lists Thomas Hardy as its author and Millgate as its editor. Millgate also wrote a traditional biography of Hardy in 1982, entitled *Thomas Hardy: A Biography*, and published a significant revision of that biography in 2006 under the title *Thomas Hardy: A Biography Revisited*. He also wrote a book of criticism, *Thomas Hardy: His Career as a Novelist*, in 1971 and served as editor for collections of Hardy's letters and his notebooks. All of these books should not be confused with Robert Gittings' two-volume biography, which, similar to the *Life*, is split into *Young Thomas Hardy* (published in 1975) and *Thomas Hardy's Later Years* (published in 1978). In addition, a version of the *Life* has been reprinted under the title *Thomas Hardy*, whose authors are listed as "Thomas and Florence Hardy." This version does not change the text but alters the attribution on the cover based on Purdy and Millgate's discoveries.[1]

This complicated history might suggest that no actual Hardy autobiography exists, but Millgate himself refers to *The Life and Work* as "Hardy's autobiography" despite the fact that, prior to the publication of that volume, Purdy wrote that the *Life* was Hardy's autobiography, Florence's contributions notwithstanding. These confusions continue to abide and, as we shall soon see, they affect and alter the ways that readers approach Hardy's poems. A number of prominent sources, including, until recently, the Poetry Foundation, refer to the *Life and Work* as "Hardy's autobiography." W. Eugene Davis in the

2010 Ashgate companion to Hardy remarked that Hardy attempted "to safeguard his privacy by writing his autobiography pseudonymously (under Florence Hardy's name)" without mentioning that Florence herself contributed to that work.[2] In other places, like U. C. Knoepflmacher's 1990 *PMLA* article "Hardy Ruins: Female Spaces and Male Designs," critics gloss this complicated textual history by imagining a simple misstatement of authorship. Knoepflmacher writes merely that "*The Early Life of Thomas Hardy* (1928; rpt. in *The Life of Thomas Hardy*, 1962), [was] attributed to Florence Emily Hardy but actually written by the subject himself," a statement that may almost be true but is not true in important ways, namely that it had both additions and deletions made by Florence, Barrie, and others.[3] These casual references to "Hardy's autobiography," a text that was never intended to exist, erases Hardy's intentions and the joint creation of the text (whether we see that joint creation as including Florence and Barrie or including Millgate).

Tim Dolin, one of the few critics to question the designation of "autobiography" for Millgate's re-creation, rightly states that a text originally written as a collaboration among unequal partners cannot fairly be reduced to the uncomplicated work of its lead author; an autobiography is quite different from a biography, and, had Hardy wanted to write one, he certainly could have. The fact that Hardy worked so assiduously to mold his public persona strongly implies that whatever "autobiography" is at the root of the *Life* and brought to the surface in the *Life and Work* cannot fully be trusted as autobiography in the conventional sense. And, of course, since autobiographies are already rather slippery and very frequently manipulate self-presentation, this one may do so in even more unfathomable ways. What Hardy apparently desired was a third-person biography of which he was the primary author. While perhaps many of the incidents and reflections would have remained identical had Hardy chosen to write an autobiography, contemporary readers have no way of knowing how Hardy would have chosen to present himself differently had the genre of the work been different.

When Millgate's *Life and Work* was published, most reviewers were ecstatically positive about it and its contributions to the study of Hardy. A few reviewers did question its being fully considered autobiography, Norman Page and J. Gerard Dollar among them. Page wrote that, because the work is written in third-person voice, it does not resemble conventional autobiographies. Third-person about oneself "is a method that comprises in a curious manner that of the fiction (where the third-person narrator – in, for example, *Jude the Obscure* – sometimes presents scarcely modified autobiography in the guise of fiction) and that of the poems, where a first-person method . . . deploys autobiographical method with apparently, though sometimes *only* apparently, greater explicitness."[4] Dollar posited that Millgate's reconstruction "brings us much closer to the book Hardy actually wrote" but noted that the text, whether in Florence's or Millgate's version, "will always remain a furtive work."[5]

Criticism

Anthologies of critical essays are an excellent place to begin exploring poetic analysis because they offer readers a variety of critical insights within a single volume. Unfortunately, nearly all of the anthologies about Hardy's work focus primarily on the novels, with just a small handful of chapters devoted to the verse. Nonetheless, the excellent *Cambridge Companion to Thomas Hardy* (ed. Dale Kramer, 1999), *Ashgate Research Companion to Thomas Hardy* (ed. Rosemarie Morgan, 2010), *Thomas Hardy Reappraised* (ed. Keith Wilson, University of Toronto, 2006), and *Companion to Thomas Hardy* (ed. Keith Wilson, Wiley-Blackwell, 2009) all include valuable chapters on the verse, and even the chapters on the novels may contribute to readers' understandings of Hardy's poetry.

Among the many articles I outlined in the previous chapter, Susan Miller's is the one that, for me, best captures the nuance and power of Hardy's poetry. A number of other articles are also quite compelling and worthwhile, though, including Dennis Taylor's "The Riddle of Hardy's Poetry" (*Victorian Poetry*, Winter 1973), which argues for the power of Hardy's verse by identifying the components which allow the poems to "transmute" and become "sincere." William Morgan's "Mr. Hardy Composing a Lyric" (*Journal of English and Germanic Philology*, July 1993) similarly aims to uncover some mystery or riddle in Hardy's verse, in this case by examining the choices Hardy makes as a poet and the rhetorical situations from which he composes his verse. Bert G. Hornback ("Thomas Hardy: The Poet in Search of his Voice," *Victorian Poetry*, Spring 1974) and Satoshi Nishimura ("Thomas Hardy and the Language of the Inanimate," *Studies in English Literature*, Autumn 2003) both explore Hardy's use of voice, considering how personal his voice is and how he lends voices to inanimate objects. William Clyde Brown's "The Ambiguities of Thomas Hardy" (*Notre Dame English Journal*, Summer 1983) demonstrates how Hardy experiments with possibilities for human happiness and love in a universe which is, at best, indifferent to human aspirations, and reads Hardy's "pessimism" as questioning and experimentation instead of a fixed bleakness. Finally, all of the wonderful discussions in the "Thomas Hardy Forum," edited by Betty Corbus and published regularly in *Hardy Review*, illustrate the kinds of conversations and debates that continue to take place about Hardy's verse and the variety of interpretations and opinions that apply to his poems.

Notes

Notes to the Introduction

1 For a consideration of how Hardy's work as a poet informs his novels, see
  Jean R. Brooks' *Thomas Hardy: The Poetic Structure* and Ted R. Spivey's
  "Thomas Hardy's Tragic Hero" in *Nineteenth-Century Fiction* 9 (1954–
  55): 179–91, where Spivey contends that Hardy was "a tragic poet . . .
  who did his work in prose" (181).
2 Webster (201).
3 Gatrell (32).
4 According to Hardy, his novels are "mere journeywork" and "have been
  superseded . . . by the more important half of my work, the verse."
  Quoted in Dennis Taylor, "Thomas Hardy and Thomas Gray: The Poet's
  Currency" (451).

Notes to Chapter 1

1 Quoted in Sankey (92).
2 This poem is too long to reprint here in full, but readers should look up
  the poem and read it alongside this analysis.
3 Sankey (86 and 96).

Notes to Chapter 3

1 Scott (275).
2 Ibid.

3 Hardy. Letter to Clodd, 22 March 1904.
4 2 February 1908.
5 This is an irony shared with the Romantic poets, who frequently address inanimate objects or animals in their odes, not expecting that an urn or nightingale might respond. Of course, that audience is not the real audience of the poems, although it is the proclaimed audience. Hardy employs a similar technique, pretending to address an audience that cannot hear him while knowing that another audience stands in the wings, listening attentively.
6 *CP* 84.

Notes to Chapter 4

1 Although Hardy wrote a number of poems about World War I, he is generally considered separately from the other World War I poets, primarily because he was at least a generation older than they and because they were soldier/poets while he never saw battle.
2 Some versions of this poem replace the word "cloud" with the word "fade," which clarifies the meaning of the final stanza.
3 Bailey (421).
4 Auden (139).
5 Whitehead, "Thomas Hardy and The First World War Companion Poems: 'Men Who March Away' and 'Before Marching And After'" (85).

Notes to Chapter 5

1 W. B. Yeats, T. S. Eliot, and other High Modernists usher in an age of poems about aging. Poets who follow Hardy, from Dylan Thomas to Philip Larkin, write about almost nothing else.
2 In this regard, he seems to anticipate the philosophy of Thomas Nagel in "The Absurd," which argues that "In ordinary life a situation is absurd when it includes a conspicuous discrepancy between pretension or aspiration and reality." Nagel posits that "In viewing ourselves from a perspective broader than we can occupy in the flesh, we become spectators of our own lives. We cannot do very much as pure spectators of our own lives, so we continue to lead them, and devote ourselves to what we are able at the same time to view as no more than a curiosity, like the ritual

of an alien religion." This very idea – of being both the people who live our lives and, simultaneously, people who observe them from above or beyond – captures at least part of what is so trying to Hardy. He wants to escape himself and to maintain some distance, but he cannot, and this tension between internality and observation is, ultimately, absurd.

3 Critics almost exclusively agree that the absent woman is Hardy's wife Emma, and they frequently write about this poem and others as though it is a fully biographical poem about Hardy's life with Emma. I purposely avoid that critical approach, and I will explain more about why I avoid it in the next chapter.

4 Heaney (30).

Notes to Chapter 6

1 Millgate, *Thomas Hardy: A Biography Revisited* (4).
2 Eagleton (94).
3 Quoted in Gittings, *Thomas Hardy's Later Years* (98).
4 Hardy, *The Life and Work of Thomas Hardy* (415).
5 Taylor, "Hardy as a Nineteenth-Century Poet" (191).
6 Ibid. (202).
7 *Collected Letters* 5 (94).
8 Brooks (8).
9 Ibid. (23–24).
10 Gittings, *Thomas Hardy's Later Years* (85).
11 Ibid. (85).
12 Tuma (1).
13 Millgate, *Thomas Hardy: A Biography* (568).
14 *The Trumpet Major* was Hardy's 1880 novel set in the Napoleanic Wars, a setting that prompted his further thinking about setting an epic work in that period.
15 Millgate, *Thomas Hardy: A Biography* (385).
16 For a fascinating discussion among professors and scholars about how autobiographical Hardy's poem "The Impercipient" might be, read Betty Corbus' "Thomas Hardy Forum" in *Hardy Review*, Spring 2008, pages 43–67. This discussion demonstrates the seriousness with which scholars approach the question of autobiography in poems and the degree to which Hardy's role in many of his own poems has been debated.
17 Morgan, "Introduction" (12).

18 *Collected Letters* 5 (67).
19 *Collected Letters* 6 (139).
20 *Collected Letters* 6 (208).
21 Gittings, *Thomas Hardy's Later Years* (155).
22 Murfin (73–74).
23 Ramazani (958).
24 Austin (5).
25 Austin (12).
26 Corbus, "Thomas Hardy Forum" (46).
27 Larkin, "The Pleasure Principle." In Larkin, *Required Writing* (81).
28 McCarty (94–102).
29 Bownas (52–61).
30 Richardson (158).
31 Beer, *Darwin's Plots* (40).
32 Henchman (38).
33 Heath (28).
34 Paulin (3).
35 Everett, http://www.victorianweb.org/authors/rb/dm1.html.
36 Taylor, "Hardy as a Nineteenth-Century Poet" (200).
37 Quoted in Flynn (91–2).
38 Flynn (92).
39 Quoted in Corbus, "Thomas Hardy Forum" (46).
40 Paulin (45).
41 Taylor, *Hardy's Poetry, 1860–1928* (xvii).
42 Cassis (290).
43 Taylor, "Hardy and Wordsworth" (442).
44 Riquelme (208).
45 Ibid. (207).
46 Ibid. (219–20).
47 Gillies (535–54).
48 Ibid. (539).
49 Ibid. (539).
50 Ibid. (553).
51 Walt Whitman.

Notes to Chapter 7

1 Howells (140).
2 Noyes (103).

3 Warren (321–22).
4 Anonymous (371).
5 Monroe (243).
6 Seccombe (496).
7 Allen (360–61).
8 Fletcher (96).
9 Leavis (57).
10 Howe (162–63).
11 Ibid. (163).
12 Ibid. (163).
13 Quoted in ibid. (168).
14 Carpenter (159).
15 Ibid. (185).
16 For instance, "Notes of the Form of *The Dynasts*" by Barker Fairley, *PMLA: Publications of the Modern Language Association of America*, 34.3 (1919): 401–15; "Mr. Hardy's Dynasts as Tragic Drama" by Charles E. Whitmore, *Modern Language Notes*, 39.8 (December 1924): 455–60; and "A 1905 Dynasts" by Richard Purdy, *Times Literary Supplement*, 14 February 1929: 118.
17 Orel (370).
18 Schwartz (124).
19 Auden (140).
20 Quoted in Whitehead, "Thomas Hardy and the First World War: Case Studies in Literary Influence" (116). Incidentally, the war poet Charles Sorley hated "Men Who March Away," but he seems to have been in the minority.
21 Ibid.
22 Larkin, *Required Writing* (67).
23 Ibid. (174).
24 Ibid. (168).
25 Eliot (59).
26 Hynes, *The Pattern of Hardy's Poetry* (vii).
27 "The Search for a Form" is Chapter 5 (74–88) in *The Pattern of Hardy's Poetry*.
28 Hynes, *The Pattern of Hardy's Poetry* (75).
29 Ibid. (88).
30 Ibid. (247–48).
31 Ibid. (248).
32 Ibid. (75–76).
33 Ibid. (88).
34 Ibid. (80–81).

35 Ibid. (82).
36 A widely-used volume of the Psalms, compiled by Nahum Tate and Nicholas Brady, which dates from 1696.
37 Hynes, *The Pattern of Hardy's Poetry* (257).
38 Taylor, "The Patterns of Hardy's Poetry" (97–98).
39 Ibid. (99).
40 Ibid. (113).
41 Taylor, "Hardy's Copy of *The Golden Treasury*."
42 Taylor, "Thomas Hardy and Thomas Gray: The Poet's Currency."
43 Taylor, "Hardy and Wordsworth."
44 Taylor, "Hardy's Use of Tennyson's *In Memoriam*."
45 Taylor, *Hardy's Literary Language and Victorian Philology* (90).
46 *Bulletin of the New York Public Library*.
47 Page, "Visual Techniques in Hardy's *Desperate Remedies*" (65–71). Page, "Hardy's Pictorial Art in *The Mayor of Casterbridge*" (486–92). Page, "Hardy's Dutch Painting: *Under the Greenwood Tree*" (39–42).
48 Page, "Art and Aesthetics" (38).
49 Page, *Thomas Hardy* (155).
50 Ibid. (262).
51 Ibid. (264).
52 Ibid. (266).
53 It is worth noting, perhaps, that the series Page lists – infancy, the pains of early love, the friendships and infatuations of a lifetime, the death of loved ones, and old age – is actually the sequence of *anyone's* life and is not particular to Hardy.
54 Page, "Art and Aesthetics" (50).
55 Page (267).
56 Miller, "Thomas Hardy and the Impersonal Lyric" (95).
57 Ibid. (97.
58 Ibid. (108).
59 Ibid. (96).
60 Ibid. (101).
61 Ibid. (97).
62 Ibid. (98).
63 Ibid. (111).
64 Ibid. (114).
65 Ibid. (112).
66 Ibid. (114).
67 Ibid. (96).
68 Ibid. (113).

Notes to Further Reading

1 The differences among these volumes may be sufficiently confusing, but there are a number of other biographies and monographs that further complicate matters. For instance, *Thomas Hardy* (by Lance St. Butler, in 1978), *Thomas Hardy* (by Harold Bloom, in 1987), *Thomas Hardy* (by Charles Lock, in 1992), *Thomas Hardy* (by Patricia Ingham, in 2003), and *Thomas Hardy* (by Claire Tomalin, in 2008) might have benefitted from somewhat more distinctive titles. These are, of course, not to be confused with Paul Turner's *Life of Thomas Hardy: A Critical Biography* (2001), Ralph Pite's *Thomas Hardy: The Guarded Life* (2007), or Andrew Norton's *Thomas Hardy: Behind the Mask* (2011). And these leave aside the volumes (this one among them) that specify a genre or title or characteristic of Hardy's writing before or after his name, as in Jean Brooks' *Thomas Hardy: The Poetic Structure* (1971), to name just one of hundreds.
2 Davis (48).
3 Knoepflmacher (1056–57).
4 Page (112).
5 Dollar (134).

List of Works Cited

Allen, Hervey. "*Human Shows, Far Phantasies, Songs and Trifles* by Thomas Hardy; *Harvest of Youth* by Edward Davison; *The Long Gallery* by Anne Goodwin Winslow; *Not Poppy* by Virginia Moore; *American Indian Love Lyrics* by Nellie Barnes." *The North American Review* 223.831 (1926): 360–66. *JSTOR*. Web. Accessed 12 June 2012.

Allingham, Philip V. "A Discussion of Thomas Hardy's Late Lyric 'Winter Night in Woodland (Old Time).'" *The Victorian Web* (2003). Web. Accessed 15 April 2012.

Anonymous. "Review in *Times Literary Supplement* of *Satires of Circumstance*." In *Thomas Hardy Critical Assessments*, ed. Graham Clarke. Vol. 1. Mountfield: Helm Information, 1993, pp. 371–73. Print.

Auden, W. H. "A Literary Transference." In *Hardy*, ed. Albert J. Guerard. Englewood Cliffs, NJ: Prentice Hall, 1963, pp. 135–42. Print.

Austin, Linda M. "Reading Depression in Hardy's *Poems of 1912–13*." *Victorian Poetry* 36.1 (1998): 1–15. *JSTOR*. Web. Accessed 24 July 2012.

Bailey, J. O. *The Poetry of Thomas Hardy: A Handbook and Commentary*. Chapel Hill: University of North Carolina, 1970. Print.

Beer, Gillian. *Darwin's Plots*. Cambridge: Cambridge University Press, 1983. Print.

Beer, Gillian. "Vision and Revision: *Time Warps* in Moments of Vision." In *The Ashgate Research Companion to Thomas Hardy*, ed. Rosemarie Morgan. Burlington, VT: Ashgate, 2010, p. 498.

Bloom, Harold. *Thomas Hardy*. New York: Chelsea House, 1987. Print.

Bownas, Jane. "Exploration and Post-Darwinian Anxiety in Thomas Hardy's *Two on a Tower*."

Hardy Review, Spring 2009: 52–61. *MLA International Bibliography*. Web. Accessed 25 April 2012.

Brooks, Jean R. *Thomas Hardy: The Poetic Structure*. Ithaca, NY: Cornell University Press, 1971. Print.

Browning, Robert, Roma A. King, and Jack W. Herring. *The Complete Works of Robert Browning: With Variant Readings and Annotations*. Athens: Ohio University Press, 1969. Print.

Butler, Lance St John. *Thomas Hardy*. Cambridge, UK: Cambridge University Press, 1978. Print.

Carpenter, Richard. *Thomas Hardy*. New York: Twayne, 1964. Print.

Cassis, A. F. "A Note on the Structure of Hardy's Short Stories." *Colby Library Quarterly* 10 (1974): 287–96. *JSTOR*. Web. Accessed 1 May 2012.

Corbus, Betty. "Thomas Hardy Forum." *Hardy Review* 10.1 (2008): 43–67. *MLA International Bibliography*. Web. Accessed 24 July 2012.

Davie, Donald. *With the Grain*: *Essays on Thomas Hardy and Modern English Poetry*. Manchester: Carcanet Press, 1999. Print.

Davis, W. Eugene. "The First 100 Years of Hardy Criticism: 1871–1971." In *The Ashgate Research Companion to Thomas Hardy*, ed. Morgan Rosemarie. Burlington, VT: Ashgate, 2010, pp. 39–55. Print.

Dolin, Tim. "The Early Life and Later Years of Thomas Hardy: An Argument for a New Edition." *Review of English Studies*, November 2007: 698–714. *MLA International Bibliography*. Web. Accessed 26 July 2012.

Dollar, J. Gerard. "The Life and Work of Thomas Hardy by Thomas Hardy; Michael Millgate." *Journal of English and Germanic Philology* 86.1 (1987): 134–36. *JSTOR*. Web. Accessed 24 July 2012.

Donne, John, and C. A. Patrides. *The Complete English Poems of John Donne*. London: Dent, 1985. Print.

Eagleton, Terry. "Buried in the Life." *Harper's Magazine*, November 2007: 89–92. Print.

Eliot, T. S. *After Strange Gods: A Primer of Modern Heresy*. New York: Harcourt Brace, 1934. Print.

Everett, Glenn. Quoted by George Landow. "Dramatic Monologue." *The Victorian Web*. http://www.victorianweb.org/authors/rb/dm1.html (March 2003). Web. Accessed 1 May 2012.

Fairley, Barker. "Notes of the Form of *The Dynasts*." *PMLA: Publications of the Modern Language Association of America* 34.3 (1919): 401–15. *MLA International Bibliography*. Web. Accessed 3 July 2012.

Fletcher, John Gould. Review of "Moments of Vision" by Thomas Hardy, *Poetry* 12.2 (May 1918): 96–101. *JSTOR*. Web. Accessed 12 June 2012.

Flynn, Suzanne J. "Hardy in (A Time of) Transition." In *The Ashgate Research Companion to Thomas Hardy*, pp. 87–99. Print.

Gatrell, Simon. "Wessex." In *The Cambridge Companion to Thomas Hardy*, ed. Dale Kramer. Cambridge, UK: Cambridge University Press, 1999, pp. 19–37. Print.

Gibson, James. "Introduction." In *The Complete Poems*. Basingstoke: Palgrave Macmillan, 2001. Print.

Gillies, Mary Ann. "Thomas Hardy: Modernist Poet." *Modern Language Quarterly*, December 1990: 535–54. *JSTOR*. Web. Accessed 12 April 2012.

Gittings, Robert. *Thomas Hardy's Later Years*. Boston, MA: Little, Brown, 1978. Print.

Gittings, Robert. *Young Thomas Hardy*. London: Heinemann, 1975. Print.

Hardy, Evelyn. *Thomas Hardy: A Critical Biography*. New York: Russell and Russell Publishers, 1970. Print.

Hardy, Florence Emily. *The Early Life of Thomas Hardy, 1840–1891*. New York: Macmillan, 1928. Print.

Hardy, Florence Emily. *The Later Years of Thomas Hardy, 1892–1928*. New York: Macmillan, 1930. Print.

Hardy, Thomas. *Collected Letters*. Ed. Richard Purdy and Michael Millgate. Oxford: Oxford University Press, 1978. Print.

Hardy, Thomas. *The Complete Poems*. Ed. James Gibson. London and Basingstoke: Palgrave Macmillan, 2001. Print.

Hardy, Thomas. *The Dynasts: A Drama of the Napoleonic Wars*. New York: The Macmillan Company, 1904. Print.

Hardy, Thomas. Letter to Edmund Gosse, 22 March 1904. The Berg Collection. New York Public Library, New York, NY. MS.

Hardy, Thomas, Michael Millgate, and Florence Emily Hardy. *The Life and Work of Thomas Hardy*. Athens: University of Georgia, 1985. Print.

Heaney, Seamus. "Place, Pastness, Poems: A Triptych." *Salmagundi*, Fall 1985–Winter 1986: 30–47. *JSTOR*. Web. Accessed 21 July 2012.

Heath, Kay. "In the Eye of the Beholder: Victorian Age Construction and the Specular Self." *Victorian Literature and Culture*, March 2006: 27–45. *MLA International Bibliography*. Web. Accessed 25 April 2012.

Henchman, Anna. "Hardy's Stargazers and the Astronomy of Other Minds." *Victorian Studies*, September 2008: 37–64. *MLA International Bibliography*. Web. Accessed 25 April 2012.

Holy Bible: King James. Goodyear, AZ: G.E.M. Pub., 2001. Print.

Howe, Irving. *Thomas Hardy*. New York: Macmillan, 1967. Print.

Howells, W. D. "Some New Volumes of Verse". *The North American Review* 174.542 (January 1902): 140. *MLA International Bibliography*. Web. Accessed 25 July 2012.

Hynes, Samuel. "Hardy and the Battle God." In *Thomas Hardy Reappraised*, ed. Keith Wilson. Toronto: University of Toronto Press, 2006, pp. 245–61. Print.

Hynes, Samuel. "The Hardy Tradition in Modern English Poetry." *Sewanee Review*, Winter 1980: 33–51. *JSTOR*. Web. Accessed 12 April 2012.

Hynes, Samuel. "On Hardy's Badnesses." In *Essays on Aesthetics*, ed. John Fisher. Philadelphia, PA: Temple University Press, 1983, pp. 247–57. Print.

Hynes, Samuel. *The Pattern of Hardy's Poetry*. Chapel Hill: University of North Carolina Press, 1961. Print.

Ingham, Patricia. *Thomas Hardy*. Oxford, England: Oxford University Press, 2003. Print.

Inglesfield, Robert. "Two Interpolated Speeches in Robert Browning's A Death in the Desert." *Victorian Poetry* 41.3 (2003): 333–47. Print.

Knoepflmacher, U. C. "Hardy Ruins: Female Spaces and Male Designs." *PMLA: Publications of the Modern Language Association of America* 105.5 (1990): 1055–70. *JSTOR*. Web. Accessed 24 July 2012.

Keats, John. *The Complete Poems of John Keats*. New York: Modern Library, 1994. Print.

Larkin, Philip. *Collected Poems*. London: Farrar, Straus and Giroux, 2004. Print.

Larkin, Philip. *Required Writing*. Ann Arbor: University of Michigan Press, 1999. Print.

F. R. Leavis. *New Bearings in English Poetry*. London: Chatto and Windus, 1932. Print.

Lock, Charles. *Thomas Hardy*. New York: St Martin's Press, 1992. Print.

Longfellow, Henry Wadsworth, and Horace Elisha Scudder. *The Complete Poetical Works of Longfellow*. Boston, MA: Houghton Mifflin, 1922. Print.

McCarty, Steve. "'That We Can Talk of Another Time': Boldwood's Madness and **Victorian** Law." *Thomas Hardy Journal*, Autumn 2005: 94–102. *MLA International Bibliography*. Web. Accessed 25 April 2012.

Miller, David. *With Poetry and Philosophy*. Newcastle upon Tyne: Cambridge Scholars Publishing, 2007. Print.

Miller, Susan M. "Thomas Hardy and the Impersonal Lyric." *Journal of Modern Literature*, March 2007: 95–117. *MLA International Bibliography*. Web. Accessed 24 July 2012.

Millgate, Michael. *Thomas Hardy: A Biography*. Oxford UK: Oxford University Press, 1982. Print.

Millgate, Michael. *Thomas Hardy: A Biography Revisited*. Oxford: Oxford University Press, 2006. Print.

Millgate, Michael. *Thomas Hardy: His Career as a Novelist*. New York: Random House, 1971. Print.

Monroe, Harriet. Review of *Satires of Circumstance, Lyrics and Reveries, with Miscellaneous Pieces*. *Poetry* 5.5 (February 1915): 240–43. *MLA International Bibliography*. Web. Accessed 12 May 2012.

Morgan, Rosemarie. "Introduction." In *The Ashgate Research Companion to Thomas Hardy*, ed. Rosemarie Morgan. Burlington, VT: Ashgate, 2010, pp. 1–19. Print.

Murfin, Ross C. "Moments of Vision: Hardy's *Poems of 1912–13*." *Victorian Poetry* 20.1 (1982): 73–84. *JSTOR*. Web. Accessed 24 July 2012.

Nagel, Thomas. "The Absurd." *The Journal of Philosophy* 68.20 (1971): 716–27. *JSTOR*. Web. Accessed 10 February 2012.

Noakes, Vivien. *The Complete Poems and Fragments of Isaac Rosenberg with a Catalogue of the Isaac Rosenberg Material in the Imperial War Museum*. Oxford: Oxford University Press, 1998. Print.

Norman, Andrew. *Thomas Hardy: Behind the Mask*. Stroud: History Press, 2011. Print.

Noyes, Alfred. "The Poetry of Thomas Hardy." *The North American Review* 194.668 (1911): 96–105. *JSTOR*. Web. Accessed 12 June 2012.

Orel, Harold. "*The Dynasts*: Hardy's Contribution to the Epic Tradition." In *The Ashgate Research Companion to Thomas Hardy*, ed. Rosemarie Morgan, 2010, pp. 355–70. Print.

Owen, Wilfred, and Jon Stallworthy. *The Complete Poems and Fragments*. New York: W. W. Norton, 1984. Print.

Page, Norman. "Art and Aesthetics." In *The Cambridge Companion to Thomas Hardy*, ed. Dale Kramer. Cambridge: Cambridge University Press, 1999, pp. 38–53. Print.

Page, Norman. "Hardy's Dutch Painting: *Under the Greenwood Tree*." *Thomas Hardy Yearbook*, 1975: 39–42. *MLA International Bibliography*. Web. Accessed 17 July 2012.

Page, Norman. "Hardy's Pictorial Art in *The Mayor of Casterbridge*." *Etudes Anglaises: Grande-Bretagne, Etats-Unis*, 1972: 486–92. *MLA International Bibliography*. Web. Accessed 17 July 2012.

Page, Norman. "*The Life and Work of Thomas Hardy* by Thomas Hardy, Michael Millgate; *Thomas Hardy: Towards a Materialist Criticism* by George Wotton." *Nineteenth Century Literature* 41.1 (1986): 111–16. *JSTOR*. Web. Accessed 24 July 2012.

Page, Norman. "Opening Time: Hardy's Poetic Thresholds." In *Thomas Hardy Reappraised*, ed. Keith Wilson. Toronto: University of Toronto Press, 2006, pp. 262–69. Print.

Page, Norman. *Thomas Hardy*. London: Routledge and Kegan Paul, 1977.

Page, Norman. "Visual Techniques in Hardy's *Desperate Remedies*." *Ariel: A Quarterly Review of the Arts and Sciences in Israel*, 1973: 65–71. *MLA International Bibliography*. Web. Accessed 17 July 2012.

Paulin, Tom. *Thomas Hardy: The Poetry of Perception*. London: Macmillan, 1975. Print.

Pite, Ralph. *Thomas Hardy: The Guarded Life*. New Haven, CT: Yale University Press, 2007. Print.

Purdy, Richard. "A 1905 *Dynasts*." *Times Literary Supplement*, 14 February 1929: 118. *MLA International Bibliography*. Web. Accessed 3 July 2012.

Ramazani, Jahan. "Hardy and the Poetics of Melancholia: *Poems of 1912–13* and Other Elegies for Emma." *ELH* 58.4 (1991): 957–77. Print.

Richardson, Angelique. "Hardy and Biology." In *Thomas Hardy: Texts and Contexts*, ed. Phillip Mallett. Basingstoke: Palgrave Macmillan, 2002, pp. 156–79. Print.

Riquelme, John Paul. "The Modernity of Thomas Hardy's Poetry." In *The Cambridge Companion to Thomas Hardy*, ed. Dale Kramer. Cambridge: Cambridge University Press, 1999, pp. 204–23. Print.

Sankey, Benjamin. "Hardy's Plotting." *Twentieth Century Literature* 11.2 (1965): 82–97. Print.

Sassoon, Siegfried. *Counter-attack and Other Poems*. London: W. Heinemann, 1918. Print.

Schwartz, Delmore. "Poetry and Belief in Thomas Hardy." In *Hardy*, ed. Albert J. Guerard. Englewood Cliffs, NJ: Prentice Hall, 1963, pp. 123–34.

Scott, Nathan A., Jr. "The Literary Imagination and the Victorian Crisis of Faith: The Example of Thomas Hardy." *The Journal of Religion* 40.4 (1960): 267–81. Print.

Seccombe, Thomas. Review of *Thomas Hardy* by Harold Child. *Modern Language Review* 11:4 (October 1916): 496–99. *JSTOR*. Web. Accessed 25 July 2012.

Shakespeare, William. *Twelfth Night*. The Norton Shakespeare. Ed. Stephen Greenblatt, 2nd edn. New York: W. W. Norton, 2008 Print.

Spivey, Ted R. "Thomas Hardy's Tragic Hero." *Nineteenth-Century Fiction* 9.3 (1954): 179–91. Print.

Swatridge, Susan, and Thomas Hardy. *Far from the Madding Crowd*. London: Macmillan, 1988. Print.

Taylor, Dennis. "From Stratford to Casterbridge: The Influence of Shakespeare." In *The Ashgate Research Companion*, ed. Rosemarie Morgan. Burlington, VT: Ashgate, 2010, pp. 123–55. Print.

Taylor, Dennis. "Hardy and Wordsworth." *Victorian Poetry*, Winter 1986. *MLA International Bibliography*. Web. Accessed 2 May 2012.

Taylor, Dennis. "Hardy as a Nineteenth-Century Poet." In *The Cambridge Companion to Thomas Hardy*, ed. Dale Kramer. Cambridge, UK: Cambridge University Press, 1999, pp. 183–203. Print.

Taylor, Dennis. "Hardy's Copy of Shakespeare's *Othello*." *Thomas Hardy Journal*, Autumn 2006: 34–47. *JSTOR*. Web. Accessed 3 July 2012.

Taylor, Dennis. "Hardy's Copy of Tennyson's *In Memoriam*." *Thomas Hardy Journal*, February 1997: 43–63. *JSTOR*. Web. Accessed 3 July 2012.

Taylor, Dennis. "Hardy's Copy of *The Golden Treasury*." *Victorian Poetry*, Summer 1999: 165–91. *JSTOR*. Web. Accessed 3 July 2012.

Taylor, Dennis. *Hardy's Literary Language and Victorian Philology.* New York: Clarendon Press, 1993. Print.

Taylor, Dennis. *Hardy's Metres and Victorian Prosody.* Oxford: Oxford University Press, 1988. Print.

Taylor, Dennis. *Hardy's Poetry, 1860–1928.* New York: Columbia University Press, 1981. Print.

Taylor, Dennis. "Hardy's Use of Tennyson's *In Memoriam*." *Tennyson Research Bulletin*, 1997: 32–41. *JSTOR*. Web. Acessed 3 July 2012.

Taylor, Dennis. "*Jude the Obscure* and English National Identity." In *A Companion to Thomas Hardy*, ed. Keith Wilson. Chichester, England: Wiley-Blackwell, 2009, pp. 345–63. Print.

Taylor, Dennis. "The Patterns of Hardy's Poetry." In *Modern Critical Views: Thomas Hardy*, ed. Harold Bloom. New York: Chelsea House Publishers, 1987, pp. 97–113. First published in *ELH* 42 (1975). Print.

Taylor, Dennis. "Thomas Hardy and Thomas Gray: The Poet's Currency." *ELH* 65.2 (1998): 451–77. Print.

Tennyson, Alfred, Lord, and Hallam, Lord Tennyson. *The Complete Poems of Tennyson. Edited with A Memoir of Hallam, Lord Tennyson.* New York: Prepared by Macmillan for W. J. Black, 1925. Print.

Thomas, Dylan. "Fern Hill." In *Collected Poems*. New York: New Directions, 1971, p. 178. Print.

Tomalin, Claire. *Thomas Hardy.* New York: Penguin, 2007. Print.

Tuma, Keith. *Oxford Anthology of Twentieth-Century British and Irish Poets.* New York: Oxford University Press, 2001. Print.

Turner, Paul. *The Life of Thomas Hardy: A Critical Biography.* Oxford, UK: Blackwell, 1998. Print.

Warren, T. H. "Review of *Poems Past and Present*." *Spectator*, April 1902: 516. In *Thomas Hardy Critical Assessments*, ed. Graham Clarke. Vol. 1. Mountfield: Helm Information, 1993, pp. 321–24. Print.

Webster, Harvey Curtis. *On a Darkling Plain.* London: F. Cass, 1964. Print.

Whitehead, J. S. "Thomas Hardy and the First World War: Case Studies in Literary Influence." In *Human Shows: Essays in Honor of Michael Millgate*, ed. Rosemarie Morgan, Richard Nemesvari, and Michael Millgate. New Haven, CT: Hardy Association, 2000, pp. 110–38. Print.

Whitehead, James. "Thomas Hardy and The First World War Companion Poems: 'Men Who March Away' and 'Before Marching And After.'" *Thomas Hardy Journal* 15.3 (1999): 85–98. *MLA International Bibliography*. Web. Accessed 29 June 2012.

Whitmore, Charles E. "Mr. Hardy's *Dynasts* as Tragic Drama". *Modern Language Notes* 39.8 (December 1924): 455–60. *MLA International Bibliography*. Web. Accessed 3 July 2012.

Wilde, Oscar. *The Picture of Dorian Gray.* Harlow: Penguin, 2008. Print.

Wordsworth, William. *The Major Works: including The Prelude.* Ed. Stephen Gill. Oxford: Oxford University Press. 2008. Print.

Index

Allen, Hervey 190, 223
Arnold, Matthew 182
Auden, W. H. 133, 186, 194, 213,
  220, 223, 226
Austin, Linda 178, 222, 226

Bailey, J. O. 119, 220, 226
Barrie, J. M. 214, 216
Beardsley, Aubrey 81, 184
Beckett, Samuel 186
Beer, Gillian 161, 181, 184, 222, 226
Berryman, John 214
Betjeman, John 195
Bible, The 92, 119, 120, 131,
  200, 228
  Ecclesiastes, Book of 119
  Jeremiah, Book of 119–21, 133
  Psalms, Book of 200, 224
  Revelation, Book of 92–3
Blackmur, R. P. 196, 201
Bloom, Harold 225, 226, 232
Boer War 110, 113, 115, 134, 136
Bownas, Jane 181, 222, 226
Brooke, Rupert 105
Brooks, Jean R. 219, 221, 225, 227
Brown, William Clyde 218
Browning, Robert 64, 182–4, 199,
  213, 220, 222, 223, 229
  "My Last Duchess" 182–3

Cambridge Companion to Thomas
  Hardy 204, 217, 228, 230,
  231, 232

Carpenter, Richard 193–4, 223, 227
Christen, Eric 184
Christianity 75, 92–3, 128, 151–4
Clodd, Edward 98, 220
Coleridge, Samuel Taylor 174,
  185, 213
Collins, Vere 175
Corbus, Betty 218, 221, 222, 227
Cornwall 169, 176, 178

Dalziel, Pamela 212
Darwin, Charles 97, 181, 213, 222,
  226
Davie, Donald 184, 186, 227
Davis, W. Eugene 215, 225, 227
dialect 6, 16–18, 42–3, 204
Dickinson, Emily 71
Dolin, Tim 216, 227
Dollar, J. Gerard 217, 225, 227
Donne, John 64, 66, 227
Dorset 6, 169

Eagleton, Terry 221, 227
Eliot, George 172
Eliot, T. S. 180, 181, 186, 191, 193,
  195–6, 213, 220, 223, 227

fin de siècle 81, 184
Fletcher, John Gould 191, 223, 227
Flynn, Suzanne 184, 222, 227

Gatrell, Simon 6, 219, 228
gender 31, 38, 47, 67–8, 164, 175

Gillies, Mary Ann 186, 196, 222, 228
Gittings, Robert 173, 176, 177, 178, 215, 221, 222, 228
Graves, Robert 105, 195
Gray, Thomas 202, 219, 224, 232
Greenslade, William 212
Gurney, Ivor 105

Hardy, Emma 47, 53, 169–70, 173, 176–8, 206–7, 221, 231
Hardy, Evelyn 99, 228
Hardy, Florence (Dugdale) 169–70, 214–17, 228
Hardy, Thomas
 Life 169–70
 Individual Poems
  "After the Fair" 13–14, 27, 42
  Afterwards" 129, 138–9, 162, 163
  "Ah, Are You Digging on My Grave?" 23–7, 31, 40, 46, 50, 54
  "Architectural Masks" 43
  At Casterbridge Fair 11–14, 15, 42
  "At Castle Boterel" 144, 147–50, 152, 157, 163, 202
  "At the Piano" 4
  "Autumn in King's Hintock Park" 165
  "Beeny Cliff" 59–61, 62–3, 64, 68, 176, 177
  "Bride-Night Fire, The" 16–19, 20, 22, 27, 29, 30, 31, 38, 41, 42
  "Cave of the Unborn, The" 104
  "Channel Firing" 69, 128–32, 136
  "Christmas Ghost Story, A" 69
  "Convergence of the Twain, The" 93–9, 100, 101, 129, 137
  "Country Wedding, The" 27–31, 41–2
  "Curate's Kindness, The" 33–7, 38, 39–40, 41, 42
  "Darkling Thrush, The" 77–81, 82, 83, 84, 85, 87, 88, 100, 129, 202

"Dead Man Walking, The" 183
"Drummer Hodge" 136
"During Wind and Rain" 139–44, 150, 152, 156
"Fiddler, The" 165
"Garden Seat, The" 165–6
"Going of the Battery, The" 110–15, 116, 134, 165
"Going, The" 154–9, 163
"Hap" 73–7, 78, 79, 81, 83, 84, 85, 87, 88, 100, 129, 202
"Haunter, The" 52–4, 57–9, 61, 66, 67, 69, 70, 71, 178
"Her Immortality" 71
"House of Hospitalities, The" 151–4
"How Great My Grief" 4
"I Found Her Out There" 43
"I Have Lived with Shades" 48–52, 53, 58, 67, 68, 69, 200
"I Look Into My Glass" 159–61, 163
"I Looked Up from My Writing" 106–10, 116, 117, 123, 135, 162
"Ice on the Highway" 14, 15, 38, 39
"In the Servants' Quarters" 42
"In Time of 'The Breaking of Nations'" 118–23, 132, 135, 136
"Man He Killed, The" 123–8, 132
"Meeting with Despair, A" 43
"Men Who March Away" 134, 194, 220, 223, 233
"Nature's Questioning" 81–6, 87, 88, 95, 98, 100, 185
"Neutral Tones" 104
"On a Fine Morning" 86–9, 90, 100, 146
"Orphaned Old Maid, The" 183
"Overlooking the River Stour" 104
"Peasant's Confession, The" 43
"Phantom Horsewoman, The" 59, 61–4, 67, 69, 176
"Pine Planters, The" 43

"Rome: Building a New Street in
the Ancient Quarter"   165
"Ruin'd Maid, The"   19–23, 38,
41–2, 124
"Self-Unseeing, The"
144–7, 150
"Sick Battle-God, The"   136
"Souls of the Slain, The"   69
"Thoughts of Phena"   69
"To an Unborn Pauper
Child"   89–93, 95, 100,
101, 104
"To-Be-Forgotten, The"   69
"Tolerance"   165
"Under the Waterfall"   176
"Voice, The"   52, 54–9, 61, 63,
66, 67, 68, 70, 71, 80
"Wife in London, A"   110,
115–18, 135, 136, 137
"Wife Waits, A"   11–12, 14,
27, 42
"Your Last Drive"   44–7, 49,
50, 52, 61, 67, 68, 69, 70,
71, 164
Poetry Collections
Collected Poems   172, 195, 197,
198, 211
Human Shows   15, 226, 233
Moments of Vision   191, 226,
227, 230
Poems of 1912–13 47, 59, 69,
71, 155, 176–8, 188, 206, 209,
226, 230, 231
Poems of Past and Present   189,
232
Satires of Circumstance   189,
226, 230
Time's Laughingstocks   183,
195, 200
Wessex Poems   172, 189
Novels
Far from the Madding Crowd   14,
169, 172, 181, 212, 231
Jude the Obscure   172, 173, 175,
203, 212, 217, 232
Mayor of Casterbridge, The   19,
22–3, 172, 205, 212, 224, 230
Return of the Native   1, 14, 22,
172, 212

Tess of the D'Urbervilles   1, 171,
172, 173, 212
Trumpet Major, The   173, 221
Other Works
Dynasts, The   98, 172–3, 184,
191, 194, 212, 223, 227, 228,
230, 231, 233
Wessex Tales   172, 212
Heaney, Seamus   166, 221, 228
Heath, Kay   182, 222, 228
Henchman, Anna   181, 222, 226
Hornback, Bert   218
Howe, Irving   192–3, 223, 228
Howells, William Dean   189,
222, 228
Hughes, Ted   186
Hynes, Samuel   186, 197–201, 207,
212, 223, 224, 229

Immanent Will   94, 96–8, 116
Ingham, Patricia   225, 229
irony   21, 34–7, 42, 50, 53, 95, 101,
105, 110, 117, 119, 124, 220

Keats, John   64, 229
Kipling, Rudyard   96, 191, 197
Knoepflmacher, U. C.   216, 225
Kramer, Dale   217, 228, 230,
231, 232

Larkin, Philip   64, 165, 180, 186,
195–6, 213, 220, 222, 223, 229
Lawrence, T. E.   195
Leavis, F. R.   191–2, 196, 223
Lock, Charles   225, 229
London   5, 116–17, 169
Longfellow, Henry Wadsworth
113, 229
Lowell, Robert   214

Mallett, Phillip   212, 231
Max Gate   169, 178
Miller, David   183
Miller, Susan   207–9, 217, 224, 229
Millgate, Michael   173, 174, 212,
214–17, 221, 227, 228, 229,
230, 233
Modernism   102, 112, 180, 186, 191,
192–3, 196, 205, 209–10, 220

Monroe, Harriet 190, 223, 230
Morgan, Rosemarie 175, 180, 217, 221, 226, 227, 230, 231, 233
Morgan, William 217
Murfin, Ross 177, 222, 230

Nagel, Thomas 220, 230
New Criticism 192
Nishimura, Satoshi 218
Norton, Andrew 225
Noyes, Alfred 189, 222, 230

Orel, Harold 194, 223, 230
Owen, Wilfred 105–6, 121, 124, 230

Page, Norman 184, 204–6, 212, 217, 224, 225, 230, 231
Paulin, Tom 182, 183, 185, 222, 231
pessimism 2–3, 21, 57, 161, 181–2, 183, 189, 195, 202
Phelps, W. L. 170
Pite, Ralph 225
Pound, Ezra 186, 193, 195
Purdy, Richard 212, 214–15, 223, 228

Ramazani, Jahan 178, 222, 231
Riquelme, John Paul 185–6, 222, 231
Romanticism 19, 73, 76, 78–81, 102, 104, 117, 180–1, 184–5, 203, 204–5, 207–9, 220
Rosenberg, Isaac 105, 121, 124, 132, 194, 231

Sankey, Benjamin 31, 32, 219, 231
Sassoon, Siegfried 105, 121, 124, 132, 194, 231
Schwartz, Delmore 194, 214, 223, 231
Schweik, Robert 212
Scott, Nathan 97
Seccombe, Thomas 190, 223, 231
Shakespeare, William 66, 71, 138, 144, 189, 202, 231, 232
    Twelfth Night 143, 231
Shelley, Mary 174
Shelley, Percy Bysshe 185, 213
"skimmity-ride" 18–19

Sorley, Charles 105, 223
Sparks, Tryphena 170
Spenser, Edmund 71
Spivey, Ted 219, 231
St. Butler, Lance 225, 227

Taylor, Dennis 137, 170, 184, 185, 201–4, 207, 209, 217, 219, 221, 222, 224, 231–2
Tennyson, Alfred Lord 64, 114, 182, 203, 206, 213, 224, 232
The Ashgate Research Companion to Thomas Hardy 175, 216, 217, 226, 227, 230, 231
The Early Life of Thomas Hardy 214, 215, 216, 227, 228
The Golden Treasury 173, 202, 224, 232
The Later Years of Thomas Hardy 215, 228
The Life and Work of Thomas Hardy 214–16, 221, 227, 228, 230
The Oxford English Dictionary 203–4
The Poetry Foundation 215
The Spectator 189, 232
Thomas, Dylan 165, 195, 220
Thomas, Edward 105, 195
Times Literary Supplement 189, 223, 226, 231
Titanic, The 94, 137
Tomalin, Claire 170, 225, 232
Tuma, Keith 173, 221, 232
Turner, Paul 225

Van Doren, Mark 193
Victorianism 102, 172, 174, 180, 181–4, 191, 193, 202, 203, 205, 207

Warren, T. H. 189, 223, 232
Webster, Harvey Curtis 3, 219, 232
Wessex 6, 17
Whitman, Walt 222
Wilde, Oscar 81, 131, 160, 184, 233
    Picture of Dorian Gray, The 160, 233

Wilson, Keith   212, 217, 229, 230, 232

Wordsworth, William   54, 73–5, 76–7, 78, 102, 138, 143, 180, 185, 199, 202–3, 206, 208, 213, 231, 233
   "Lines Composed a Few Miles Above Tintern Abbey"   76, 202

"World Is Too Much With Us, The"   54, 73

World War I   105–6, 110, 118, 120–1, 124, 128, 134, 194, 197, 213, 220

Yeats, W. B.   81, 186, 191, 220

Printed in China